A Great Day in Cooperstown

A GREAT DAY IN
COOPERSTOWN

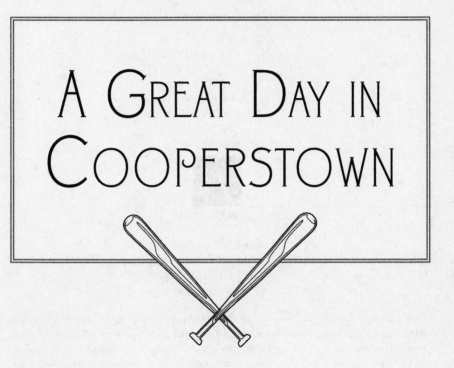

The Improbable Birth of Baseball's Hall of Fame

JIM REISLER

CARROLL & GRAF PUBLISHERS

NEW YORK

A Great Day in Cooperstown
The Improbable Birth of Baseball's Hall of Fame

Carroll & Graf Publishers
An Imprint of Avalon Publishing Group, Inc.
245 West 17th Street
11th Floor
New York, NY 10011

AVALON
publishing group incorporated

Cover photo: First in their class: Gathered June 12, 1939, in Cooperstown were (front row, left to right) Eddie Collins, Babe Ruth, Connie Mack, and Cy Young; and (back row, left to right) Honus Wagner, Grover Cleveland Alexander, Tris Speaker, Napoleon "Larry" Lajoie, George Sisler, and Walter Johnson. Ty Cobb was late and missed the photo session. (Courtesy of the National Baseball Hall of Fame, Cooperstown, NY)

Library of Congress Cataloging-in-Publication Data is available.

ISBN-10: 0-7867-1869-2
ISBN-13: 978-0-78671-869-6

9 8 7 6 5 4 3 2 1

Book Design by Maria E. Torres

Printed in the United States of America
Distributed by Publishers Group West

For Tobie and Julia

☙ CONTENTS ☙

PREFACE • xi

CHAPTER 1:
"So This Is Where All the Grief Started" • 1

CHAPTER 2:
The Plan—"An Interesting Museum (with) Funny, Old Uniforms" • 14

CHAPTER 3:
"Dear Mr. Spalding . . .
The American Game of Baseball Was Invented by Abner Doubleday" • 35

CHAPTER 4:
"In the Beginning, a Vision and It Came to Pass" • 54

CHAPTER 5:
"I Am Overwhelmed" to Make the Hall of Fame • 87

CHAPTER 6:
"The Point Is to Get Baseball into the
Other Pages as Well as the Sports Page" • 130

CHAPTER 7:

An "Embarrassing Revelation" for Baseball ♦ 144

CHAPTER 8:

"I Hope It Goes Another One Hundred Years" ♦ 171

CHAPTER 9:

A "World Series with the Score Tied Nothing to
Nothing in the Ninth Inning" ♦ 190

CHAPTER 10:

"I Wouldn't Have Missed It for Anything" ♦ 203

ACKNOWLEDGMENTS ♦ 225

BIBLIOGRAPHY ♦ 227

INDEX ♦ 231

"Lemmings head for the sea. The swallows come back to Capistrano. The buzzards somehow find their way to Findlay, Ohio. The geese follow their instincts south. And baseball fans go to Cooperstown."

—Dan Chabot, *Milwaukee Journal*

PREFACE

The idea, hatched back in 1958, was novel: Gather as many of the world's greatest jazz musicians as possible in one place for an *Esquire* magazine group photo. It sounded easy enough; the trick was getting them all there and keeping them long enough to take the photo.

So the photographer, Art Kane, sent out a note to sixty of the era's top jazz musicians, waited, and hoped that they'd show up as asked to the corner of 120th Street and Eighth Avenue in Harlem at 11:00 A.M. on a weekday morning. For most everyone, that time is reasonable, but for jazz musicians—a population used to jamming all night and sleeping most of the day—it is either very early or very late, depending on their perspective.

On shoot-day, Kane arrived two hours early to set up his camera—and waited. Somebody thought to bring a movie camera—and the various comings and goings, who was talking to whom, and all the details of what we now recognize as a wonderful moment in our cultural history, was fortunately preserved. First came the anxious moments when few musicians had even arrived, and Kane wondered if the whole idea was going be a washout. Then, with minutes to spare before the scheduled start of the shoot, something miraculous happened: cars started pulling up, depositing night-crawling musicians, most of whom hadn't yet gone to bed. They greeted one another like long-lost relatives, and as the cars kept coming, a who's-who of '50s-era jazz musicians—Dizzy Gillespie, Thelonious Monk,

Sonny Rollins, Marian McPartland, Gerry Mulligan, Milt Hinton, and Coleman Hawkins among them—kept spilling out, wanting to schmooze. The ultimate alumni reunion was shaping into form.

By shoot-time, Kane's challenge was getting the hundred or so musicians' attention long enough to actually take the photo. The scene had become so crowded that Kane had to move his camera back across the street to accommodate the bulging crowd. It all worked magnificently, and the photo, which has since been commemorated in a well-known poster called a "Great Day in Harlem," shows a veritable Hall of Fame of well-known musicians grabbing every available space on a tenement stoop and fanning out to the sidewalks in a kind of reverse "T." There are even several little boys, who probably lived in the building, looking out from a second-story window and another dozen or so kids lining the sidewalk curb, next to a smiling Count Basie.

The day the Baseball Hall of Fame opened in Cooperstown, New York, was a little like that. In the planning stages for two decades, the Hall in 1939 was an unusual idea that even months before had seemed doomed to failure. Would the organizers acquire enough items to actually start the museum? Would anybody show up for the opening ceremonies? Would the famous players and pioneers they invited—men like Babe Ruth, Connie Mack, Ty Cobb, Honus Wagner, Eddie Collins, and Grover Cleveland Alexander—even bother to make it to the tiny upstate New York crossroads of Cooperstown?

The answers to those questions were "yes," "yes," and "yes" again. Not only were the organizers able to receive and display some extraordinary contributions of baseball's early days, but ten thousand spectators showed up, as did the famous players and pioneers. The museum was attractive and stately—looking more like a library and fitting snugly into the character of the small town, along Main Street, across from the post office. That everything went swimmingly amidst the grimness of the Great Depression when weary Americans were frankly more interested in just trying to find jobs is a tale of a small band of unsung heroes who started with a vision and succeeded against great odds. How they did it—using a fabricated story that baseball was invented in Cooperstown—was the birth of the game's mythology.

The story of the National Baseball Hall of Fame and Museum is a triumph of public relations, organization, and old-fashioned persistence. On the day it opened, even the weather held up—and the famous photo of the players, a straight-ahead wire-service shot of the Hall's first group of living members, has become a classic, a kind of baseball equivalent to Art Kane's shot of the jazz greats. All in all, it was a "Great Day in Cooperstown" and arguably one of the best days in baseball history, all at a time when America needed a break. Here's how it happened.

CHAPTER 1

"So This Is Where All the Grief Started"

By 8:45 A.M., the crowd could no longer squeeze into the one-room train station. They filled up the waiting room of the old weather-beaten wooden freight shed, once grandly called the Delaware & Hudson Station for the names of the railroads that originally fed passengers into town, and spilled out onto the platform and even down the tracks, all of them eagerly waiting for the arrival of the town's first passenger train in five years.

The hamlet of Cooperstown, New York, some two hundred miles north of New York City, wasn't the destination of many people in the summer of 1939. Cooperstown, some twenty-five miles northeast of Oneonta and perhaps seventy miles due west of Albany, fit snugly at the foot of lovely Lake Otsego, among the northern foothills of the Catskills. Best known as the home of the early nineteenth-century novelist James Fenimore Cooper who based some of his works there, this town of three thousand wasn't on the way to much of anywhere. So few were the visitors to Cooperstown that the train station, closed since 1934 and subdivided into city offices, had to be cleared of weeds and given a quick overhaul to accommodate the expected train.

By then, the Great Depression, which hit with the force of a freight train in the stock market crash of 1929, had ravaged America for close to a decade. Considering the hard times, it would have seemed Cooperstown residents would have other things than base-ball on their minds. A dry spring was one thing people worried about in this farm-rich community; a report in May from the U.S. Department of Agriculture at Cornell University had said a sus-tained period of warm, wet weather was essential if farmers were to salvage a good season for oats, onions, and potatoes. Dairy farmers also had concerns about the dry weather: Pasture conditions in New York had been steadily deteriorating, according to reports, and milk production for May was off 13 percent from the year before, only the sixth time the figure had declined since 1865 when reports had started.

But this train was unusual. It was the "Centennial Special," a car-avan of thirteen Pullman cars that had assembled to carry the guests to Cooperstown for the centerpiece of a four-month gala celebra-tion to commemorate baseball's first century and the opening of a novel idea—a museum or "hall of fame" for the storage and archiving of artifacts for the public to see. Pieced together with trains from New York, Boston, and Chicago, the train had left the previous evening, Sunday, June 11, from New York's Grand Central Terminal, filled with unusual cargo. Aboard were the greatest legends of baseball's first century. As the train chugged along the New York Central line northward on old rails that people in the small towns had cleared of foliage, residents along the way turned out to watch it go by and try to catch a glimpse of the notable figures aboard.

At 9:00 A.M. on the dot, the train pulled into the Cooperstown station on Railroad Street, a half block south of Main Street, where most of the festivities were scheduled to take place. The train stopped, and in the first act of what would be a momentous day, the conductor jumped down, ready to assist some of the more elderly passengers on the platform. It wasn't choreographed, but it seemed so: One by one, the retired heroes of the game stepped off the train, smiling and waving as they hit the platform, as if swallowed up by the appreciative crowd, pressing close. Some, like the moon-faced Babe Ruth, whose image had adorned the nation's newspapers, newsreels, and Wheaties boxes for close to twenty years, were instantly recognizable. Ruth, only forty-four and the youngest of the immortals to be elected to this Hall of Fame, was his charismatic self—a good thirty pounds beyond his playing weight, and only a year from a brief stint as a coach for the Brooklyn Dodgers—but playful and instinctively aware of how to work the crowd. The oldest? He was easy to spot—the seventy-seven-year-old, rail-thin, ramrod-straight Connie Mack whose lean 150-pound frame on a 6'1" body made him seem a half foot taller. Born Cornelius Alexander McGillicutty in the second year of the Civil War, Mack had broken into baseball as a catcher with Washington, and had devoted more than a half century to baseball, most of it as manager and owner of the Philadelphia A's for whom he also managed from the dugout, usually dressed in a suit and skimmer.

Even at a time when few had ever seen these legends up close and there was no television to beam their likenesses, the crowd knew them all. It wasn't hard to miss the stocky frame of the great Pittsburgh shortstop Honus Wagner: Now sixty-five with snow-white hair, a substantial beer gut, and a tie that was way too short, the great Wagner, twenty-two years retired, had stayed in the game as a Pittsburgh Pirates coach, and could silence any crowd by habitually taking pregame infield practice and gracefully pegging the ball to first base from just about anywhere. There was the lanky, angular Walter Johnson, known as "The Big Train," the fastest and most feared pitcher of his time. Now fifty-one, the soft-spoken Washington Senators legend was dressed like a banker but was in fact a Maryland farmer. Looking like he could still step to the plate and smoke a double into the gap was forty-six-year-old George Sisler, twice a .400 hitter with the St. Louis Browns, and now a St. Louis baseball executive. Fifty-two-year-old Eddie Collins, the great infielder, was there as well, taking a break from his duties as general manager of the Boston Red Sox, and looking positively dude-ish in a double-breasted suit and two-toned shoes. As was the great pitcher Grover Cleveland Alexander—only two months older than Collins, but looking like he could use a shave and a nap. Postbaseball life had been hard for the great "Alex" as he was known, and it showed; the 374-game winner and star of the 1926 World Series had fallen on hard times, and at the time was living in Hells Kitchen and subsisting as a performer at a Times Square Flea Circus.

Curiously absent was the leading vote-getter of the Hall of Fame balloting by sportswriters—the magnificently cantankerous Ty Cobb, the great Detroit Tigers batsman, said to be driving into the event with two of his five children from his home in Menlo Park, California. "So where is he?" asked ballplayers, officials, and fans alike.

Very much present were a good many of the day's baseball stars—

each major-league team had been asked to supply two players—ready to play later in the day in an exhibition ballgame at the little ballpark, Doubleday Field, that had been built using WPA funds. Among them were sensational Detroit Tigers slugger Hank Greenberg; the Pirates hitting brothers, Paul and Lloyd Waner; Casey Stengel; Pepper Martin; Carl Hubbell; and Mel Ott of the New York Giants, and Cincinnati Reds twenty-four-year-old lefty star Johnny Vander Meer, who a year before had secured a unique spot in baseball history—pitching two no-hitters in a row. Best of all, the immortals would attend, some even suiting up.

Already, the gathering amounted to the greatest assemblage of baseball talent in a single place ever—the ten Hall of Famers to be honored as well as the current players, many of whom would be elected themselves one day, assembled on the platform of Cooperstown's one-room train station. Today, such Hall of Fame reunions are routine, with every move choreographed by ESPN cameras. Have a question for the Hall of Famers, particularly the newly elected ones? You'll have to wait until the press conference, which is before or after the parade of limos swoop in to take the retired ballplayers off to their annual golf tournament or closed-door banquet. Not that it can be helped these days, with upward of thirty thousand visitors roaming about on a typical induction weekend. But all of that was far into the future on a pleasant morning in Cooperstown in the early summer of 1939 when nobody had given much thought to logistics or scripts. So to get into town, the retired players and guests would just have to walk, trailed by several hundred residents, many of whom seemed to be small boys asking for autographs; at least it was all in the neighborhood.

Many more people other than just players continued to pile from the train. There were scouts, baseball writers, radio announcers, still and newsreel photographers, and a score of baseball officials, team owners, and a lot of hangers-on. Blanche McGraw, widow of the great John McGraw, the longtime manager of the New York Giants, descended from the train, as did another widow, Jane Mathewson, whose husband, Christy, was McGraw's star pitcher, the greatest of his era, and for a time, a roommate. Both had been elected posthumously to the Hall of Fame. Of the officials, most notable was the wiry commissioner of baseball, the silver-haired, exquisitely-named Kenesaw Mountain Landis, a federal judge and public relations showboat, who had become the game's first and only commissioner in the wake of the 1919 World Series scandal, and ruled ever since with an iron fist. Adding some levity to the proceedings was the comedian Joe Cook, who had made the trip north from New York, and emerged from the train, waving a baseball.

"An authentic copy of my prize possession," he announced with a flourish, "exactly like the original in my safe at home: the only souvenir baseball not autographed by Babe Ruth!"

Those within earshot roared with laughter, and Cooperstown's big day of Monday, June 12, 1939, was underway. It was the start to the grandest birthday of the only team sport that mattered then, a celebration of baseball's first century and the ceremonial election to its Hall of Fame that Ruth, Wagner, Johnson, Sisler, and others were present to join. Despite their public lives, much of which were spent crisscrossing the country to play baseball, few if any of these players, past and present, had ever been here, and until a couple of years before, had ever heard of Cooperstown, New York. But the army of reporters and photographers still piling off the train combined with the forthcoming festivities ensured that Cooperstown would soon be known to the world.

◆ ◆ ◆

With all points in Cooperstown within walking distance, the base-ball stars really had no choice but to descend into the thick crowd of well-wishers, many of whom came armed with pens and commemorative first-day stamp covers, released that morning from the Cooperstown Post Office, to ask for autographs.

So they did the only thing possible: comply, and begin the day by signing their names to the stamp covers, slips of paper, and just about anything else residents thrust in their faces as they trudged toward town. The crowd followed, and the small mob of baseball stars, offi-cials, reporters, and autograph hounds left the station, made a left onto Chestnut Street, crossed Main and onto the grounds of the stately, old Cooper Inn, where there was to be an early luncheon, prior to the noon kickoff of the program.

Built in the early nineteenth century, the Cooper Inn was an old mansion, known as "Willow Brook," built by local newspaper pub-lisher Henry Phinney. Opened as a hotel in 1936 with the addition of a wing, the spacious halls and colonial authenticity of the inn served as perhaps the town's most appropriate venue to host the trav-eling caravan of stars before they headed to the ceremonies out on Main Street. Even the weather was cooperating, and sunlight streamed through the inn's wide windows, making it a perfect day for a ballgame—and conversation.

Quickly filling the hotel dining room, the mob soon occupied every table and chair, with so many old-timers and current stars wasting no time in talking shop—and a handful of writers with stories to file for the next day's papers, eagerly soaking up the atmosphere.

At one table huddled two current stars, Joe Medwick and Terry

Moore, teammates on the great "Gashouse Gang" St. Louis Cardinals of the early 1930s, talking about the rise of the Cincinnati Reds, first place for now in the National League. Joining the conversation was Vander Meer, one of the reasons for their success. "I'll pay you to join Cincinnati for two weeks," Medwick called out to the adjoining table occupied by Reds manager Bill McKechnie.

"Pay him enough to take care of his hospital expenses," cracked Vander Meer.

At the next table sat two former National League presidents, John Heydler and John Tener, also the ex-governor of Pennsylvania and a one-time National League pitcher with Chicago and Pittsburgh. "This is a great and precious thing," said Heydler of the Hall of Fame, "but nobody except outstanding players should be voted [in] . . . while [they are] living."

Nearby, one of those voted into the Hall, the great Napoleon Lajoie, now sixty-five, and looking every bit the big-league veteran with a .338 lifetime batting average, glowed with a broad smile. "I never had such fun meeting my old opponents!" he said.

Milling about outside the hotel and staring toward the crowds starting to assemble in town, Carl Hubbell, the grim-faced screw-balling ace of the Giants, and five times a twenty-game winner, broke into a smile.

"So this is where all the grief started," he muttered. Hubbell's wry humor hid how he and other present-day stars, some of whom had grumbled at having to be there, were getting sucked in by the moment and humbled to be in the presence of these legends. He hesitated for now in walking the half mile or so to visit the new Hall, cracking that "they may want to keep my left arm up there." In time they would try; Hubbell would retire in 1943 after sixteen big-league seasons and 253 wins, and be elected to the Hall in '47.

Somebody noted that the first inductees had played every position but third base—and that Pie Traynor, here as the Pirates manager and recently retired third baseman known for his quick hands and lethal bat, should take advantage of the opportunity to sit for his Hall of Fame bust. "If they want to sculpt," the thirty-nine-year-old Pie said, "they better get me now while I still look like something. Another three months and Ol' Traynor'll never look the same."

In another part of the Cooper Inn dining room, Honus Wagner held court. Picking up one of the commemorative bats that he and the other immortals had received, he dared Grover Cleveland Alexander to throw him some heat. "Every time you grab one of these things," Wagner said of the bat, "you still think you can hit."

So it went the rest of the morning, with ballplayers, past and present, baseball officials, and all those fans milling about from the hotel, around the streets and down on Main Street, where festivities would soon begin. Positively bursting at the sudden, improbable glare of attention focused on little Cooperstown was its mayor, Rowan D. Spraker, absolute in his power, having won 698 out of 700 votes in the last election—entertainer Charlie McCarthy and radio personality Graham McNamee got the other two—and hopeful that the attention would help transform his hamlet into a tourist haven.

So started the memorable first day at the new National Baseball Hall of Fame, where good-natured frivolity and a dose of down-home nostalgia, heavy on the patriotism, dominated—a freeze-frame of a Norman Rockwell painting, and in real contrast to the hyper-competitive nature that these immortals had displayed on the ball field. "Usually when ballplayers assemble, there is horseplay and stinging banter," wrote baseball historian Ken Smith. "But that note was missing in this unique roundup. Rather it was a friendly, family picnic. An air of nostalgia subordinated the customary jockeying and teasing. Reminiscence caught hold and held on."

It would be like that all day long, and by the time newspapers had run long, detailed pieces about every aspect of the glorious day, Cooperstown would be branded on the nation's conscience as the birthplace of baseball. That it was all based on a fabrication didn't particularly bother anyone. The small band of disciples who had made it happen, led by an heir to a fortune built by the oddest of tycoons, could sit back and bask in their luck.

◆ ◆ ◆

No novelist would dare create a character as unique, eccentric, and wholly American as Isaac Merritt Singer. Born to modest means in 1811 in the town of Oswego, one hundred miles or so west of Cooperstown, Singer was a restless soul—running away from home at the age of twelve and supporting himself as an itinerant laborer with an eclectic battery of hobbies and a knack for things mechanical.

For starters, Singer was an exhibitionist, joining for a time a Shakespearean acting troupe. Married with two children, he had a roving eye and lived with three women at the same time, trying to support each household and the fourteen children from these relationships. Born with a restless, probing mind, Singer was also a tinkerer, and by the age of twenty-eight, had invented a wood carving machine for which he sought the help of Cooperstown lawyer Edward S. Clark in securing the proper patent. That didn't work, but Singer trudged on, next fixing his sights on a new device that would force him to the edge of bankruptcy and then make him very rich.

Singer's idea was to perfect the sewing machine, which by 1850 had been around for a half century, but never caught on because it couldn't consistently stitch an even, single-thread pattern. His break-through wasn't inventing yet another sewing machine; it was improving an earlier version patented by Elias Howe just a few years earlier. Using parts from earlier sewing machines, Singer figured out a simple, up-and-down action that didn't break the thread.

But Isaac Singer would have been remembered as a historical foot-note if it hadn't been for his next plan: reaching again for Clark as a partner in going to court to fight for patents and to get the product built and to market. Clark proved he was just the man for the job by deftly arranging a court settlement in which he, Singer, and an asso-ciate formed a company for the mass production of the new Singer Sewing Machines that paid royalties to the various patent holders. Next, Singer and Clark bought out their associate for $6,000, but when Clark, recognizing the potential of the invention, refused a cash settlement for his services, settling instead for a 50 percent share of the profits, the two men became business partners for life.

Singer and Clark were the mid-nineteenth-century Odd Couple of American business tycoons. Edward Clark was everything Singer wasn't—calm and cultured, he was a Williams College graduate who went into law and worked on Wall Street. He and Singer formed their company in 1863, and within a few years had earned a fortune that Clark then poured into philanthropic projects in Cooperstown, his wife's hometown. Clark bought a grand summer house there, bought up properties in the area, and became one of the town's civic leaders.

Clark displayed his flare for business—continuing to lead the company through constant legal battles and always seeming to find new sources of financing, and new markets in Europe. Clark also showed a knack for advertising—and his self-styled ad campaigns mocked husbands who did not buy a Singer Sewing Machine for their wives. To build demand, he targeted women with influence, offering half-price machines to ministers' wives, and created what may have been industry's first installment plan—$5 down and $5 a month for the $100 machine.

A year later, revenues had tripled. But even with business booming, the relationship between Singer and Clark was not. Not friends to start with, and fueled by business haggling and Singer's general unpleasantness, they became bitter enemies. Singer called Clark at one point "the most contemptible-looking object I ever saw with his wig off." That was par for the course for the unsavory Singer—his death in 1875 brought a predictably messy and pro-tracted estate settlement, sliced up among his far-flung family of twenty-three surviving children.

Singer's death left Clark as company president, a post he held until his own death in 1882. After his death, his estimated $40 million for-tune, most of it in Singer stock, was passed to his only surviving child, the thirty-eight-year-old Alfred, a Cooperstown resident. Apparently, Alfred inherited his father's business acumen: When he died sixteen years later, he had tripled the family wealth, and divided that amount equally among his four sons who shared their family's abiding passion for their community.

One of those sons, Edward, was known as the "Squire" around Cooperstown, and encouraged by a friend and local physician, Mary Imogene Bassett, built a hospital in town and named it after her. He raised prize herds of Guernsey cattle—living in a house once occu-pied by James Fenimore Cooper—and called the property his "cow palace"—which later became the Farmers Museum. Edward also built the elegant Otesaga Resort Hotel overlooking Lake Otsego, as well as the Alfred Clark Gymnasium, the town's recreation center named for his father.

Meanwhile, two other sons, Frederick Ambrose, known as "Brose," and Robert, didn't stick around Cooperstown, but became benefactors as well, with Robert and his wife helping to establish the Clark Art Institute in Williamstown, Massachusetts, in 1955. The fourth son, Stephen, did stick around, and soon became the family's true leader of philanthropy in Cooperstown—and the driving force behind the vision to create a reason for people to journey to the area: a National Baseball Hall of Fame and Museum.

CHAPTER 2

The Plan—"An Interesting Museum (with) Funny, Old Uniforms"

By 10:00 A.M., most of the luminaries had left the inn and fanned out across town, wearing their commemorative red, white, and blue baseball caps, perhaps looking for a barber to get a shave and killing time before the noon festivities. Joe McCarthy, manager of the American League-leading New York Yankees, lounged on a park bench, greeting passersby as he waited for his wife to return from window-shopping along Main Street. Along came Pie Traynor.

"You look worried, Joe. Club going bad?" he asked, fully aware that the standings showed the Yankees, as usual, with a healthy lead— in this case, nine games.

"When you start to worry in this game, you might as well get out," McCarthy said, drawing a deep breath on his ever-present cigar. Then he laughed. "I take a day off and we win two. That shows how much they need me. I might as well go to Atlantic City for the summer!"

Reds manager Bill McKechnie stood in the shade of an awning in front of a grocery store, and with one foot propped on a bushel basket of potatoes, he was telling Eddie Collins how Bill Werber had chased Johnnny Hudson across the plate in yesterday's game.

"Reminds me of the 1917 World Series when Heinie Zimmerman pulled the same chase on me," Collins remembered. "It's a wonderful feeling—for the one in front."

Holding court by Mohican Garage on Chestnut Street, Walter Johnson told a group of fans and reporters about the time he and Ty Cobb were arrested for speeding in Detroit.

"The cop told Ty he might let him off," Johnson said, "if he would hit a couple of homers the next day. I made the mistake of ribbing Ty about it, and what a mistake, because, by George, he did hit two against us!"

Grover Cleveland Alexander had drawn a crowd as well, giving players and fans alike an impromptu clinic on the grip he had used to win 373 big-league games.

"I threw my fastball with a twist that rolled the ball off the inside of my middle finger," he said. "Sort of a screwball. But when I reached spring training, my finger was tender and a blister always formed. I'd have to take it easy until the blister broke and a callus could form. Well, when the blister broke, the team always went out for a beer celebration. It meant that Ol' Pete was ready to start throw'n' 'em hard."

The concept of these baseball icons spreading out throughout the flag-decked town was unprecedented. It was the world's largest rolling fraternity party, carnival, college alumni reunion, and Elks

Lodge bash rolled into one. Schools had closed at 10:00 A.M.—stores would stay open until noon—leaving many of the neighborhood kids to prowl the streets trying to collect as many ballplayer autographs as they could. That seemed appropriate, thought many of the legends and current players themselves, and before long, they, too, were collecting signatures of one another with all the eagerness of the kids.

Some were even taking home movies, a novel concept at the time. Johnny Vander Meer did his best to capture the morning on camera, as did slugging Tigers outfielder Hank Greenberg, and Red Sox catcher Moe Berg. Continuing to chronicle this impromptu baseball country fair were the newspaper reporters, an all-star cast themselves, each hoping to add detail to their summaries for the next day's papers.

This meant that little if anything that these famous ballplayers could say or do in Cooperstown would be off the record. Every trip to the grocery store or newsstand on this day was news—rare for reporters who in those days seldom wrote about the lives of ballplayers away from the field. At Gage Barbershop, in fact, business was so good—rare for a Tuesday morning—that a line had formed when Babe Ruth popped in, hoping to be next for a shave. But not even The Babe, with his chronic bustle and impatience, could butt in. He'd have to wait in line like everyone else.

That wouldn't do, and as suddenly as The Babe, dressed in a light suit, open collar, white shoes, and socks that wouldn't stay up, entered the barber shop, he was gone, as were the trail of children he always seemed to attract. The barber just shook his head: "To think I almost shaved Babe Ruth," he said with a sigh.

Not losing a step, Ruth then disappeared into a drugstore to replenish his cigar supply. "Funny thing is," The Babe said to no one in particular and perhaps thinking ahead to what he'd say at the ceremony, "I pitched my first big-league game just twenty-five years ago, minus one day."

That was pretty good for The Babe, who had trouble remembering names and dates—he still called his wife, Claire, "Clara"—but seemed to be getting into the nostalgic spirit of the day. So was Boston Bees manager Casey Stengel as he gazed on the phenomenon of the great second basemen Collins and Napoleon Lajoie, killing time by jawing with Charley Gehringer and Billy Herman, perhaps the two best second basemen of the day.

"Since when," says Stengel, gesturing to the four, "did you see four second basemen as good as those fellows collected in one spot?"

◆   ◆   ◆

Traffic came to gridlock as more and more spectators streamed into town, leaving the cars on the edge of the road and heading to Main Street for the festivities. Reaching this remote part of upstate New York had been a tad complicated for some of the ballplayers, particularly those from American League teams that had played out west the previous day, some of whom had reached Cooperstown by rental car after taking the train to Albany or Utica.

Recognizing the historical significance of the day, they were happy to be there. Indeed, the presence of these baseball gods had humbled many a baseball figure. On the train to Utica was the great Cy Young, traveling from his farm in central Ohio. Sliding into an open seat next to the 532-game winner was baseball's commissioner, Judge Kenesaw Mountain Landis, on his way to Cooperstown from Chicago and a man whose wiry frame masked a titanic ego.

"May I sit beside you?" the Judge asked Young with a rare humility that baseball officials were still buzzing about the next day.

Young looked at Landis, and nodded. "If you behave yourself," he said.

But Landis wasn't killing time before the formal festivities on Main Street kicked off. After breakfast, he hustled with grave purpose down to the Cooperstown Post Office, directly across from the new Hall. Striding through the front door, Landis encountered another mob—several lines, actually—gathered to buy the special-issue postcards bearing the hundredth-anniversary, three-cent stamp with the Cooperstown postmark. Gruffly excusing his way to the front of the line, Landis, his small head dwarfed by the red, white, and blue baseball cap, was forgiven: It seemed right that the high ruler of baseball should be in front. And with that, Landis, forever with a stern sense of occasion, plucked down three copper pennies, pushed the money under the grill, and bought the first stamp celebrating baseball's Centennial, also known as the Cavalcade.

Selling him a postcard was Postmaster General Jim Farley, who had arrived on the train from New York, but skipped the breakfast in order to get to the post office early. Farley's presence put a government seal on the proceedings—and he had been an enthused participant from the get-go, overseeing preparation of the stamp with considerable gusto and ceremony.

The idea of a commemorative stamp had been kicking around since 1937 when members of the Board of Directors of the Cooperstown Chamber of Commerce had developed the idea with the enthusiastic backing of the local Leatherstocking Stamp Club. Given the proper advertising, they saw creation of the stamp as a genuine moneymaker—figuring the stamp club could sell twenty thousand of the first-day covers, and turn over most of the profits to the Chamber. As it turned out, their estimate was low, and in the end, more than 450,000 baseball stamps and as many first-day covers were sold in one day—second only to the record 585,000 first-day New York World's Fair covers sold earlier in the year.

Farley had been met at the train by Cooperstown postmaster Melvin Bundy, and had immediately doffed one of the red, white, and blue baseball caps before heading directly to Gage Barbershop for a shave, and then to the post office. The postmaster general was an early advocate of the special stamp, having jumped on board back in February when he gave up a trip to the West Coast in order to formally announce the issuance of the Centennial stamp—the first to commemorate a sport. Speaking to more than eleven hundred people at the annual dinner of the New York baseball writers at the Commodore Hotel in Manhattan, Farley had reminded his audience that U.S. stamps cannot use the likeness of a living person, and threw open the competition for a stamp design.

Several designs had been considered, perhaps the most popular an artist's rendition of the late Christy Mathewson, with his striking good looks and regal bearing. But just before the start of the 1939 regular season, Farley wisely avoided any whiff of favoritism by selecting a rectangular image of baseball as it would have been in the early days. It showed a group of boys playing baseball on a village green with what appears to be a barn, a house, and a church in the background. To the left of the drawing was a small window with the superimposed image of a catcher's mask in the center, crossed bats in the back, and the inscription, "1839 to 1939."

Most liked the stamp's nostalgic take on the game. But in a letter to the *Sporting News,* one fan grumbled that this seemingly early depiction of a baseball game showed fielders wearing mitts whereas most players in those days went bare-handed. The fan wasn't done, and went on to point out that, in the early days, a mitt-wearing catcher was branded a "sissy."

But those details were all but forgotten amidst the crush at the post office to buy the commemorative postcard. Postal officials had prepared well—bringing in sixty extra men and women who had started Sunday and used a special canceling machine to prepare the orders, many of which came in from stamp dealers across the country. Not only did it seem that most of the estimated 15,000 people in Cooperstown that day wanted a first-day cover for themselves, but they wanted Farley to sign it. The postmaster general did his best, quickly letting the post office clerks take over the sales, and standing to the side, signing every cover thrust his way—and marking an early foray into the baseball memorabilia craze. He did so until well after the ceremonies had started, saved only by his merciful departure for a political gathering—a lunchtime clambake for the Otsego County Democrats.

◆　◆　◆

Old photographs of Stephen C. Clark, Jr. show a gruff, unsmiling man who looked as if he'd rather be anywhere but in front of the camera. But for all Clark's apparent discomfort with getting his picture taken, he was a gracious, patrician figure who took his family's philanthropic heritage to heart and became the true guiding light behind baseball's gala celebration and its Hall of Fame.

Clark was born in an era and to a class in which wealth and public service were synonymous. Whereas his siblings dropped most of their ties to Cooperstown, Stephen Clark maintained a deep and abiding interest in helping his hometown, and certainly came well prepared for the role: A graduate of Yale and Columbia Law School, he was a true renaissance man, later serving in the New York State Assembly, as vice president of the Safe Deposit Company of New York, and as a director of the Singer company. In World War I, he rose to the rank of lieutenant colonel and earned the Distinguished Service Medal. Back home after the war, he expanded upon an early interest in art and joined his brother Robert on an art-buying trip to Europe.

But Stephen Clark's heart wasn't in Europe, or even in New York City, where he became a well-known art patron and for a time used the top floor of his apartment on East Seventieth Street as a gallery. It was in Cooperstown, whose economy and long-term sustainability he set forth to expand and secure for the future. Quietly and diligently, Clark created the foundation that bears his family's name and poured funding into the town's recreation center, hospital, and scholarship program for local high school graduates; other branches of the far-flung family ran "Clark's Clothing Store" at 88 Main Street and "Clark's" luncheonette at the entrance to Doubleday Field. Meanwhile, Stephen Clark built museums and worked to preserve the town's rural small-town charm—so much so that, today, it's hard to find a neon sign in town, the result of a tough ordinance, on the books for years. Indeed, nightfall in Cooperstown really is a throwback, with Main Street lit with only the aid of storefronts and streetlamps.

When, in 1920, blight ravaged the region's hops crop, Clark started looking for alternatives to farming for economic stability in and around Cooperstown. Tourism was his answer—and the key to creating the Hall of Fame. How ironic, then, that for all his wide-ranging interests, Clark knew next to nothing about baseball, and at first needed to be convinced that the sport was a means to draw tourists to the area. Enter one Alexander Cleland, a Glasgow-born social worker who very much had Clark's ear.

Cleland had known Clark since 1931 when he took over as director of the Clark House, a settlement house on the Lower East

Side of Manhattan. Founded by the Clark Foundation, the house provided new immigrants with temporary housing and aid in finding a job. It was while working there that Cleland found he shared Clark's genuine passion for charity work, and developed a real admiration for the community commitment of his wealthy employer. They shared something else as well: Cleland never much cared for baseball, either.

Cleland had immigrated to the United States in 1903, taking a job in Chicago as industrial secretary for the central YMCA. Three years later, he arrived in New York, where he plunged into immigrant issues—taking a series of positions for the Dillingham Federal Immigration Commission, the New York, and eventually the New Jersey immigration commissions. By 1913, he had moved on to prison reform, and during World War I, oversaw the distribution of food, lodging, and entertainment for soldiers stationed in and around New York City. It is likely that Cleland's work would have continued along similar patterns, even after he took over the Clark House, had it not been for a fateful trip to Cooperstown in 1934.

The trip started out routinely enough—a quick jaunt by train to Cooperstown to visit Clark to discuss Clark House matters. What the two men spent most of their time talking about that pleasant Saturday in May is lost to history. What endured is Cleland's epiphany after leaving Clark and taking a leisurely stroll through town before catching his train back to New York City.

Passing the ball field just off Main Street in the center of town, Cleland noticed several construction workers hauling dirt on to the property. They were working on the renovation of Doubleday Field, named for former resident and Civil War general Abner Doubleday, who was said to have invented baseball in town. As Cleland stopped to watch, one of the workers asked what he thought of the village's plans for celebrating baseball's Centennial, still five years away. Cleland admitted he hadn't heard much about it, so really couldn't provide much of a response. Well, that was a shame, the construction worker added, because people in town were really looking forward to the celebration should Cooperstown actually pull it off.

On the train back to New York, Cleland found himself thinking about what the construction worker had said. He asked himself: What exactly was being planned for this baseball celebration? Had the game really gotten its start in Cooperstown? Could it be that this celebration of baseball, of all things, might attract tourists to the area? What about adding something permanent to the Centennial like a baseball museum? Cleland wondered if the baseball establishment would ever support such an idea.

Cleland pondered those questions the rest of the weekend. By Monday, he had crystallized his thoughts: Convinced that baseball could boost Cooperstown's fortunes, Cleland believed that a museum created to celebrate the history of the game could be a real lure for the game's fans. Back in the office Monday, Cleland wrote up a proposal for Clark focusing on "a building on Doubleday Field where a collection of all past, present, and future historical data of the game could be shown." And he outlined "an interesting museum" full of photos and "funny old uniforms," along with ceremonial baseballs thrown out by presidents and the bats of baseball heroes.

Cleland figured he could present the idea to the Baseball Writers Association of America who could help generate enthusiasm for the idea. To cover the construction costs and maintenance of such a museum, he proposed that the baseball establishment provide a portion of the profits from the World Series or through a benefit game similar to the major league All-Star Game started two years before by Chicago sportswriter Arch Ward.

The idea of a museum dedicated to a sport was a stretch in the mid-1930s, but Cleland had some degree of precedent on his side—the thematic Hall of Fame for Great Americans museum in New York City. Opened in 1900 by New York University chancellor Dr. Henry Mitchell MacCracken, the "Hall of Fame," as it was dubbed, was an elegant 630-foot open-air colonnade designed by the celebrated architect Stanford White that housed the bronzed busts of ninety-eight distinguished Americans from George Washington to Robert E. Lee, Alexander Graham Bell, and Eli Whitney. The Hall of Fame, still viewable at what it now Bronx Community College, showed that an offbeat museum could be done with elegance and style.

Cleland wasn't a baseball fan, but he was a sportsman with a keen appreciation for the pull of the game on the nation's conscience. As a youngster in Scotland, his hero had been one Sandy McMahon, star forward of the Glasgow Celtic, the New York Yankees of Scottish soccer. Years later while traveling across the Atlantic, Cleland encountered McMahon waiting tables on an ocean liner. It had been a long, sad fall for the onetime hero of Scotland, but Cleland and some fellow passengers were thrilled to have the time to chat, and McMahon, once known as the "Prince of Dribbles," had been engaging and tickled to be remembered. Before leaving the ship, Cleland helped put together a small purse to help McMahon regain his feet, and the experience stuck with him: Perhaps his Cooperstown plan could include some way of remembering and helping older, indigent ballplayers.

With the memory of meeting Sandy McMahon very much on his mind, Cleland poured heavy doses of nostalgia into his proposal, arguing that fathers would flock to Cooperstown to "show the building to their sons and perhaps throw a baseball or two on the

Field." He anticipated that the concept, with proper publicity, could raise funds for old players, while attracting "hundreds of visitors . . . to the shopping district right in the heart of Cooperstown." The village would benefit, he said, as would the baseball clubs "from a publicity point of view."

That virtually everything detailed in Cleland's report came true made his organizational blueprint a remarkable document. Just as important were Cleland's skills in striking the right chords with those who could make the dream happen. Clark quickly endorsed the plan, and together with Cleland, set forth on the considerable task of trying to win over baseball's hierarchy.

◆　◆　◆

Just before noon, everything for the ceremony was nearly set. Crossing the street from the post office to the handsome red-brick edifice of the Hall of Fame and National Baseball Museum, Judge Landis ambled through the throngs—police were now estimating that 15,000 people—five times the population of Cooperstown— packed the little town. Earning one of the day's long-distance awards was eighteen-year-old Frank McCusky, who had spent most of the week since he'd graduated from high school in Minneapolis hitchhiking the 1,200 miles or so to Cooperstown just to see the festivities; arriving in Cooperstown at 10:00 P.M., Saturday, he had spent two nights at the home of Mr. and Mrs. Albert Coleman at 14 Delaware Street. Most stood, but others in the back climbed trees and sat on car tops for a better view of the raised wooden platform caked with red, white, and blue bunting outside the museum, where just about anyone who was anyone in the baseball world was about to congregate.

The sheer volume of the crowd would be enough to overwhelm Cooperstown's two-man police force—a day and a night officer—so a handful of officers were brought in from Utica as well as the state police. But baseball officials had thought ahead and imported several plainclothes Pinkertons to roam the crowd and look for pickpockets. That all of four people were arrested—all were from New York City and with long criminal records—is testament to the atmosphere of mostly well-behaved fans. All four men were taken to Otsego County Jail, fined $50, and released the next day.

The plan was for Landis, other baseball officials, and the new Hall of Famers to emerge one by one from the doors of the new museum to a platform and say a few words into the NBC microphones, due to carry the ceremony nationwide. Afterward, they'd take their seats, and pose for photos. For a few minutes prior to noon, then, the baseball legends, by now inside the Hall, killed time by wandering among the rooms of vintage baseball relics—and wondering when Ty Cobb was going to show.

The live broadcast was a compelling reason to start on time. So were Landis's dictatorial powers and perpetual frown—enough to prompt everyone into action. It worked, and bang on the stroke of noon, the gathering instantly turned formal when the Cooperstown High School Band launched into "The Star Spangled Banner." Then Charles "Chilly" Doyle of the Pittsburgh *Sun-Telegraph*, and president of the Baseball Writers Association of America, stepped to the microphone and soberly announced, "Today in Cooperstown, New York, home of baseball, we gather in reverence to the game's immortals—living and dead," before launching into a story of how a Civil War-era Union general named Abner Doubleday had invented baseball in Cooperstown. Who cared that the tale was pure hokum? It had served its purpose—and baseball's great day had started, with only a parade of officials to get through before the crowd was allowed a look at the immortals. Mayor Spraker spoke briefly, inviting the world to visit Cooperstown. Then former NL president John Heydler introduced Landis, who with great ceremony, stepped forward and announced the Hall of Fame as officially open.

"Nowhere, other than at its birthplace, could this museum be appropriately situated," thundered the seventy-one-year-old iron-fisted overseer of baseball. "To the pioneers who were the moving spirits of the game in its infancy and to the players who have been nominated into the Hall of Fame by the Baseball Writers Association of America, we pay tribute. But I should like to dedicate this museum to all America."

When first approached to throw his support to the concept of the Hall of Fame, Landis was not enthused. But once he realized the public relations benefit it could bring to a sport that could use a boost, he had become a champion. Landis was an old hand at using his steely gaze and blustery, sandpaper voice to earn respect with a touch of fear. Late in 1920 with baseball consumed by a gambling epidemic, big-league owners had turned to Landis, convinced his hard-boiled manner was just the tonic the game needed to regain its integrity. He took the job.

The son of a Civil War Union surgeon who had lost a leg to a Confederate cannonball, Landis was named for the Georgia battle-field where his father had served. Wiry and slight in stature, Landis had a chiseled face and a gravelly voice that made everything he said sound important. He seldom smiled and had a titanic ego that reflected what baseball historian Robert Smith called "a pathological urge to flaunt his power." Appointed to the bench in 1905 by President Theodore Roosevelt, Landis issued rulings that were hard to categorize. His list of dislikes was long, ranging from big corporations to organized crime. He loathed socialists and union organizers, whom he labeled "filthy, slimy rats." And perhaps most of all, Landis had it in for business tycoons like John D. Rockefeller, whom he browbeat on the stand in 1916 in a case that led to a $29 million antitrust judgment against Standard Oil. When the sentence was reversed by a higher court, Landis was unmoved: "To hell with the law," he sniffed. "I know what's right."

As commissioner, Landis demanded and received dictatorial powers, unparalleled in any other sport—and a lifetime contract with an annual $100,000 salary to go with it. Landis quickly and decisively dealt with the guilty White Sox, dubbed the "Black Sox"—overlooking their acquittal in court and imposing a lifetime ban on the seven ballplayers, including the great Shoeless Joe Jackson, who admitted they had lost intentionally. He also banned one more, Sox third baseman Buck Weaver, who knew about the fix, but had played his heart out in the Series and swore to his dying day that he had never taken a dime from gamblers. To Landis, Weaver's offense was that he hadn't finked on his teammates; continually applying for reinstatement until he passed away in 1956, Weaver was turned down every time.

Landis's hard line on gambling earned admirers and restored much of baseball's luster. But the commissioner's reaction to race was more unfortunate: Black players would simply not appear in a major league game as long as he was around. That meant gifted Negro Leaguers like Josh Gibson, Cool Papa Bell, and Judy Johnson, who would have been stars in the majors, would never get the chance to play for a big-league team. The commissioner died in November 1944; only eleven months later, Branch Rickey of the Dodgers signed Jackie Robinson.

Back in Cooperstown, Landis kept his remarks brief. Then the Cooperstown High School Band broke into "Take Me Out to the Ballgame" and the league presidents, Will Harridge of the American League and Ford Frick of the National League, put their fingers through two pairs of scissors and snipped the red, white, and blue ribbon across the door to the museum in half. The Hall was officially open for business.

A few pieces of ceremony remained. Cooperstown Centennial Committee Chairman Theodore Lettis presented a ceremonial key to the museum. Up hopped Chilly Doyle, who to muffled drums, read off the names of deceased players and officials elected to the Hall of Fame. There were the officials, Morgan G. Bulkeley and Ban Johnson; player-manager John McGraw; builders like Albert Spalding, Alexander Cartwright, Charles Comiskey, and "Father" Henry Chadwick; and players, Buck Ewing, Candy Cummings, "Old Hoss" Radbourne, and Cap Anson. And with that came one final name—a manager, a builder, a former player, and very much alive . . . "Connie Mack," intoned Doyle, just as the door to the Hall of Fame suddenly swung open, and the tall, thin, neatly-tailored figure of the seventy-six-year-old Mack headed rigidly toward the microphones. So this is what everyone had come to see.

♦   ♦   ♦

On the surface, Henry Chadwick and Albert Spalding had little in common. Yet it was the enduring friendship of these passionate baseball entrepreneurs—and their very public disagreement about its origins—that set the stage for the birth of the game's mythology and the baseball museum that followed.

Chadwick was the older of the two. A native of Devonshire,

England, the sports-minded Chadwick had emigrated in 1837 as a teenager with his journalist father and family to Brooklyn. By the early 1850s, the twenty-something Chadwick was a journalist himself, covering cricket matches for a number of New York area papers. Then, in 1856, as Chadwick was on his way to Jersey City to cover a cricket match, he saw something that would change his life—a group of young men playing "base ball." This fresh American version of what had been rounders so captivated Chadwick that he would dedicate the rest of his professional life to promoting it.

By 1858, Chadwick had become the young game's missionary, a "Johnny Appleseed" of baseball publicity and chronicler of this new American phenomenon. Traveling to all points of New York to cover baseball, he supplied most of the area's major papers with so much baseball coverage under the moniker "Unkle Harry" that he wore them out; whereas in the early days, most papers took three or four lines on each game, Unkle Harry's efforts for more than twenty newspapers and magazines proved so exhaustive that by the 1870s most papers had hired their own baseball reporters. But Chadwick didn't stop there, and helped by his gregarious and engaging personality, was soon advising anyone who would listen about changes in the rules, how to combat gamblers, and even developing one of the staples of baseball—the box score. His 1868 study, *The Game of Base Ball*, is considered to be the first book on the game.

As the first great pitcher of this new game, Albert Spalding was the recipient of Chadwick's glowing praise for his conduct on and off the field. A star from the start, Spalding burst onto early professional baseball in 1871 at the age of twenty, became the first pitcher to win two hundred games, and led the Boston Red Stockings to four consecutive championships. "Big Al," wrote Chadwick, "is intelligent and gentlemanly . . . [and] conducts himself in a manner well calculated to remove the public's bad impressions as to professional ball tossers, created by swearing, gambling specimens from the black sheep of the flock."

At a time when many professional players were frowned on as ne'er-do-wells and unwelcome in better hotels, Spalding was different —more than just an extraordinary player, he was a responsible ambassador and a role model of the game. It also didn't hurt that he was handsome in a stern, manly kind of way—"his face is that of a Greek hero," the *New York Times* wrote—and had a quick mind that saw entrepreneurial possibilities in baseball that would flourish well beyond his career on the diamond. An icon in baseball-mad Boston, Spalding in 1875 went an unfathomable 54–5—at one point, winning twenty-four games in a row—and, lured by a $500 raise and a promise of a quarter of the gate receipts, bolted Boston for the Chicago White Stockings, where in 1876, he won another forty-seven games.

Spalding's star was bright. But as quickly as he had enjoyed what the game had to offer, the wear and tear started to take a toll at a relatively young age. In 1877, Spalding, only twenty-six, pitched four games—winning one—and abruptly quit to take his chances as a full-time baseball promoter. Borrowing $800 from his mother, Spalding opened a sporting goods business on Broadway in New York City, using his considerable connections and business sense to pay the National League $1 for every dozen balls its teams used so he could plug his product as the "official" league ball. Before long, he was producing hats, uniforms and mitts, as well as equipment for golf, boxing, croquet, and even clog dancing.

The Spalding Sporting Goods Company boomed—and along the way, Al Spalding became not just a business magnate, but a master of spin control for the strenuous, healthy life, a kind of notable, quotable forerunner to the gospel of exercise as preached later by President Theodore Roosevelt. "The pursuit of baseball is that of a healthy, recreative exercise, alike for the mind and body, suitable to all classes of our people," Spalding gushed. "To the adult as well as the mere boy, there can be no longer room for surprise that such a game should reach the unprecedented popularity that the American game of baseball has attained."

Spalding brought in his brothers, opened a store in Chicago and "depots of supplies" across the country. Meantime, he kept his hand in the game as manager of the White Stockings, running his team and his business from a private box in Chicago's Congress Street Grounds, outfitted with a gong to summon servants and a telephone. After the 1888 season, Spalding and his mother led the White Stockings and a group of all-stars on an unprecedented baseball tour around the world in which they tried throwing baseballs over the Great Pyramid in Egypt, met the Prince of Wales in Britain, and were toasted by Mark Twain on their arrival back in New York.

Critical to Spalding's soaring success was the company's annual baseball guide. Edited by Chadwick, the guide was the game's first stat sheet, and featured everything from the big-league schedules to features on top players, the rules, and of course, ads for Spalding equipment. The guide did for Spalding what the catalog did for Sears—spreading his name and products to every nook and cranny of America.

The game thrived. So did Spalding, whose guides became an annual rite of spring. For years, Chadwick had free reign on the content, even when it came to the origins of the game, which he argued had sprung from the English game of rounders. Nobody seemed to mind very much until 1903, when in that year's Baseball Guide, Chadwick launched into detail to commemorate what he claimed was the game's seventieth anniversary. As it turned out, his essay would become the opening salvo of a protracted debate about how baseball had started.

Chadwick traced the game's origins back to 1833 in Philadelphia and what he claimed was the first organized baseball club, the Olympic Town Ball Club. In hindsight, Chadwick was mostly right: While the Philadelphians weren't yet playing what we would recognize today as modern baseball, his evolutionary theory of the game and time period were on target. In fact, there were several versions of what became baseball at the time: Generally called "town ball," the game had been played from the 1820s throughout New England, using a four-sided field with bases at each corner, with the rule that runners were out if struck by the ball. It was a suitable forerunner to the similar "New York" game that a young Manhattan shipping clerk named Alexander Cartwright would perfect a decade or so later.

Chadwick knew what he was talking about. He had played rounders as a young man in England, and seen baseball take off in the United States and considered it the most American of games. All he was emphasizing was the game's British origins—a fact that Spalding chose to highlight and dispute. While the two remained friends—Chadwick bequeathed his extensive baseball library to Spalding in hopes he'd write a history of the game—their argument had gone public.

Just why Spalding was so adamant in his denial that baseball was anything but purely American in origin was mostly personal. As a business tycoon, he had grown used to following his gut—and didn't tolerate dissent. Scholarship be damned; the game that had made him rich and famous simply had to be American, he figured, and probably evolved from "old cat," the old colonial stick and ball game.

"As no other form of sport," Spalding wrote, "[baseball] is exponent of American Courage, Confidence, Combativeness: American Dash, Discipline, Determination," and so forth. Spalding even threw in "American Vim, Vigor [and] Virility," but offered little evidence or scholarship to support his claim. He was right, he said, and that was that.

Spalding was also a man of his time. The cricket theory challenged his platform as an American role model, and underscored the country's growing swagger as a world economic power, which included hefty doses of flag waving and anti-British sentiment. "To deny the native roots of America's foremost game was equivalent in the minds of many to ideological blasphemy," writes James Vlasich in his scholarly book about the Hall of Fame, *A Legend for the Legendary*. And quite possibly, Spalding may have still been miffed at the mixed reception his 1888–89 Round-the-World all-star baseball tour had received in England, where the Prince of Wales had watched them play: The pitcher had such an overwhelming advantage against the hitter, one critic had written, "that our English love of fair play is offended . . . [and] for this reason, baseball will never be popular in England."

So just where did baseball begin? Spalding intended to use his considerable influence to explain it his way.

⚾ CHAPTER 3 ⚾

"Dear Mr. Spalding . . . The American Game of Baseball Was Invented by Abner Doubleday"

Walking stiffly to the podium, seventy-seven-year-old Connie Mack was an appropriate person to kick off baseball's greatest day. Gangly and dignified in his stiff collar and dark suit, he looked more like a church deacon than a baseball icon. In a sense, he was—a man whose conservative ways and formality had always clashed against baseball's rowdier elements, and triumphed, having guided his Philadelphia A's to nine American League pennants and five World Series titles.

"I feel greatly honored in being here today where our first national game was started," Mack said. "I want to express my appreciation to the people of Cooperstown, New York, for having the game of baseball started here. And I want to express my sincere thanks for having my name enrolled with the other great stars of baseball and with all of those who have taken part in promoting the interest of baseball for the past hundred years. And I am quite positive in the years ahead that we can look forward to the game progressing. . . . Thank you."

Pick an early baseball event, and it's likely Mack was there. When, in 1888, the Washington Senators became the first big-league team to travel to Florida for spring training, "four of the fourteen players were reasonably sober, the rest were totally drunk," as Mack, then an obscure young catcher on the team, put it. "There was a fight every night," he said of the trip to Jacksonville in which the team stayed in a fleabag hotel on the edge of town. "The boys broke a lot of furniture."

But not Mack. "When he set out," wrote Wilfrid Sheed, "ballplayers were considered lower than even actors, and Mack was the type who could get them into the hotel and assure you they were all good boys and get them out by midnight." It was a sign of things to come—taking over as manager of the Pirates and later the A's, he always wore a suit while managing his team from the dugout, giving him the look, as Shied wrote, of "a funny kind of saint," a man who seemed more like the local pharmacist than a crafty big leaguer.

At 6'1" and only 150 pounds, Cornelius Alexander McGillicuddy of East Brookfield, Massachusetts, seemed too slight to be a ballplayer. While the young man went against his father in choosing his career—"Why don't you get into something more lasting?" McGillicuddy the elder had told him—he always carried with him the quality of small-town New England rectitude. Mercifully shortening his name to "Connie Mack," the young catcher caught on in 1884 with Meridan, a midsize city in the Connecticut State League, and reached the big leagues two years later as a catcher with Washington.

From the get-go, he was different. He drank, but not a lot. He didn't smoke or swear. Most of all, Mack used his smarts to compensate for being a beanpole by developing an arsenal of tricks, from freezing the baseballs overnight to keep an opponents' best hitters from slugging the ball to chatting up the batters to distract them, and occasionally even tipping the bat just before the hitter swung. Mack proved an early testament to why substitute catchers often make good managers—they sit, watch, and study the pitchers. Mack proved so adept at all of the above that the Pirates, to whom he was traded in 1891, made him their manager three years later. Mack served as Pittsburgh's player-manager for three years, never rising above sixth, and retired after eleven years with a .245 lifetime average when the Pirates fired him.

Mack would never again be fired. In 1897, Ban Johnson, then running the Western League, asked him to manage the Milwaukee club. Looking to brighten the game's image, Johnson thought Mack had just the right blend of dignity and baseball smarts to take the position. Mack managed there for four years—staying on when Johnson wheeled and dealed, and in 1901, turned his minor league into the American League. Johnson awarded the Philadelphia franchise to Mack, who had become enough of an operator himself that he arranged with team owner Benjamin Shibe to bite off a one-quarter ownership share of the team.

By 1939, Mack had managed the A's nonstop for thirty-eight years, becoming a baseball legend in the process. Some years his teams were bad—really bad—while other years, they were great—extraordinarily great—especially the A's from 1910 to 1914, the heart of which was their "$100,000 infield" of Eddie Collins, Frank "Home Run" Baker, Stuffy McInnis, and Jack Barry. Players respected Mack because he treated them like men, and tolerated a lot—having a particular soft spot for eccentrics like Rube Waddell, the great pitcher who chased fire trucks, bolted the team for days on end, and was probably retarded. The great A's team of 1929 cussed so excessively and so loudly that it was clearly audible to fans in the stands, and Judge Landis issued an edict for them to calm down. But for every foul-mouthed ruffian, Mack went to campus to look for college-educated ballplayers, among them Eddie Collins of Columbia, Jack Coombs of Colby College, Eddie Plank of Gettysburg College, and Chief Bender of the Carlisle Indian School. All were "boys who knew their geometry and trigonometry," Mack said, "ballplayers" who "put intelligence into the game" and helped make winners of the A's.

Mack's contribution was a quiet, steady hand—and a style all his own. Managing while dressed in a tie and a skimmer, Mack directed his players by pointing with a rolled-up program and never seemed ruffled. Most of all, Mack earned respect, and in contrast to a feisty, vulgar manager like John McGraw of the Giants, got an audience when disputing an umpire's call with class.

Once, when umpire Bill McGowan called an A's runner out in a close play at third, Mack strode out to discuss the situation. "That man looked safe to me, Mr. McGowan," said Mr. Mack, offering the odd sight of a man in street clothes on the ball field.

"No, Mr. Mack, he was out," said Mr. McGowan. "I wouldn't lie to you, Mr. Mack."

Well, that sounded reasonable, figured Mr. Mack. "No, you wouldn't, Mr. McGowan," he said. "Thank you, Mr. McGowan."

His distinctive style gave Mack the reputation of baseball's great puritan, helped by his solid Yankee roots. Some of it was deserved—his players never called him "Skip" but simply "Mr. Mack"—and he was universally regarded with awe. But Mack wasn't a saint, as he was so often portrayed, and had both a temper and a brusque assessment of baseball talent. As carefully as he took years to build a powerful team, he was just as apt, some said, to rid the A's of any player even rumored to be on a gambler's take. Asked by a reporter at Yankee

Stadium about the rumor that the A's were after Detroit outfielder Dick Wakefield, Mack, still managing at a time when most people his age had long since retired, snapped he wasn't worth even thinking about.

"I don't want him," Mack said with evident crankiness. "He's half a ballplayer. I don't want half a ballplayer."

On the other hand, Mack could be remarkably magnanimous— partial to his own players, particularly those from his early years, and quick to praise those he felt deserved it. Asked to evaluate the young Joe DiMaggio, who by 1939 had become the game's great young star, Mack said simply, "DiMaggio is the best . . . he's the greatest team player I've ever seen."

It was vintage Mack, as were his brief and understated remarks, delivered in his distinctive New England accent to the crowd that now stood cheek by jowl all the way down Main Street past the flag-pole in the middle of town. Thunderous applause greeted the end of his minute-long delivery, and he went to take a seat on stage. It had become clear what the program would entail—with each of the leg-ends, the ultimate lineup, set to emerge from the doors of the Hall and give some remarks.

For baseball fans, even thinking of their collective contributions inspired awe, more so than any all-star team before or since. Today it seems that for every two or three players who make it to the Hall of Fame on the first ballot comes the borderline Hall of Famer for whom membership takes years and requires the intervention of the Veterans' Committee. Not so this group, whose credentials were downright unworldly, occupying an honored place in baseball's strat-osphere. Of these ten living legends beyond Mack—it would have been eleven except that Ty Cobb still wasn't there—three were pitchers who had cumulatively won 1,296 games—an *average* of 432—thrown four no-hitters, and each played at least twenty-one big-league seasons. Numbers of the six men, elected as position players, were just as scary—an average lifetime average of .337, playing careers between twenty-one and twenty-five years, and an astounding collection of records, from Babe Ruth's 714 home runs to Eddie Collins's record fourteen World Series stolen bases. (For the record, this group wasn't the first class to be voted into the Hall of Fame, but comprised all eleven of the living immortals of the first twenty-five elected to date. Voting had kicked off in 1936, when Cobb, Ruth, Wagner, and Johnson had been among the first five elected. Lajoie, Young, Speaker, and Mack made it in '37; Alexander in '38, and Sisler and Collins in '39.)

Ranging in age from Ruth at forty-four to Mack's seventy-seven, they looked to the uninitiated like any gathering of Rotarians—middle-aged and older men; mostly well dressed, particularly Eddie Collins with his dudelike, multicolored shoes and double-breasted suit. They were comfortable in the public glare—though not prone to speeches—and mellowed by age and comfort. Larry Lajoie even had a good suntan. But they were baseball royalty, and suitably for this most American of games, natives of New England, the industrial heartland, the rural South, and the Midwest. They comprised several ethnicities, as many regional accents—and the sweep of baseball history dating clear back to 1890, Young's first season when Benjamin Harrison was president and ballplayers wore tiny mitts that looked like flimsy mittens. The Hall had been built and they had come. All in all, baseball's big day was shaping up nicely.

◆　◆　◆

The dictionary defines a "legend" as "a story handed down for generations and popularly regarded as history." Legends can begin most anywhere, and spread by repeated telling or rumor, particularly when delivered by a forceful personality. So it went with Albert Spalding's contention that baseball could not have started anywhere but in America.

In 1903, when Henry Chadwick put forth his theory that the game developed from the English game of rounders, Albert Spalding was no longer just an ex-ballplayer selling sports equipment. He was a bona fide big shot, a business tycoon used to getting his way and given to windy pronouncements on how to succeed in business and in life. "The magnate must be a strong man among strong men," he said. "Everything is possible to him who dares."

In the 1905 *Spalding's Official Baseball Guide*, Spalding delivered his formal rebuttal to Chadwick—timing his revisionist argument to mark the sixtieth anniversary of the Knickerbockers baseball club of New York, but offering no real evidence to his claim. Arguing that the original Knickerbockers should be the ones "honored and remembered as the founders of our national game," Spalding then took another step—deciding to establish a self-appointed committee to agree or renounce his theory. Their answer, he said, "would be accepted by everyone as final; and conclusive."

Or so it seemed. The committee Spalding assembled was a powerful collection of sportsmen-turned-business leaders who happened to be men he knew well. Its chair was Abraham G. Mills, a Civil War-era ballplayer, National League president from 1882 to 1884, attorney, and Otis Elevator Company executive. Joining him were two U.S. senators, Maryland's Arthur Gorman and Connecticut's Morgan Bulkeley, the National League's first president. Rounding out the committee was another former National League president, Nicholas Young; the president of the Amateur Athletic Union; and sporting goods mavens Albert Reach and George Wright, a former

Cincinnati Red Stocking; James Sullivan, who published Spalding's guides, was secretary.

As impressive as this collection appeared on paper, they were the classic "rubber stamp" committee. Back in 1889 at a New York banquet welcoming home Spalding's 'round-the-world baseball tour, Mills had thrown his support behind the antirounders crowd, stating, "Patriotism and research had established the fact that the game . . . was American in origin." Acting more like bleacherites at the Polo Grounds, his audience loudly agreed, greeting his remarks by crying, "No rounders!" So much for an "unbiased" view.

For all the group's success, you could hardly expect them to dispute Spalding, a man regularly referred to as the "baseball messiah" in the press. Nor were they prepared to devote the kind of diligence and attention to detail that this essentially academic exercise required. They gave their project lip service anyway, and with his essay in the 1905 *Guide*, Spalding invited anyone and everyone to write in and give their theory so "the actual origin and early history of the great American national game . . . may be settled for all time."

Chadwick had little faith his theory would be accepted, describing the commission's work as a "piece of special pleading, which lets my dear old friend Albert escape defeat." He plodded on anyway, sticking to his rounders theory in a 1907 letter to the commission. Arguing that rounders was played by two sides and used a ball that was pitched or tossed to an opposing batsman, Chadwick said that was more than enough to constitute "the basic principle of the American national game" of baseball.

Spalding held firm. Baseball "is so thoroughly in accord with our national characteristics and temperament," he said, "that this fact in itself tends to confirm my opinion that it is of purely American origin." Adding that "no other game or country has any right to claim its parentage," Spalding then resorted to his old theory that baseball stemmed not from rounders, but from the colonial game of "one old cat." How did he know? He just did, claiming that in playing one old cat, "some ingenious American lad naturally suggested that one thrower be placed in the center of the square."

You would think that for all the prestige of what became known as the Special Base Ball Commission, they would have hired researchers to examine old newspaper files, memoirs, and even children's books on games. But they did none of that, and in the end, chose to rely on Spalding's considerable sway, supported by anecdotal evidence in letters from old-timers scattered around the country.

But the Mills Commission even ignored most of the letters, except for one from an elderly Colorado miner named Abner Graves. The information provided in his letter gave weight to Spalding's claims, and became baseball's missing link, the DNA that for the Mills Commission confirmed its American origins in the tiny upstate New York hamlet of Cooperstown.

◆　◆　◆

The suit worked for Connie Mack. But it didn't fit the man who followed him out of the doors of the Hall of Fame and ambled toward the podium. The shoulders on Honus Wagner's black suit were too big, the shirt across his barrel chest a bit tight, and his tie's front loop was short, giving him the slightly disheveled look of your favorite eccentric uncle.

Honus Wagner wasn't meant to wear a suit. He had been the complete ballplayer, a man who should have been born in a baseball uniform, his cheek swollen with tobacco, and a Pirates cap slung at an angle across his forehead. Like Mack, Wagner didn't have the natural build of a ballplayer: At 5'11" and 200 pounds, he was considered too

husky to have much speed and was bowlegged—yes, bowlegged—
but led the National League six times in stolen bases. Equipped with
oversized, powerful hands and long arms, he looked more like a
blacksmith, and only became a shortstop in his seventh big-league
year, after stints at first, third, and the outfield. Once, Wagner took
two called strikes against a young Cardinals fireballer, and then rattled the pitcher by leaning over the plate and catching the next pitch
with his bare hand before throwing it back to the startled young
pitcher with the deflating comment: "Changeup, huh?" The umpire
called Wagner out, but the pitcher was so unnerved by the gesture
that he walked the next five batters, and the Pirates took the game.

John McGraw called Wagner the best all-around player he'd ever
seen, better than Cobb or Ruth. When a brash young Giant pitcher
asked McGraw how to pitch Wagner, the Giant skipper shrugged
and advised him to "just pitch—and duck." Wagner won eight
National League batting titles, too—standing deep in the batter's box
with a squatlike stance that made him look like he was sitting on a
barstool. Driving the ball to all fields, Wagner seldom slumped, and
in twenty-two years in the big leagues, compiled a lifetime average
of .329. To him, ending a rare slump was simple: "I'd look at my
feet," he said, "shift my feet a bit, and the hits would start coming."
In the field, Wagner was the game's most graceful shortstop, a man
with the tendency to go deep in the hole and uncork both the ball
and a handful of dust on a line to nail the runner at first.

These days, Honus—in Pittsburgh, he was just "Honus" and often
had trouble getting down the street for all the people who wanted to
stop him to talk baseball—liked nothing less than to talk shop with his
trademark modesty. Retired since 1917, Wagner certainly had the time
to talk, which he did with relish and a glint in his eye. In his first few
postbaseball years, he had prospered—marrying Bessie Smith of

Pittsburgh with whom he fathered two daughters, and continuing to play baseball and even basketball as a barnstormer. He coached both sports at Carnegie Tech in Pittsburgh for a time, and even did a stint working for the state legislature in Harrisburg. Then came the Depression, and a failed partnership with Pie Traynor at a Pittsburgh sporting goods company, a case of bad timing that showed Wagner was no businessman. He could have done more to trade on his famous name, but considering it beneath his dignity, he wasn't much interested. By 1933, the business had left him nearly destitute, when Pirates owner Bill Benswanger, the son-in-law of former Pirates owner Barney Dreyfuss, came calling to ask if he'd like to rejoin the club as a coach.

Would he ever. Back with the Pirates, Wagner became a popular pregame attraction. As he worked with the Pittsburgh infielders, scores of National League spectators took to showing up at the ballpark hours early just to watch infield practice and hoping they could catch a glimpse of the white-haired old man, his bow legs even more pronounced, uncork a few to first. It became a kind of game outside the regular game—and Wagner would often retreat after practice to the grandstand, where he'd sign autographs. He'd sign more—and tell more stories—on the banquet circuit at just about every Kiwanis Club or VFW outing in western Pennsylvania, making him, next to Babe Ruth, the game's most beloved ambassador.

Wagner's stories, well honed from the banquet circuit and occasionally true, spilled forth. Of the great Philadelphia A's pitcher and a former roommate, Rube Waddell, Wagner told of the time that Rube insisted on sleeping with the water running in the bathtub. Waddell, who lived near a roaring stream in Pennsylvania, contended that the splashing of water soothed him.

So, did Wagner choose to continue rooming with Waddell? "Not by a damn sight," said Honus.

Wagner insisted he'd once lost a home run because the ball he'd hit over the fence was coughed back onto the field by the huffing and puffing of a steam engine as it rounded the edge of the outfield. Then came the time when his dog ran onto the field, just as a ground ball was headed his way during a pickup game, and he heaved the dog instead of the ball to first—and "darned if the umpire didn't call the runner out!" More than schmaltzy, the stories revealed the surprisingly gentle character of a man who had triumphed in a hard game. Like Mack, Wagner had seldom argued with an umpire, a policy he preached to young players, and which was underscored in a story about a young Pirate pinch hitter named "Booe."

"What's your name?" asked the umpire, Bill Klem.

"Booe," the player answered.

"What did you say?" the umpire asked.

"Booe" came the reply, after which Pirate manager Fred Clarke, seeing what was happening, hastened to home plate, where he brandished a scorecard bearing Everett Booe's name to Klem.

When a Pirates rookie told Wagner he simply couldn't believe his stories, Honus didn't disagree. "That may be so, sonny," he said, "but I never told you anything that you can't tell your mother."

Not using a script in Cooperstown, Wagner peered from the lectern and started. "I was born in 1874," he said, sounding as though he was about to launch into another story, "and [professional baseball] started in 1876. When I was just a kid, I said to myself that 'I hope someday I'd be up there playing in this league. And by chance, I did.'"

That much was true. Born outside Pittsburgh in the town of Carnegie, then known as Mansfield, Wagner was one of nine children of a Bavarian immigrant, a coal miner, and at the age of twelve had followed his father in the mines. Earning $3.50 a week for loading coal, Wagner tried following a brother into barbering, but in

1895 leapt at the chance to play baseball professionally for $35 a week as a pitcher for Steubenville, Ohio. But, forced to absorb the cost of his gloves, shoes, and uniform, Wagner had an expensive introduction to professional baseball; after that first week, he had all of $3. The story goes that Wagner moved to shortstop after he'd thrown so hard that he had already used up three catchers, one of whom had two broken fingers. There he became a star—in large because, as a batter, he simply had no weaknesses. "[Honus] takes a long bat, stands well back from the plate, and steps into the ball, poling it," said an admiring Christy Mathewson, against whom Wagner hit for a .324 lifetime average. "He is what is known in baseball as a free swinger, and there are not many free swingers."

"Now Connie Mack," Wagner continued, gesturing to the man who had just sat down. "I remember walking fourteen miles just to watch him play ball for Pittsburgh, walking or running or hitchhiking a ride on a buggy. In them days, we didn't have no automobiles. I certainly am pleased to be here in Cooperstown today. This is just a wonderful little town; it puts me in the mind of Sleepy Hollow [New York]. And I'm pleased to be here."

The crowd erupted in applause and laughter. The unscripted Wagner was at it again, spinning free-flowing yarns—and instantly blowing the lid off any formality. The great day was right where it should have been all the way along—back in a homespun atmosphere suggesting a simpler, romanticized time, an era of horse-drawn buggies, lemonade, picnics, and boys playing baseball. And with that, Wagner took his seat in what may have been his shortest story since '33 when he'd been taken back as a Pirates coach. Even so, Wagner's remarks "brought a catch to the throat," remembered Hall of Fame historian Ken Smith. "Hard-bitten newspapermen admitted they had choked up."

Wagner's remarks provided the day with a soft glow. It was

becoming a day of remembrance, baseball's first major collective dip into nostalgia—aided enormously by this inaugural group of Hall of Famers, mellowed by age and fueled by a wealth of stories enhanced by long, successful careers in the spotlight.

Controversies and rivalries were promptly forgotten, shoved under the rug for this day of gentle remembrance, all of it G-rated and told with language suitable for the kids. Among them was the long-simmering contempt between two of the featured guests—Ruth and Cobb, the latter of whom hadn't taken the train, saying he was driving instead, but still hadn't shown up. There was even a touch of mystery about Wagner and the real story of his famous 1909 baseball cigarette card, the so-called "T206" that on account of its scarcity is thought to be the most valuable card in history. One story is that Honus, despite his fondness for cigars and chewing tobacco, objected to his likeness on a tobacco card because he didn't want boys to start smoking. In another version of the story, Wagner didn't want poor kids coaxed into buying cigarettes just to get the card, so he complained and convinced the Piedmont Cigarette Company to pull it from the market; kids still could buy cigarrettes in 1909 because it wasn't until the following year that the Pennsylvania legislature outlawed the sale of cigarettes to anyone under twenty-one. Still another version of the tale is more blunt—Wagner objected because he hadn't been paid for his image on the T206-model card. Whatever the real story, Wagner would undoubtedly be floored to find his card to be among the rarest, most valuable pieces of sports memorabilia. For a time, hockey star Wayne Gretzky was part of a partnership that owned the card. Finally, in 2000, the Wagner T206, typically called the "Mona Lisa of Baseball Cards," sold on eBay for approximately $1.2 million.

How could anyone not laugh at Wagner's stories? Honus had an endless supply of them that he told throughout the day. Looking back to the Pirates first World Series triumph, against the Tigers, in 1909, Wagner recalled, "Things were changing fast by that time [because] women were beginning to come to the ballpark." Why? He added, "We had to stop cussing."

So why, somebody asked Wagner, did he never manage? Actually, Honus did, late in 1917 after the Pirates fired Jimmy Callahan and gave him the job he didn't want. Wagner took it anyway, won his first game, then lost four in a row, and resigned, preferring to finish out the season as a player. The new manager, Hugo Bezdek, who was hired after Wagner recommended him, seemed a bit lost—he'd been the Penn State *football* coach—and often consulted his shortstop on strategy. One day, with a young Pittsburgh pitcher loading the bases in the late going at the Polo Grounds, Bezdek headed to the mound, summoned his infielders, and asked Wagner what to do.

Honus just smiled, happy that it wasn't his decision to make. "I'd say," said Wagner, "that *you've* got a helluva problem on your hands."

◆　◆　◆

"Dear Mr. Spalding," so began the letter, dated April 3, 1905, and postmarked Denver. "The American game of base ball was invented by Abner Doubleday of Cooperstown, NY. . . . The pupils of Otsego Academy and of Green Select School were playing the old game of Old Town [which] Doubleday then improved."

Here was just the evidence that Spalding needed for his American theory of baseball. Abner Doubleday? That the supposed "inventor" earned fame as a Union general during the Civil War added a touch of class to the story. So did the picturesque hamlet of Cooperstown, New York, which had earned fame years before as the home of writer James Fenimore Cooper. That the letter had come from a rather dubious source was quickly overlooked. It was all too appealing to pass up; the decision of the Mills Commission was essentially made.

The letter writer, Abner Graves, was a Cooperstown native and said he was childhood friends with Doubleday. Graves claimed that, as a boy, he had played town ball, which Doubleday had then taken upon himself to improve by designing a whole new set of rules. Doubleday, as Graves put it, had engineered a considerable number of improvements to the game—limiting the number of players on a side from up to fifty to eleven to avoid collisions, creating four bases, including a home plate and three that a runner must touch before scoring a run, and calling it "baseball." Graves described a feature called "soaking," or retiring a runner by socking him with the ball. He even said that Doubleday designed a six-foot ring where the pitcher could stand to deliver the ball, underhanded, to the batter, and placed a catcher behind home and infielders between the bases.

Graves couldn't pin down an exact date when all this had supposedly happened. It was either "the spring prior to or following the 'Log Cabin and Hard Cider' campaign of General William Harrison for the presidency," he said. Pressed by Spalding in a follow-up letter, he later set the date as the spring of 1839—a year or so before Harrison's campaign—and added that he remembered that Doubleday had drawn a diamond in the dirt while explaining the game to a bunch of kids playing marbles in front of a Cooperstown tailor shop.

Positively smitten with this romantic theory of baseball's origins, Spalding forwarded Graves's information to Mills with a cover note asking that the chairman give "special attention" to its contents. Spalding knew full well that Mills would be easily swayed to adopt the Doubleday theory; as members of the same New York veterans' organization, he and Doubleday had been close friends, so close that Mills had served on the general's funeral honor guard back in 1893.

So the Mills Commission's decision was all but made: Baseball started in Cooperstown, they ruled, and as Spalding wrote, "has no relation to or connection with any game of any other country, except in so far as all games of ball have a certain similarity and family controversy." Virtually ignored was Chadwick's scholarly assessment that baseball had descended from rounders—a game, like baseball, with two opposing sides, the use of a pitcher and a batter, and a similar way of going from base to base to score runs and win the game. Contrasting Spalding's claim that baseball has originated from the colonial game of old cat, Chadwick wrote that lacrosse, played by Native Canadians, and the British game of cricket were the primary ball games played in America in colonial days.

Spalding disagreed. Studying a rule book for rounders, he found "very little similarity between the two games," arguing that the rounders field was square, not diamond-shaped, with the bases some fifty to sixty feet apart and not the ninety feet of baseball. And instead of bases, rounders used three-foot-high sticks marked by flags at the tops. The ball was roughly similar in weight, but not the rounders bat, which was flat, like a cricket bat. Not only was rounders more like cricket, Spalding said, but any comparison to baseball "only tends to belittle both games."

The episode made a minor celebrity of Graves. In choosing to accept his claims verbatim, the Mills Commission ignored something else— the rackety, somewhat unsteady life of the letter writer himself. At the time, Graves was seventy-five, and his smiling face, beard, hat, and teeth planted firmly on a cigar as preserved in a photo, underscored his colorful life. Born in 1834, which would have made him only five at the time his "friend" Doubleday allegedly invented baseball, Graves left Cooperstown for good at fourteen in the wave of prospectors headed to California to mine for gold. He didn't strike it rich, and later served as a pony express rider and worked on the transcontinental railroad. By his early thirties, Graves had settled down and prospered—marrying for the first time, having a son, and farming cattle near Cedar Rapids, in Iowa, where he served as county judge and treasurer.

But in the early 1880s, when hard times hit Iowa, Graves lost his business. His personal life unraveled, too—he and his wife separated, and Graves moved back West, this time to Denver where he resumed his mining career. A year after the Mills Commission issued its report, the seventy-six-year-old Graves married again, this time to the thirty-three-year-old Minnie. The marriage seemed a good match, but three years later, Graves and his wife quarreled after he accused her of trying to poison his coffee. So the nearly eighty-year-old man pulled a gun and shot her dead. After a trial, the court found Graves to be criminally insane, and sent him to the Colorado State Insane Asylum at Pueblo, where he died two years later.

Life turned out a lot better for the "other" Abner—Doubleday—lionized as a national hero for his distinguished military career, but never once recognized as the inventor of baseball until long after his death. An 1842 graduate of West Point, Doubleday served with distinction with the cavalry in the Mexican War of 1846. He then secured a spot in the history books early in the Civil War as an artillery commander at Fort Sumter, and, after he was promoted in 1862 to general, at Gettysburg. It was during the first day of the epic battle at Gettysburg that Doubleday and his corps reinforced the cavalry after General John Reynolds was killed, and held the federal left just enough to allow substantial amounts of the Union Army to enter the fight. Although Doubleday and his troops were eventually forced to retreat, they had played a crucial role in giving the Union Army time enough to secure a decisive defensive position and win the battle.

Doubleday's star continued to rise after the war. He was promoted to the rank of major-general and took on government positions for a time both in Texas and San Francisco, where he received a charter for the country's first cable car system. Doubleday retired in 1873, after which he contributed articles on a wide range of subjects including everything from military matters to how best to supply water to growing cities. Doubleday died in 1893 at eighty-nine, and was buried at Arlington National Cemetery. A monument recognizing his heroism was erected at Gettysburg.

It wasn't until years later, after Doubleday's name had cropped up in connection with his supposed invention of baseball, that any details emerged about his interest in the game; at his death, Doubleday left behind more than twenty journals covering his widespread interests, but none mentioned baseball. Nor could he have had anything to do with baseball in 1839 when West Point cadets were not allowed off campus. According to Doubleday's son, quoted in various newspaper accounts, it's possible that Doubleday played baseball around 1840, which may have occurred when the future general was in Cooperstown on break from his studies. His son said young Doubleday had played one of the two shortstop positions, and, as he was prone to take command, may have dabbled in setting up the sides and even creating the rules. But even if that seems conceivable, the account of Colorado miner Abner Graves does not; he was fifteen years younger than Doubleday, making it virtually impossible that they had attended rival schools at the same time. Could it be that one of the other Cooperstown Doubledays, of which there were quite a few, including another "Abner," had been the one? And that, if so, an elderly man who hadn't been in his hometown in a half century just got confused?

Whatever the answer, it wouldn't be until the early 1930s that the Doubleday myth gained traction.

⚏ CHAPTER 4 ⚏

"In the Beginning, a Vision and It Came to Pass"

Baseball's great day was rolling. Sustained applause had met Honus Wagner's remarks followed by anticipation about which baseball legend would be popping out next. Would it be Ty Cobb? Where was he, anyway? Speaking rapidly, MC Chilly Doyle raced into the next introduction with little embellishment. It wasn't Cobb or Grover Cleveland Alexander, but Tris Speaker, he intoned: "Greatest defensive player of all time and a great hitter!"

The radio announcers were equally as terse and excitable—and talking even faster. "Here he comes, ladies and gentlemen, the great 'Grey Eagle,'" NBC announcer Tom Manning told the national audience as the proceedings started taking on the air of a fashion runway shoot. "He looks as fit as a fiddle, as though he could go out there and put a glove on, and go and get 'em now! He's dressed in grey, with his grey hair. And now to the microphone."

At fifty-one, the "Grey Eagle," as Speaker had been known since the teens for his premature greyness and ability to run down almost any fly ball, was every inch his nickname. Dressed formally in a double-breasted suit, he conveyed the courtly gregariousness of a contented senator with a handshake and easy greetings for all—but in fact was a hard man to know. Speaker's athletic gifts had made his success look easy, but it was in fact his very aloofness when combined with an iron will, self-confidence, and tendency to speak his mind as both a player and as a manager that made him great.

"I'm not going to take up a great deal of time—Connie Mack really made a speech for all of us," Speaker said in a flat Midwestern accent that hardly sounded like somebody from Texas. "I'm very happy indeed to have been chosen by the sportswriters as a member of this great Hall of Fame. Our time is limited, so I'm going to let someone else come on."

Today, there would be conference calls and press conferences. But back then, no one had thought of that. Having these men there was enough for most. So Speaker's remarks were three sentences. But that was typical of Speaker whose very bluntness had marked his career beyond his twenty-two big-league seasons, a lifetime .344 lifetime batting average, and unparalleled defensive skills. The native Texan had gotten a sliver of a break in baseball in 1906 at the age of eighteen while pitching for a store team in Corsicana, Texas, when the owner of the Cleburne club of the North Texas League had stopped off to scout an outfielder on the same team.

The owner, Doak Roberts, saw Speaker pitch, get the win, and also hit two home runs. Quickly forgetting about the outfielder, he offered Speaker a contract and a dollar for the fifty-mile train trip to

Waco, where the team was playing. Pocketing the dollar and hopping a freight train, Speaker reported as directed.

Awaking the team's manager, one Benny Shelton, at 6:30 the next morning, he was angrily told to wait in the hotel lobby until 9:30 when he was taken to the ballpark, given a workout—and then told he'd be pitching that day. So he pitched—and held a 2–1 lead into the ninth when Shelton, playing first base, held the ball to protest a close play at the bag, and allowed both the tying and winning runs to score.

So the next morning when owner Roberts appeared in Waco, he found second baseman Mickey Coyle waiting for him at the train station, launching into a diatribe against the rookie pitcher. "He's cussed out Shelton and challenged everybody on the ball club to fight, including me," complained Coyle.

At breakfast in the hotel, Roberts found Speaker. "What's the idea of insulting Shelton?" he demanded.

"*Who* insulted him?" the young ballplayer snapped. "All I said was he was a butter-brained bum standing around holding the ball, and that monkey-faced second baseman stuck his nose into it, and I told him I could lick him, which I can."

"Come upstairs," said Roberts. "We've got business to talk."

And with that, Speaker inked a $50-a-month contract with Cleburne, provided he apologize to Shelton. He did, and the manager accepted the apology—enough so that Speaker found himself on the mound the next day as a full-fledged professional baseball player.

But Speaker wasn't a pitcher. He gave up twenty-two runs that day before Shelton replaced him. Later in the game, when right fielder Dude Ransom was hit in the face with a pitched ball that broke his cheekbone, Speaker volunteered his services.

"Put me in right field," Tris said. "I'm the best right fielder in the league."

And so he was. A year later when Roberts moved his club to Houston and joined the Texas League, Speaker batted .314 and had already piqued the interest of big leaguers. Jimmy McAleer of the St. Louis Browns was one of them and had asked Roberts to let him know when he thought the young star was ready for the majors.

Roberts tried twice but never heard back. He tried again, wiring McAleer that Speaker could be his for $1,500, along with two hundred acres of prime Texas farmland "if [he] does not make good." There was still no reply, so the next day, Speaker was sold to the Red Sox for a pittance of $800—and no land.

But then the Red Sox nearly muffed it. Called up in September 1907, Speaker had three singles in nineteen at-bats and attracted so little attention that the team didn't send him a contract in 1908. But Speaker's grit came through again; without a contract, he paid his own way to spring training in Little Rock, where the Sox finally signed him, but didn't take him north. So he stayed in Little Rock, busted up the Southern League by hitting .350, stealing twenty-eight bases, and finally earning the full attention of the Sox, who brought him up for good at the end of '08. In '09, his first full big-league season, Speaker hit .309 to begin a streak of seven phenomenal seasons in Boston that included World Series titles in '12 and '13.

By then, Speaker, in center, had joined Duffy Lewis in left and Harry Hooper in right as baseball's greatest outfield of the dead ball era. His outfielding abilities were unmatched. "An old-timer spent a couple of afternoons watching the Lone Star Ranger patrol center," Damon Runyon wrote, "and he remarked: 'If I had a ball club, consisting of just Speaker, poor old Rube Waddell, and a catcher, I could win the pennant in either league. The opposition couldn't ever hit Rube, and if they did, they couldn't hit past Tris.'"

"Shifting his position with every batsman to such a degree of nicety that he never once failed to call the turn, Tris showed that he studies the opposing hitters with remarkable care," Runyon wrote. "A great artist, this Texas fellow, when it comes to playing his field, so great that he stands out almost all alone in that department."

Speaker's specialty was playing a shallow center to drastically cut down the batter's field in those deadball days when long flies were rare, and using his remarkable speed to tear back and still reach long flies. Speaker credited his Hall of Fame mate Cy Young with much of the credit for developing his outfielding prowess and ability to anticipate where balls would be hit. "Cy was a veteran near the end of his playing career around the time I got my big-league start in Boston," Speaker recalled years later. "The old fellow took a fancy to me, and said he'd help make a slick outfielder out of me."

By the hour, Young hit fungos to Speaker, developing his skills. "I got to watching and studying his fungo swing," Speaker said. "By doing that, I could start after the ball before he actually hit it."

Speaker applied that knowledge to his game. By watching the arc of a batter's swing, he could tell generally whether the ball was headed to right or left, gauge the ball's distance—and usually be there before it landed. Four times in his big-league career, Speaker threw out thirty or more men in a season, twice reaching thirty-five, still the American League record. Even after 1920, when a newly stitched baseball helped unleash an unprecedented era of power-hitting and send Speaker a little deeper into the outfield, he still managed to throw runners out from the outfield.

Twice in a single month—April of 1918—Speaker pulled off an unassisted double play at second—spearing a low line drive for one out, and racing to second where he doubled up the runner. He even worked as a pivot man in a double play—taking the throw from the second baseman or shortstop and throwing on to first. No wonder players routinely referred to Speaker as a "fifth infielder."

At the plate, Speaker would certainly have been more recognized had his close friend Ty Cobb not won twelve of thirteen American League batting titles between 1907 and 1919. Cobb was simply a hard man to surpass at bat, which Speaker managed only once, in 1916, when in his first year with the Indians, he hit a league-leading .386 to Cobb's .371. Playing all or parts of twenty-two seasons as a regular, he never fell under .300—and for years, held the American League record for doubles, with 793.

When Boston unloaded Speaker to the Indians, it marked the start of many decades of Red Sox front-office miscalculations and blunderings. No, this wasn't eventual owner Harry Frazee peddling Babe Ruth to the Yankees in 1920; in Speaker's case, it was Joe Lannin who was determined to retrench, and sent his star outfielder a contract for half the $18,000 he'd made each of the previous two seasons. Again showing his chutzpah at a time when players had little leverage with team owners, Speaker held out, saying he wouldn't settle for a penny under $15,000. Playing without a contract, he reported to spring training anyway, and two days before the season, went to Cleveland with infielder Fred Thomas and $50,000 for pitcher Sam Jones. Speaker refused to go—unless he received $10,000 of the purchase price.

His stubbornness paid off. Speaker got the money, and established himself as the Indians' premier player. In 1919, he became the team's player-manager, and led them to the 1920 World Series title. Using the tragic death that August of the team's second baseman, Ray Chapman, from a beaning by Carl Mays of the Yankees, Speaker made his team's pursuit of a tight three-team pennant race that year with the White Sox and Yankees into a vindication of sorts for the popular infielder. It worked, and the Indians beat Brooklyn in an emotional best-of-nine series. It was Cleveland's first title—capped off by Elmer Smith's grand slam in game five, the first in Series history, which Speaker called his greatest moment in baseball.

Speaker was an Indian until 1926, abruptly retiring to go into business in Cleveland. At the same time, Ty Cobb resigned as player-manager in Detroit, prompting the only unpleasant incident of Speaker's entire career. As it turned out, Speaker and Cobb had been quietly forced to resign amid allegations from Detroit pitcher Dutch Leonard, a Boston teammate of Speaker's as well as a member of Cobb's Tigers, that the two stars had contrived to fix a game back in 1919. Commissioner Landis's investigation found that Leonard's charges were off base and he reinstated the two. But the bogus story took its toll, forcing the resignation of American League founder and president Ban Johnson for believing the tale and dragging the game's reputation through the mud.

But the Grey Eagle was nearly done anyway—spending '27 in Washington, and in '28, finishing up with Cobb and the A's in Philadelphia, before calling it quits at forty. In his last at-bat, on August 30, 1928, against the Red Sox, Speaker struck out. In the A's lineup that day was not only Cobb, who retired two weeks later, but other future Hall of Famers, Mickey Cochrane, Al Simmons, and Jimmie Foxx. Pitching against them that day: another eventual Cooperstown inductee, Red Ruffing of the Yankees.

In retirement, Speaker managed and played a little at Newark of the International League, and worked as a broadcaster in Chicago. In 1933, he joined Kansas City as a manager and part owner, but the Depression-era venture didn't pan out, so Speaker went back to Cleveland as an Indians broadcaster. Cleveland was happy to have him back: "There is no manlier man than Tris Speaker," wrote sportswriter Joe Williams. No one disagreed.

◆ ◆ ◆

How to jump-start the myth that Abner Doubleday invented base-ball to help Cooperstown was the challenge facing Stephen Clark in early 1935. With America some three years into the Great Depression, the thought of something so frivolous as baseball's birthplace seemed like bad timing.

By 1935, the economic malaise that had gripped the country showed few signs of easing. President Franklin Roosevelt and Congress had created a blizzard of legislation and agencies designed to break the 20 percent rate of unemployment. Workers were promised a "New Deal" of social and economic measures that distributed funds to the unemployed, created jobs, raised crop prices, and set wage and production standards for industry. But hard times continued to wear away at the fabric of the country, with farmers in the Dustbowl facing crippling windstorms and a drought that ensured crop failure, and drove them west as migrants. Roosevelt did his best, creating more and more job-creating agencies, each with colorful acronyms like the AAA, CCC, and TVA. And hanging over the specter were unsettling stories from overseas of a rearming Germany and a hostile Japan. This was hardly the environment in which to build tourism in a small town in upstate New York.

In fact, efforts to use baseball to lure tourists to Cooperstown had kicked off some years before. Back in 1917, five men from nearby Ilion kicked off the idea of a "national" baseball field for the village, as well as a home for retired players to be financed by donations. Calling themselves the Doubleday Memorial Fund, the five, who included a couple of elderly former Detroit infield teammates, Deacon White and Hardy Richardson, started the group modestly— by each pitching in a quarter of the amount. Then they went to work drumming up publicity, principally by tapping the support of another old teammate, eighty-one-year-old Sam Crane, by then a sportswriter with the New York *Evening Journal*.

As a journeyman big leaguer, Crane spent seven seasons with four teams, hitting .208. And though Crane was a pedestrian writer, he was an enthusiastic booster of the Cooperstown idea, and wrote numerous articles urging that organized baseball throw its support behind the project. His efforts worked a little—another former big leaguer and retired National League president John Heydler became a backer—but it was mostly the efforts of Cooperstown business leaders who got the ball rolling. The idea of an old-folks' home for retired ballplayers wasn't as far-fetched as it sounds; although at the turn of the century, big-league salaries averaged about $3,000 a year, which was more than teachers and on par with doctors and lawyers, it was after their playing days in the prepension days that many ex-ballplayers found it difficult to make ends meet.

The businessmen set their sites on raising funds for a ballpark on a property just off Main Street in the center of town on the exact spot where Abner Graves had said baseball probably started. It was a piece of swampy pastureland still being used as a playground and owned by one Alexander Phinney, a descendent of former newspaper publisher Elihu Phinney. Led by a local dentist, the appropriately-named Ernest Pitcher, the group raised more than $3,700 for a two-year lease to the property.

So starting in 1919, workmen removed a barn from the pasture, and cleared it of cows. Then they filled in the swampy parts with dirt, actually grew some grass, and laid down base paths for a ball field. A year later, on September 6, 1920, the new park, christened Doubleday Field, opened with a game between clubs from Cooperstown and nearby Milford. Accompanied by a street fair, the game netted another $450.

But progress on anything more than a nice ball field named for Abner Doubleday moved slowly, very slowly. In 1923, Cooperstown voters approved a ballpark supplement of $1,238, which went into the construction of a playground and a wooden grandstand that included bleachers behind home plate and down the lines. In 1926, another appropriation went to buying the land between the lot and Main Street, where the ballpark entrance and parking is today. And in 1933, with the help of funds allotted by President Roosevelt's Work Relief Program, the entire field was graded and landscaped, a new diamond put in, and the area fenced. Cooperstown finally had a ball field of note, and in 1934, New York lieutenant governor William Bray rechristened the little field where baseball was allegedly first played.

But a ball field alone wasn't enough for Stephen Clark. Convinced by Cleland that a museum full of vintage equipment and the "funny old uniforms" would bring the pilgrims to Cooperstown, he still needed something concrete to link baseball's origins to the area. Joining him in this dream were another collection of like-minded locals, but this time, they were people with some clout: members of the Cooperstown Board of Trustees, the Chamber of Commerce, and the Otsego County Historical Society. Calling themselves the Doubleday Field Association, they first met in April 1935 at Clark Gymnasium and vowed to continue to publicize and promote the museum idea but serve as the community's eyes and ears for Clark and Cleland, back in New York City.

The Doubleday Field Association hoped to convince major league officials to help with fund-raising. They sought to use Doubleday Field for that purpose, and shrewdly appointed Clark as its vice president and Cleland as executive secretary. One member of the Association, the managing editor of the *Otsego Farmer*, Walter Littell, went a step further—regularly shuttling to

New York to let Clark know of any developments related to the museum.

Later that month came the break members needed—a brief item in the *Farmer* about the demolition in nearby Fly Creek of a house once occupied by Abner Graves, the Colorado man who had created the Doubleday story for the Mills Commission. In the attic of the house was an old trunk that had belonged to the former Graves, and inside were a few of his things, including an undersized, weathered old baseball—homemade and stuffed with cloth.

Littell was intrigued. Could the fact that the ball had belonged to Graves, who had left the area in the late 1840s, make it among the first ever used? That way, it would certainly qualify as among the baseballs used by Doubleday, he figured—and quite possibly as *the very first* baseball, or at least one of the earliest. It was a stretch, but for an organization anxious to attract disciples to Cooperstown with the myth of baseball's start, it would do.

Clark, his eye for a deal already honed from his developing interest in collecting art, was thrilled. To him, the lopsided, weather-beaten old baseball was precisely what they needed, "the missing link," as baseball historian James Vlasich put it, to jumpstart the project. Keeping it all low-key, Clark offered the farmer $5 for the baseball, which was eagerly accepted. In hindsight, it was a bargain for an object—still viewable in a special case at the entrance to the Hall's second-floor galleries—that would become so vital in convincing America that baseball could be traced back to Cooperstown.

◆   ◆   ◆

Connie Mack, Honus Wagner, Tris Speaker, and now . . . Larry Lajoie. The famed second baseman, a man so beloved in Cleveland that they renamed their team "the Naps" from the "Indians" in his honor, was next in the parade of speakers. Anyone heard from Cobb? Chilly Doyle had, and reported he was on his way from Utica but delayed in traffic. And where were the pitchers?

Could it be that the organizers had put the most talkative Hall of Famers first, and saved the biggest of the big names 'til last, squeezing in those least likely to say much in the middle? Possibly. No one questioned Lajoie's massive contributions to baseball—a lifetime .338 batting average in twenty-one big-league seasons, a three-time American League batting champion, and such pinpoint bat control that he could pull off the hit-and-run play by swinging the bat *with one hand*. But what was always a bit of a mystery about Napoleon "Larry" Lajoie was his reserve, which many partook for arrogance.

"I'm very glad to be here today, and to meet all the old-timers who a lot of you have probably watched playing baseball, some of the greatest men who ever walked on a ball field," said Lajoie. "I am glad to have the honor to be here today, and join with them. I hope everybody enjoys it as well as I do because we're having a great day." And that was that. A man of few words, Larry Lajoie took his seat. It was in keeping with his character: For a time, baseball Centennial organizers had some trouble even finding the sixty-three-year-old Lajoie to invite him to Cooperstown. Letters to his winter home in Florida had gone unanswered. They did some digging, and sent him another letter, this one addressed to his home in Mentor, Ohio, outside Cleveland. This one, Lajoie answered. Greatly relieved, officials asked Lajoie why it had taken him so long to commit. Well, he had never received the first letter, he explained.

But arrogance wasn't the reason for Lajoie's personality. He was simply a quiet man—"[not] a bit stuck up, but ... not a good mixer," a Cleveland newspaper columnist put it early in Lajoie's career. "He doesn't care for the crowd. . . . He's loyal to a few cronies and chums. . . . He is never what they term 'a good fellow,' never 'one of the boys.'"

Reporters were, in fact, among those cronies and chums, and along with football coaches, became his poker companions, and took to calling him "Bashful Larry." No scholarly explanations of why Lajoie was so reserved exist, but chances are it had something to do with being the youngest in a large family born to French Canadian parents in the mill town of Woonsocket, Rhode Island. Speaking French at home as a child meant English was a second language for Lajoie—pronounced "Lazhoway"—who always chose his words carefully.

As a boy, Lajoie helped his family by driving a horse-drawn taxi and working in a livery stable. Baseball came easily—as a teenager, he emerged as the Woonsocket club's star who hit for power, found the gaps, and fielded flawlessly. A ballplayer with no conceivable flaws other than a lack of speed, he was signed at twenty-one by the Fall River, Massachusetts, team in a contract written on the back of an envelope. Later that year, in 1896, he made his big-league debut with the National League's Philadelphia Phillies.

Lajoie's impact was immediate. He hit .328 in thirty-nine games that year, and .363 in his first full season the following year. Never a carouser as many ballplayers were in that era, Lajoie was simply a star dedicated to playing the best he could. All those poker games were in the winter—he rarely played cards during the season, choosing to focus on baseball. Nor would he read on trains or go to movies for fear he might injure his batting eye. And he always insisted on three square meals a day.

Lajoie's swing was smooth, fluid, and was the hardest in baseball.

He once sent a line drive to left that struck and killed a pair of sparrows. Third basemen hated to play Lajoie tight in bunt situations for fear they'd be drilled by one of his liners. In New York, Lajoie lined a shot to the outfield that stuck in the wire fence, which outfielder Willie Keeler tried to extract as Lajoie ran around the bases. He needn't have strained himself; the ball plopped outside the fence for one of baseball's weirdest home runs.

In 1901, Lajoie was still making the National League minimum of $2,400, and happily jumped to the upstart American League for $4,000—insisting that the money be deposited in a bank for fear the new league wouldn't last. He picked up where he left off for Connie Mack's crosstown A's—batting an unworldly .405 against the slightly inferior pitching in the new league. Lajoie was so feared a hitter that on May 23, the White Sox intentionally walked him with the bases loaded.

Jumping back and forth between the American League and the National League was common in those days, inciting a war between the two leagues. So with Lajoie stealing headlines with the A's, owners of the cross-town Phillies went to court to prevent him from playing in Philadelphia. When the Phillies obtained an injunction that kept him from playing for the A's, American League president Ban Johnson came up with a creative solution: He simply reassigned contracts for Lajoie and another jumper, Bill Bernhard, to the Cleveland Blues.

In Cleveland, Lajoie developed another nickname—fans there called him the "Peerless Lajoie" who rapidly became the team's rock. In 1905, the Naps, as they were now known, named Lajoie manager, and though his club came close several times to winning the pennant, they never did. That Lajoie never played in a World Series is the only unfortunate statistic of his long career.

Among Lajoie's greatest strengths was seldom making a mistake in the field or at bat. At 6'1", he would be on the small size these days; but a century ago, Lajoie was among the tallest of big leaguers and wasn't afraid to crowd the plate to reach outside pitches and expand his strike zone. Pitchers threw inside to keep him off the plate, but Lajoie refused to be intimidated—seldom hitting the ground and instead just casually drawing his head back as if to emphasize that an 85-mph beanball was no big deal. Once, when an excitable White Sox rookie told the great spitballer Ed Walsh that he had discovered Lajoie's weakness, the veteran listened attentively and agreed.

"Why, I discovered Larry's weakness long ago," he said.

"You did?" asked the rookie.

"Sure," said Walsh. "I just throw the ball down the middle of the plate and duck."

Just what it was that made Lajoie so good was a continual source of interest to writers. Grantland Rice called him "the greatest hitter we have ever seen"—a whopper of a statement given the writer's long friendship with Cobb. But Rice gave Lajoie the nod because "he had to make his hits cleanly—not having Cobb's speed to beat out the infield tap." And that wasn't the end to platitudes from Rice for whom Lajoie was also "the greatest infielder the world has ever known when it came to making a hard chance look as easy as an accommodation bounder."

"Eddie Collins can cover a bit more ground than Lajoie," Rice said. "But Eddie nor any other man ever had that knack of shuffling over easily and half-lazily in front of a hard chance and picking it up without even the semblance of an effort."

When Lajoie resigned as Cleveland's manager after 1909, preferring to focus on being a player, the team lost its nickname as well, and would forever after be known as "the Indians." Lajoie was once again just a player, and continued to chalk up impressive numbers with extraordinary consistency—placing second or third in the batting race most years behind Cobb. Then, in 1914, at the age of thirty-eight, he slipped below .300—batting .289—and was shipped back to the A's where he finished his career in '16.

Lajoie finally got his pennant—managing Toronto to the International League title in 1917. He then managed Indianapolis until the league disbanded during World War I and then left baseball to return to Cleveland, where he went into business as a tire salesman for trucks. In the early '20s, Lajoie picked up golf, and became good at that, too—developing the same graceful swing as he had in baseball, and consistently shooting between a seventy-five and an eighty-two.

Just as he had while playing, Lajoie made infrequent public appearances, splitting his time with his wife, Myra, between Cleveland and Florida. Baseball sometimes intruded, as in 1934, when at the age of fifty-nine, Lajoie made a film of his batting style, just as graceful as it had been thirty years before. And for all his shyness, Lajoie was a fierce defender of players from his era, even during the '20s when Babe Ruth and his home run assault made many records of the dead ball era seem small by comparison.

"Just go look at the old-timers' records," he said. "They say some of us old-timers are jealous of these home run hitters. Well, I'm not. I just compare the records, that tells me."

◆　◆　◆

Newspaper editor Walter Littell had a good sense of spin, circa 1935. To build the idea of the Baseball of Hall of Fame and help drum up the story of baseball's origins into people's heads, Littell labeled the discovery of the Abner Graves baseball as the "Doubleday ball." He also got to work chronicling other discoveries of baseball memorabilia for the planned museum: One early find was a handsome china plate, won by the 1889 National League champion New York Giants, with etchings of each player, several of whom like John Ward, Buck Ewing, Tim Keefe, and "Smiling" Mickey Welch were among the game's first great stars. The plate was donated by the son of the original owner, an old-time fan from New York City.

By February, several other items had dribbled in, including a 21-inch-by-38-inch framed print of Union prisoners during the Civil War playing baseball in Salisbury, North Carolina. Sketched in 1863 by one Major Otto Boetticher, presumably a prisoner of war himself, it was thought to be one of the earliest baseball images. The Hall acquired another image—this one a Currier & Ives print from 1866 showing a "grand match" at the Elysian Fields in Hoboken, New Jersey. The prints, along with the Doubleday ball, and three other early baseballs donated by A's owner Thomas Shibe, went on display in the ground floor of Main's Village Club, now home to the town offices.

Word was getting out of the efforts underway in Cooperstown. In June, Clark Griffith, a onetime star pitcher, the first manager of the Yankees, then known as the Highlanders, and the president of the Washington Senators, donated a framed portrait of Abner Doubleday, secured through friends at the U.S. War Department. Griffith sent some other items as well—several prints of various U.S. presidents throwing out the first pitch of the season at National (and, starting in the 1920s, Griffith) Park in Washington, D.C. National League president Ford Frick pitched in, too, donating another item from the '89 Giants, a silver cup engraved with the names of the players.

In July, Cleland's inaugural efforts to collect items for the museum landed an article in the *Sporting News*, giving Cooperstown nation-wide publicity. Meantime, several team photos turned up, including shots of the Knickerbockers, generally regarded as baseball's first team, and the powerful Cincinnati Red Stockings of 1869. Letters filled with morsels of baseball history piled in from all over, including one from Harry Wood of Irvington, New Jersey, who related the sad tale of the great Wee Willie Keeler, who had retired from baseball in 1910, having put away a considerable nest egg of more than $100,000, only to see it stolen by unscrupulous "sharks," as Wood put it, and leaving the great player destitute upon his death in 1923. The Village Club, meant to be a temporary repository of items before a permanent museum could be built, was getting so tight that billiard tables in the West Room had to be moved to accommodate the memorabilia.

The growing number of items gave Cleland the credibility he needed in contracting baseball officials with the idea of raising funds for a museum. To do so, Cleland aimed right for the top by sending Judge Landis a folder that described the museum, and floated a new idea—a big celebration in 1939 that would commemorate baseball's first century and inaugurate the museum. Cleland's search for administrative support kept him mum about another idea—having sportswriters elect famous players into the Hall, where they would earn plaques that commemorated their careers. That idea alone, specifically getting writers to vote during the winter, would become crucial to keeping the Hall in the minds of baseball fans year-round.

Appealing to Landis's vanity, Cleland proposed making the commissioner the head of another committee to be composed of baseball officialdom and a group of influential sportswriters to get the word out about the collection of artifacts. Indeed, he had already laid the groundwork for the committee, having composed a list of possible candidates including John Heydler, National League president Ford Frick, American League president Will Harridge, and Julian Curtis, the chairman of Spalding & Company. Much to Cleland's disappointment, Landis deferred any decision or endorsement to the December baseball meetings.

But in the end, Cleland's earlier canvassing would be his ace in the hole. Heydler was an early enthusiast of the baseball museum, and became the guiding light to backing up the Hall of Fame with a yearlong celebration to be called "The Cavalcade of Baseball," in which baseball Centennial events would be celebrated around the major and minor leagues throughout 1939. And although most baseball officials eventually got behind the Hall of Fame, especially after Landis did, none signed on with anything close to the enthusiasm of Ford Frick. In the end, the Hall of Fame would owe its existence as much to the vision of Clark and Cleland as to Frick's immense drive and innate knowledge of how to get things done.

At forty-four, Frick had already risen far and fast in the baseball establishment—proving eminently capable of juggling multiple careers and having a knack for ending up in the right place. An Indiana native, he played baseball at DePauw University, and then became a high school and college English teacher, before working as a sports and editorial writer in Colorado Springs and Denver, while dabbling part-time in advertising.

Chances are Frick would have entered the advertising business for good had Arthur Brisbane, the powerful editor of William Randolph Hearst's *New York American,* not happened to read one of his articles. Impressed with the young man's prose, his boundless drive and background, Brisbane brought him to New York in 1922 as one of his paper's sportswriters where he would become a colleague of Damon Runyon. A year later, Frick went to the *New York Journal,* and had the good fortune of establishing a close friendship with Babe Ruth with whom he served for years as the ballplayer's ghostwriter. In 1930, Frick moved again, to radio, to host two daily sports shows. In 1934, he tacked on yet another job, baseball administration, as a public relations representative of the National League Service Bureau. Continuing in radio, he was among the first to call games.

Then, in December 1934, Heydler, now sixty-five and in failing health, retired after eighteen years as National League president. Wasting little time, the eight club presidents voted the forty-year-old Frick as the National League's new president—handing him a range of pressing Depression-era challenges from how to resurrect several nearly bankrupt teams to setting the groundwork for night baseball games.

Like just about every other business in the mid-1930s, baseball faced crushing problems. In Frick's case, three National League teams—the Philadelphia Phillies, Brooklyn Dodgers, and Boston Braves—were particularly hard hit. Attendance wasn't at rock bottom as it has been in 1932 and 1933, the early years of the Depression, but it was still slumping, causing Casey Stengel, who as Brooklyn's new manager in 1934 inherited a mediocre sixth-place team, to proclaim that indeed, "the Dodgers were still in the league."

They were, but barely. The Dodgers weren't very good in 1935, either—finishing fifth—causing Stengel to wonder if they should change their nickname. Calling them the "Caseys," though, wouldn't do it—back in the '20s, the team went by "Robins" after its manager, Wilbert Robinson—because that would remind people of "that guy who struck out."

In Brooklyn, attendance, which from 1927 to 1930 exceeded one million spectators a year, had been halved by 1934. Other teams were in free fall as well; the woeful seventh-place Phillies drew a shade above 200,000 in '35, with the cellar-dwelling Braves only slightly better at 232,000. Even the pennant-winning Cubs were having troubles; the team drew 692,000, less than half what they had drawn five years before.

The teams responded as best they could—lowballing players at negotiation time, cutting salaries, and in the case of the notoriously cheap Cardinals, cutting the laundry bill and forcing their players to take the field in steamy St. Louis in dirty uniforms. Some teams, like the New York Giants, took to renting their ballparks for prizefights, college football, and Negro League games. Players with the nerve to hold out in negotiations found themselves virtually blacklisted; when, near the end of the 1930 season, Dick Bartell of the Pirates asked for railroad fare home to California as his contract specified, he was suspended by owner Barney Dreyfuss who denounced him for his "impertinence." The next spring, Bartell found himself with the last-place Phillies.

Everyone suffered. Jimmie Foxx was asked by the A's to take a $5,300 pay cut—after his 1933 American League MVP season of forty-eight home runs and 163 RBIs. He refused, and eventually haggled a measly $1,700 raise to $18,000. Others faced graver problems: Mickey Cochrane, the great A's catcher and team leader, lost $80,000 in a 1931 Philadelphia bank failure. Four-time American League batting champion Harry Heilmann of the Tigers and Tony Lazzeri, the Yankee second baseman, lost everything.

Considering his many weighty problems, Frick must have felt a relief when Cleland came calling in the spring of 1935, asking only that the league mount an all-star game in Cooperstown to attract publicity for the Centennial. Having written a newspaper piece some years before about Cooperstown, Frick was well aware of the town's supposed link to baseball history. Underscoring his enthusiasm for the project by donating the 1889 Giants' silver cup, he not only got on board quickly, but then went a step further—suggesting the more comprehensive idea of incorporating a place within the museum where the retired stars of the game could be remembered.

Frick called the idea a "Hall of Fame"—the same that New York University used for the Hall of Fame for Great Americans, which by chance, he had visited just days before. In fact, the term had been used in baseball as far back as 1905, just as the Spalding-Chadwick controversy went into high gear and the sport developed a sense of its past. Pitchers who threw a no-hitter would often be labeled as "having entered the hall of fame," and sportswriters, then as now, filled out rainy-day copy with their personal favorites or "hall of famers."

No doubt Frick remembered an earlier baseball foray into the idea of a hall of fame—a proposal back in the early 1920s when organized baseball had approved a plan to build a $100,000 baseball monument in the Potomac River in Washington, D.C. The monument was to list the names of the sport's greatest players, but Congress had never delivered any funding. The idea was tabled at the 1924 Winter Meetings and never went a step further.

Frick's concept was just the breakthrough that Clark and Cleland needed—the baseball establishment's rousing endorsement so crucial to seeing their vision become a reality.

Central to Frick's enthusiasm was his recognition that there was real marketability to the new concept of baseball nostalgia. While the baseball memorabilia trade was relegated in those days to a few signed bats, balls, and pictures given away in auctions and fund-drives—and nothing like the multimillion-dollar business of today—there was still a great deal of interest in old-time baseball players.

The autograph craze was starting to catch on, and seldom did Ruth venture anywhere without being asked to sign something—so different from his early days in the league when a crowd of kids would meet him after the game just to shake hands or say "hello" to their favorite player. Nor could Frick have helped but notice the news from the spring that sixty-eight-year-old Cy Young, twenty-three years removed from active baseball, was headed again to spring training—as part of an old-timers' tour.

Little is known of how the conversation went that day. All Frick would ever say of it was a line in his memoirs that "in the beginning, the Hall of Fame was a vision—and it came to pass." But in his enthusiastic support of Cooperstown, he gave baseball officialdom's stamp of approval, with Clark and Cleland staying in the background, wily enough to let the young baseball magnate get the credit. Overnight, Frick's support moved the idea for a baseball museum from the dreams of a group of small-town boosters to baseball's highest office.

Moving quickly, Cleland, Frick, and the baseball committee determined the most equitable way to ensure that the game's best players and top officials be chosen for this Hall of Fame. They proposed a national contest in which baseball fans would choose the top fifty players of all time, but figured it risked becoming too much of a popularity contest, something that could overlook the contributions of nineteenth-century players and pioneers. In the end, the committee chose two methods that endure to this day—deciding that members of the Baseball Writers Association of America, those who covered the sport as a beat, should be the ultimate decision-makers. So ballots were mailed to 226 writers, with the plan for the top ten vote-getters, provided they received 75 percent of the votes, to form the inaugural class of the Hall of Fame. To ensure the pioneers were remembered, the committee asked a group of older baseball men, the forerunner to today's Hall of Fame Veterans' Committee, to select five players from a further list of pre-1900 players and officials.

The pace was quickening: Frick signed on to Cleland's committee, and on August 15, 1935, he invited Cleland to meet other baseball officials. Then Frick announced his plans for a hall of fame and museum to the Associated Press, which immediately reported the news about the voting process. The response was immediate, with reporters and fans alike rendering immediate, strong opinions on who deserved to get into the Hall of Fame, and who didn't. The Cooperstown publicity machine was starting to kick into gear. It looked as though the idea was going to work after all.

◆   ◆   ◆

No question that the Baseball Centennial was a treat for Cy Young—an acknowledgement of his remarkable 511-win career and "rubber" right arm that in a twenty-two-year career, the great pitcher recalled, was never sore or even rubbed down.

But it's a shame that the enduring image it left of Young was of a doddery, slow-moving old man, seemingly more intent to cradle his pipe and stare skyward at the trees than at the swarm of photographers. Few images exist of the younger Denton Young—nicknamed "Cy" for the cyclone-force delivery of his pitches. Born two years after the close of the Civil War, Young combined a Roger Clemens-like bulk, pinpoint control, and smarts to rack up an astounding 511 wins, although by 1939, whole segments of the crowd weren't even alive twenty-eight years before when he'd thrown his last big-league pitch.

Indeed, the seventy-two-year-old Ohio farmer, considerably

thinner than in his later playing days, took his time reaching the podium. Then he spoke—slowly. "I match the old boys who preceded me," he said. "I'm glad to be here today in honor of this Hall of Fame, and that I was able to go through twenty-two-odd years and do what I did, and to have my name on the record. Nothing pleases me better than to be about and to see and know that the young generation today is following our footsteps. Baseball is one of the greatest games, and I do hope and wish that a hundred years from now, the game will be greater."

It was vintage Young. Like most of his fellow Hall of Famers, Young had been a public figure for most of his life, and had perfected folksy stories and an easy irreverence that he displayed at reunions or when newspaper reporters came calling at his farm in Newscomerstown, Ohio. Young wasn't as quotable or long-winded as Honus Wagner, but like his fellow inductees, he had a detailed memory for all that had happened in his baseball career, retained a keen interest in the current game, and was supremely confident that his skills would be just as effective in the present.

"I had excellent control," he told reporters, "throwing with four different deliveries and wheeling on the batter to hide the ball. I saw some fast ones—Amos Rusie, Walter Johnson, Lefty Grove, and Bob Feller, among others—but I was among them, too. My favorite pitch was a whistler right under the chin . . . and I had a couple of good curveballs, an overhanded pitch that broke sharply down, and a sweeping, side-armed curve."

Young was crafty, too. "I could throw a 'tobacco' ball, a pitch that was dirtied and a ball that wasn't so lively," he would say, fully aware that he wouldn't have had that same opportunity after 1920, when baseball resorted to a livelier ball made of tighter stitching and started using multiple balls in a single game. Still, he appreciated the modern game, following the Cleveland Indians on the radio, and often driving the sixty miles north to Cleveland to see the twenty-year-old phenom Bob Feller, already in his fourth big-league season, pitch for the Indians.

Young went so far back that he was almost too old to have been in a World Series. After going 28–9 in 1903 for the Boston Pilgrims, he won two more in that season's Series, the first one, to upset Wagner and the Pirates. His salary at the time was $2,400—not bad for the era but considerably less than the $20,000 a gambler offered him to throw the Series. Young had refused, telling the gambler that "if you put any value at all on money, bet me to win."

By then, Young was already a veteran of more than a dozen big-league seasons. The son of a Civil War Union soldier, the 6'2", 210-pound right-hander had started his baseball career in 1890 pitching fifty miles from home for Canton of the Tri-State League. It is said his teammates took one look at him, dressed in a jacket too short and his clothes crammed into a cardboard suitcase, and laughed. They laughed some more when, dressed in blue coveralls, he walked to the mound and began warming up by throwing the ball against the tin outfield fence. He threw so hard that his pitches dented the fence, and the laughing stopped.

But Young was more than a hard thrower. He proved durable from the start—and as the story goes, was picked up later that season by the National League's Cleveland Spiders after the team's owner, Davis Hawley, had bought the Canton owner a suit of clothes. Not so, said Young, who insisted his sale was a cash transaction—$250. In his first game, against Cap Anson and his Chicago White Stockings, Young wasn't nervous or scared—just mad, after Anson had tried intimidating the twenty-three-year-old rookie by calling him names like "a big farmer" and "Rube." But the insults didn't work, and only inspired him. "I wanted to show him up more than anything else in my life," Young would say.

So he did. Not yet having an effective curveball, Young blazed fast-balls by Anson, striking him out on the way to his first big-league win. Hard to believe that the strike zone was only fifty feet away— it would increase in 1894 to the current sixty feet, six inches—or that Spiders catcher Chief Zimmer wasn't even wearing a padded glove that day. Young himself didn't wear a glove until 1897, instead catching the ball by cupping his hands over it like a clamshell. Young took note, saying that use of the glove changed the game signifi-cantly by improving both the infielders' reach and range.

The increased pitching distance was a temporary setback. From a thirty-four-win season in 1893, Young dipped to twenty-six wins in '94, and then got right back to where he had been—in '95, winning thirty-five, and twenty-six the next year. The whole time, his dura-bility was unworldly—in nineteen of his twenty-two big-league sea-sons, Young pitched in at least thirty-eight games a season and almost always in excess of three hundred innings while walking only about two men a game. Along the way, Young, a lifetime Republican, pitched three no-hitters—one each during the presidential adminis-trations of fellow Republicans McKinley, Roosevelt, and Taft.

His secret? None, really. Young kept it simple and stuck to routine. To stay in shape, he ran, particularly in the spring before he picked up a ball. He also worked hard all winter on the farm from swinging an ax to hauling lumber—and keeping his back and shoulders in rock-hard condition. "My arm would get weak and tired at times," Young admitted, "but never sore, even though I worked with just two days' rest and often with only one. . . . I credited it to my legs and my off-season conditioning."

In 1898, Young won twenty-five games, but wasn't enjoying himself much. Spiders owner Frank Robison had his team playing virtually all their games on the road, and after the season, actually bought another team—the Cardinals—and proceeded in '99 to ship most of his star players, including Young, to St. Louis. Cy enjoyed himself even less in St. Louis, disliking both the city and particularly its sultry summers, and was in a receptive mood when Ban Johnson of the new American League called in 1901, offering him a $600 raise to jump to the Boston Red Sox, then known as the Pilgrims.

Spiders owner Robison sneered, figuring Young, by then a paunchy thirty-three-year-old, and having dipped the year before to his first sub-twenty-win season in a decade, was finished anyway. "Young is through," sneered Robison. "In that bush league, he may last another year, but we couldn't have used him."

Robison was right on one account: In the early going, the new league probably wasn't up to National League standards, a disparity that stars like Young and Larry Lajoie exploited. But Young was hardly finished—steadily peeling off thirty-three, thirty-two, twenty-eight, and twenty-seven-win seasons for the Boston Red Sox.

In 1908, the forty-one-year-old Young, by then so wide in the waist that bending for bunts was difficult, was in the midst of his final twenty-win season when the Red Sox decided to have a day for him at Huntington Avenue Grounds, their pre-Fenway home. With twenty thousand cramming the old ballpark—ten thousand were turned away that day—Young received cash gifts of nearly $7,500, more than his annual salary. He even got a traveling bag from the American League umpires and a trophy from fellow pitchers—all of which left him misty-eyed with gratitude.

After the season, the Sox sold him back to Cleveland, now part of the American League, and in 1909, Young enjoyed a final success, winning nineteen games, but only seven each in 1910 and '11—the last four back in Boston, for the National League Braves. Finally, in the spring of 1912, when that extraordinary right arm started bothering him, Young told Braves manager Johnny Kling, "I guess I'll have to call it a career."

So he did, heading back to Ohio and his big white house with pillars, where he resumed farming, and squeezed in frequent trips to baseball reunions. There he would enjoy a nip or two—"Cripes," said New York saloonkeeper Toots Shor after a bash, "the old man was the only guy in the joint who could drink more than I did"— and spin the yarns. Asked for his thoughts on how the game had changed, Young harbored few regrets, saying, "I'm happy to have blazed the trail for the young, fine fellows carrying on today."

Don't think for a moment that the game was any easier in the old days, Young would say. No, sir. "Whenever I got into a city, I'd find they had saved their ace for me," he said, "so that record of mine was piled up against fellows like Walter Johnson in Washington, Addie Joss in Cleveland, and Rube Waddell in Philadelphia. I once pitched a twenty-inning game and allowed no passes, but lost to Waddell because of two errors behind me."

Sure, the game had changed, Young would say, without "so much stress on playing for one run, the livelier ball and closer fences—but it's all a natural evolution on the sport, and it's been healthy progress."

Small wonder that, given his enduring interest in baseball, Young would be the first Hall of Famer to make a donation to the Hall of Fame. In response to Cleland's 1937 letter-writing campaign, the great pitcher donated several of the trophies he'd received through the years, as well as the 1908 game ball from his five-hundredth career win.

Predictably, Young was more than happy to donate the items. "I don't need them," he said.

◆   ◆   ◆

"No, no!" insisted Ford Frick. "That isn't madness," he said, gently dabbling his lips with a holiday handkerchief. "That's cream cake. But this all-star stuff is ridiculous. It's a mistake—a blunder—the idea, which was ours by the way, as to . . ."

Tough crowd, these sportswriters as they peppered the National League president with accusations that Frick's idea of this Hall of Fame was just a ploy to stock the ballot with a lot of National Leaguers. And to do so, of all places, at Frick's own 1936 New Year's Party at Radio City Music Hall in New York amidst the pastries, punch, and sandwiches.

You couldn't blame the sportswriters for bringing up supposed discrepancies in the balloting. Of the thirty-three players listed on the first ballot, nineteen had spent all or the majority of their careers in the American League. That the list of potential Hall of Famers was stacked in favor of the American League—younger than the National League by seventeen years—revealed a deep sense of competition between the two leagues. And it just didn't seem right.

The list had been the work of Henry Edwards, secretary of the American League's Service Bureau, and a native of Cleveland, an American League city. Small wonder, then, that Edwards tipped the scales in favor of his own league, a process the *New York Times* called "the American League steam-roller process"—a reference to Edwards's insistence on dragging in player statistics at the expense of old-timers, most from the National League for whom few numbers were available. Not that anyone would disagree at naming American Leaguers to several positions—Ty Cobb, Babe Ruth, and Tris Speaker in the outfield certainly, Walter Johnson on the mound, with Eddie

Collins and Larry Lajoie manning the infield—but failing to defer to the Nationals was shortsighted.

Nor did the rules surrounding the formation of Edwards's second list defer—the pre-1900 players, only five of whom, or half the number of the modern players, would be selected for the Hall. There were twenty-six names on that list, among them obvious choices like Albert Spalding, Cy Young, Cap Anson, Mike "King" Kelly, and Willie Keeler. But Edwards's ballot choices included other question-able names, like catcher Silver Flint, a career .239 hitter and marginal fielder; and one Matches Kilroy, a left-hander who started out strong, winning seventy-five games in his first two seasons for Baltimore, but then, in Mark Fidrych-like form, came back to reality and five years later was barely hanging on. Another former player, Ross Barnes, ended his career at shortstop with a respectable .319 career batting average—in a four-year career.

Frick said he was surprised by the names on the ballot. "I guess it was our mistake to let Henry draw up that list," he admitted. "[He] made a mistake in a lot of the names of National Leaguers that he left off the list. I'll refresh his memory as soon as I see him." Basically, the National League president had been caught napping during a temporary blip in a string of otherwise upbeat coverage. It put Frick in a temporarily delicate position as he reminded sportswriters that they wouldn't be voting for an all-star team but for a Hall of Fame— "men who had meant something to the game," as he put it, "men who have made lasting contributions." Edwards's list, he reminded his audience, was merely meant to be suggestions in the event voters might overlook any worthy candidates.

But from the get-go, the process had stirred considerable debate: Wasn't this a slight against the true pioneers, only five of whom would be chosen for the Hall, as opposed to ten post-1900 players, argued writers and fans? Thomas Shibe, in a letter to American League president Will Harridge, argued that the nominees should actually go back even further than 1869 to include Abner Doubleday himself. On the other extreme were current stars like Dizzy Dean, Hank Greenberg, and Paul Waner. Certainly, they deserved to be honored.

Frick did the best he could under the circumstances. Growing flustered at the incessant questioning at his New Year's party, he reiterated that this wasn't an all-star team. "If that had been, I assure you that the National League would have had a sufficient number of worthy candidates." Then he turned to the topic of food: "How about one of those turkey sandwiches? Or a dash of caviar?"

But for all the crankiness of the sportswriters, the controversy amounted to tremendous publicity for the Hall of Fame. With the ballots mailed right after the New Year, news of the impending vote gave baseball scribes a lot to write about in the dead of winter when baseball news often received little press. First appearing in the papers on Christmas Day, the story about the vote as well as the Hall of Fame generated an onslaught of articles in more than four hundred daily newspapers across the country. "Publicity of such a character and of such value has never before been accorded this village," the *Otsego Farmer* reported in the understatement of the decade. "It is a tremendous impetus to the work of making the nation conscious of the coming Centennial celebration in 1939 and in drawing interest to the Museum."

The upcoming vote generated tremendous interest, as did the follow-up columns, many of which delved into the plans in Cooperstown. "The suggestion to start the Hall of Fame with five oldtimers and 10 from the so-called 'modern era' . . . with the addition thereafter of five players each season, strikes me as being close to an absurdity," wrote George Daily in the January 5 edition of the *New York Herald-Tribune*. "The addition of one name every four or five years would be more equitable. In fact, no stated time should be set for an addition. Baseball should wait until some player proves himself worthy of a place with the original 15—so it seems best to limit the field."

Weighing in with more sympathetic analysis was the January 2 edition of the *Sporting News*. "Obviously, in order to make the honor worthwhile, there had to be some discrimination shown, as choices could not be made willy-nilly without a set standard," it wrote on its editorial page. "Just how to arrive at such a standard, proved somewhat of a snag at the outset . . . the solution [of which], as finally decided upon, calls for the separation of baseball history into two periods."

Acknowledging the "drawbacks" of the process, the *Sporting News* nonetheless sided with the process set up by the baseball establishment, arguing that the development of the old-timer committee actually democratized the process and made it fairer for players who would have otherwise been forgotten. "Many of the younger scribes were in no better position to pass on the merits of old-time stars than were the fans," the paper editorialized. "The maturity of this committee's personnel assures careful consideration of all eligibilities, and there should be little criticism of their choices."

Frick, ever the sportswriter in spirit, was apologetic for the rocky parts of the balloting process. "I am sorry that there has been a general misapprehension about the Hall of Fame idea," he said as the ballots were mailed out. "It looks as if we will have to make a new start. We want to make it as difficult as possible to get into this Hall of Fame. We are not going to provide any automatic system for piling up additions."

CHAPTER 5

"I Am Overwhelmed" to Make the Hall of Fame

The retired immortals were keeping it pithy. Not that Walter Johnson, the "Big Train," was ever particularly flashy anyway. Humble, self-deprecating, and on the quiet side, Johnson had let his thunderbolt of a right arm speak for him.

"I'm very proud to have my name enrolled in the Hall of Fame," he told the crowd. "And I'm very happy to have my name enrolled with these men."

That was that, and Johnson went to take his seat. Having won 413 games in his twenty-one years of pitching—second only to Young—all of them with the mostly-doormat Washington Senators, along with an unreal 212 shutouts, including two no-hitters, Johnson could afford to be succinct.

His greatness had been recognized early. The Senators found the gangling nineteen-year-old Johnson in mid-1907 while pitching for a team in the tiny town of Weiser, Idaho, quickly signed him, and shipped him to Washington. Thrown into his first game, on August 2 against the Tigers, he faced Ty Cobb four times, and limited the great batter to only one drag bunt of a single.

When the game ended, a loudmouthed fan leaned over the fence and yelled at Cobb: "What's the matter, Ty, that big busher got your number?"

"No," said Cobb, "but you can't hit 'em if you can't see 'em."

A new phrase had been coined, and it was usually associated with Johnson. The next year, on Friday, September 4, against the Yankees, then called the Highlanders, at the Hilltop Park in New York, Johnson pitched a six-hit shutout. With the Senators' pitching staff a tad depleted by injury, Johnson was given the start on Saturday as well. He pitched a four-hit shutout. There was no Sunday baseball in New York then, so with the next game set for Monday, the first of a Labor Day doubleheader, Senators manager Joe Cantillon figured Johnson could go again. He did—shutting out the New Yorkers again, this time on a stingy two hits.

Johnson had thrown three shutouts in four days. "I must have been a big green pea of a country boy, or I never would have tried it," Johnson said years later of the accomplishment, almost unfathomable in today's game. "Yet at the time, it didn't seem extraordinary. A pitcher is supposed to pitch, isn't he?"

Perhaps the most impressive moment of that weekend had come late in the Saturday game when Highlander spitballer Jack Chesbro plucked Johnson on the right arm while batting. The game was called and the Senators' trainer feared at first that he had broken his arm. But it was a false alarm; the Big Train took a few minutes, dusted himself off, and resumed play.

But Johnson himself seemed a tad surprised when he was picked to pitch the first game of the Labor Day doubleheader. "About five minutes before the game, Cantillon said to me, 'Walter, how you feel?' Then, like a dummy, I answered, 'All right, I guess,' and he handed me the ball again. So I warmed up and pitched.

"By this time, I realized something unusual was going on. Three games in a series with only one day's rest. . . . When we went out for the last half of the ninth inning, [teammates] Jim Delahanty and George McBride came over to me and said, 'Just go along like you're going, Walter. We'll get them for you. Put that ball in there. Fire it past him.'"

So he did, and had his third shutout. "The boys thought that was fine, and when the game ended, they pounded me on the back and told me that no one ever would break the record."

No one did. And throughout his life, Johnson would talk about himself and his remarkable feats with all the flair of somebody reminiscing about a career behind the counter of the hardware store. That he was able to throw as hard in 1923 as in 1908 made him, like Nolan Ryan a generation later, a baseball rarity with an ability to throw thunderbolts for a long time and do so relatively pain free. Said Cobb when asked for his most embarrassing moment in baseball: "Washington on any dark afternoon with Walter Johnson pitching."

Johnson is thought to have thrown a baseball harder than anyone in history, faster than Bob Feller, Bob Gibson, or Roger Clemens. For much of his career, cranking up and throwing hard was all he had to do—Indians shortstop Ray Chapman once dropped his bat after strike two and returned to the dugout, muttering to himself that waiting for Johnson's next pitch "wouldn't do me any good." But even Johnson admitted that it took him years to become a true craftsman on the mound, a pitcher able to mix in curves and off-speed pitches. "I was a thrower," he said of his early years.

But he was a magnificent thrower. From 1910 to 1919, Johnson won at least twenty games a year, reaching thirty-two in '12 and thirty-six in '13, a year when he also pitched fifty-six consecutive scoreless innings. He struck out 3,487 batters, a record since broken by Ryan, appropriately; once struck out six batters in a row; and fanned more than two hundred men in seven consecutive years.

Similar to the other immortals, there are stories about teams that let him slip through their fingers and failed to sign Johnson despite the reports of his greatness. Born in 1887 on a farm near Humboldt, Kansas, Johnson moved to Southern California, where he attended high school, and began striking out batters. Fast from the get-go, Johnson signed his first baseball contract at the age of seventeen for an independent club in Anaheim, and in 1906, at eighteen, with Tacoma of the Northwest League. But after Johnson lost a ten-inning exhibition game to Aberdeen, a benefit for San Francisco earthquake sufferers, Tacoma let him go because of inexperience, and as baseball historian Fred Lieb wrote, "lost the pitching jewel of the country."

So Johnson took his fastball to the semipro, mining town of Weiser, Idaho, where he arrived at the train station on a spring afternoon in 1907. A boy looked at his big bag, and asked if he were a ballplayer; indeed, he was, Johnson told him. "I'll bet you're gonna play with the high school, because the town team is no good."

He pitched eighty-five consecutive shutout innings for Weiser, before information started leaking out about the young man who could throw a baseball so fast you couldn't see it. At the time, most big-league clubs carried a single scout or none at all, and depended on friends to send them information on prospects deep in the sticks.

But when a traveling salesman who was a Pirates fan wrote Barney Dreyfuss of the Pirates about this young fireballer in Idaho, Dreyfuss figured the reports were so glowing that they were exaggerated, and passed. So had the Giants the year before, but they passed when John McGraw's scout reported that Johnson had speed, but couldn't hold runners, the few there were, on base.

The Senators, however, paid attention. When they sent injured infielder Cliff Blankenship to Wichita, Kansas, to check out a young prospect of an outfielder named Clyde Milan, they asked him to go to Idaho as well to watch Johnson. "While you're out that way, you might as well take a look at the strikeout kid," manager Joe Cantillon instructed Blankenship.

It was a worthwhile trip. Blankenship saw Johnson and knew instantly he was special. Introduced to him, Blankenship told Johnson he'd like to take him to Washington to pitch for the Senators. But the young pitcher, who had never been east of Kansas, seemed hesitant. Did he want more money? "No," said Johnson. He wanted a train ticket home if it didn't work out.

Johnson then signed one of the more memorable contracts in baseball history—on the back of a piece of brown paper that wrapped some meat. And by chance, he and Milan, who Blankenship also signed with the Senators, became friends and roommates.

Perhaps the only pitcher of his era comparable in skills to Johnson was Christy Mathewson of the Giants. "Matty was the only fella I knew who was even like Walter," said longtime Senators owner Clark Griffith. "But he wasn't the pitcher Johnson was. Matty was an artist, but Johnson was a powerhouse."

Griffith was stingy, and never paid Johnson a penny more than $10,000 a season—half the salary of Ruth in his early seasons with the Yankees. Johnson had other opportunities to pick up extra income—handy for a man with five children and a farm in Maryland—but wasn't much interested. When a cigarette company offered him $10,000 to endorse the product, Johnson turned it down.

"I don't smoke them," he earnestly explained. "Although I don't object to anybody else using them, a lot of kids might start smoking them too soon and hurt their health."

Nor did Johnson ever show up a teammate. While some pitchers grow exasperated when a teammate commits an error, Johnson developed the curious, calming habit of not so much as even looking at the offending infielder, but reaching to the ground, picking up a pebble, and tossing it away. He had the same patience with fans, as Clyde Milan was to discover one evening as the two men hurried to the theater.

When a stranger approached, Johnson stopped to chat, and had to run to catch up with Milan.

"Why do you let a stranger hold you up like that when we're trying to get to the theater?" Milan asked him.

"He told me he knew my sister," Johnson said.

"Your sister?" Milan asked. "I didn't know you had a sister."

Johnson shook his head. "I haven't," he said.

Critics said Johnson lacked aggressiveness, that he had no edge and was too easygoing and friendly to back hitters off the plate. But even that criticism was mild: "They knew Johnson's target was the plate, not them, and took full advantage of his sportsmanship," Washington sportswriter Joe Williams wrote of his opponents. "And even then, they seldom saw the ball." Johnson saw it differently, acknowledging that, with anything but pinpoint control, he could hit and hurt a batter. He also rarely got rattled or excited, instead letting his skills take over. "I had no weight across the chest and no bulging arm muscles," Johnson once said. "A pitcher needs whip, and the way my arm hung on my shoulder, I got that whip into every pitch. My speed came from the tremendous leverage I got from a full pivot and long arm."

But most of the time, even Johnson couldn't help the Senators, who finished in the bottom half of the standings in fifteen of his twenty-one years with the team. The Big Train waited eighteen years to reach a World Series, and as it was, needed some luck to record his first Series win, in 1924, against the Giants. The thirty-six-year-old Johnson had already been twice beaten by the Giants when he entered the ninth inning of game seven with the score knotted at three, and the team's first title on the line. He shut down the Giants for four innings, striking out five until the twelfth when Earl McNeely's ground ball down the third-base line struck a pebble and leapt over the head of third baseman Fred Lindstrom, sending in Muddy Ruel from second with the winning run. Washington had a party to remember; even umpire Billy Evans was happy, pleased that the big guy finally was on a winner. "This is the biggest kick I've ever gotten out of baseball," said Evans, using a handkerchief to wipe real tears from his eyes.

Johnson followed up with two wins in the 1925 Series, shutting down the Pirates 4–1 with ten strikeouts in the opener, and taking game four as well, a 4–0, six-hit shutout. But these being the Senators, they blew a 3–1 Series lead, losing the Series to Pittsburgh despite being four runs up in game seven. The Big Train's career World Series stats—a 3–3 record and a 2.34 ERA—were decent for most anyone but him.

However, Johnson was approaching the end of the line. His twenty wins in '25 was his last twenty-win season. In 1926, he went 15–16 for his first losing record in more than twenty years. On

August 13, 1926, against the Yankees, the Big Train had a particularly galling day—giving up two home runs to Lou Gehrig—the only batter *ever* to take him yard twice in a single game. Though Johnson spent much of his career in the deadball era when players didn't generally hit for power, it was nonetheless astounding that, in more than eight hundred games, he gave up only ninety-seven home runs.

The end came September 30, 1927, with a 4–2 loss to Ruth, Lou Gehrig, and the rest of the Yankees at Yankee Stadium. Then he retired to his 552-acre farm near Bethesda, Maryland, where he supervised the milking of his forty cows and indulged in his lifelong hobby of hunting.

Johnson returned to baseball for a spell, managing the Senators from '29 through '32, and the Indians from '33 to '35, compiling a respectable .551 percentage. And though he rarely attended games after that, Johnson still dabbled in the game, as on the cold day of February 22, 1936, when he was called on to duplicate General Washington's feat of throwing a silver dollar across the Rappahannock River as part of the Washington Sesquicentennial.

Johnson's second toss landed forty feet beyond the far river bank, a fact he begged newspapermen to ignore, saying it looked like he was showing off. "I think the river is a lot narrower now than when Washington was around," he said.

By then, Johnson was a full-time farmer, and single as well—his wife, Hazel, had died back in 1930 at only thirty-five.

But as is the case with many athletes, politics called. In 1936, Johnson plunged into the presidential election as a local spokesman for Republican nominee Alf Landon, running against Franklin Roosevelt. Two years later, Johnson ran for commissioner of Montgomery County, Maryland, as a Republican. On the surface, Johnson's candidacy seemed curious for this most private and modest of men; on the other hand, his name was a draw, and he'd had a taste of politics as a boy through his father who had been a county commissioner in Montgomery County, Kansas.

Running a low-key campaign, Johnson was elected easily to a two-year term, as the lone Republican commissioner in a heavily Democratic area. He had spent just fifty cents during the campaign to pay a printing bill. Not much is remembered of his first term in office, discounting the grumbling of his colleagues, who claimed their work was constantly disrupted by the large numbers of well-wishers visiting the offices to meet him.

◆   ◆   ◆

Ty Cobb was on the golf course February 1, 1936, near his home outside San Francisco when he got the news. Given the former Detroit star's cantankerous, unpredictable personality, it was a surprise to many that he was so gracious when a newsman informed him that he'd been the top choice in balloting for the inaugural class of the Hall of Fame.

"I am overwhelmed," the Georgia Peach said. "I deeply appreciate the honor. I am glad [the writers] feel that way about me. I want to thank them all." His son, Jimmy, would say later that his father was prouder of the Hall of Fame vote than of anything else in his long baseball career.

The writers proved as tough in their voting for the Hall as they had been in their questioning of the process at Ford Frick's New Year's Party. Cobb was named on 222 of the 226 votes cast, which begs the question as to who were the four writers to actually have the nerve to leave him off their ballots. Four others were elected as well—Babe Ruth and Honus Wagner, each with 215 votes; Christy

Mathewson, who received 205; and Walter Johnson, with 189. As the only five to receive the required 75 percent, or 169 votes, needed for selection, they formed a formidable first Hall-of-Fame class.

At least the writers left the door open a crack for those players who had missed. Lajoie, Speaker, Young, Rogers Hornsby, and Mickey Cochrane ran in that order for the other "moderns"—how could anyone leave them off the ballot, either, come to think of it?— but they would receive other chances to garner 75 percent of the votes again in '37 and, if necessary, in '38, both well before the planned Centennial.

The '37 vote put Lajoie, Speaker, Young, and Mack over the top, with Grover Cleveland Alexander elected in '38, all by his lonesome; and George Sisler, Willie Keeler, Eddie Collins, Rube Waddell, Rogers Hornsby, Frank Chance, and Ed Delahanty making it in '39.

No question, each and every one of these immortals was deserving of their election. But the manner in which each was named and the fluctuation of how the tide changed in balloting from year to year demonstrated how each election was a fluid process. Take Sisler, Collins, and Keeler: Of the three, Sisler received the majority of ballots in '36 with Collins second and Keeler third. But in '37, Collins drew the most votes with Keller second and Sisler third. But Sisler pulled ahead, again, in '38 and '39, with Keeler and Collins flip-flopping.

If that was confusing, the vote on the veterans—the pre-1900 players—was more so. Nobody received the 75 percent of votes, although Buck Ewing and Cap Anson earned the most, with a little more than half of the seventy-eight votes cast, with fifty-eight needed for election. If that was hard to fathom, consider than Keeler, with a lifetime .341 batting average, received only thirty-three votes, and Young, with his 511 victories, only received thirty-two and a half.

Earning even less support were John McGraw (seventeen votes) and Albert Spalding (with all of four). To compensate, the top ten vote-getters were resubmitted for another tally; all would make it in time for the Centennial.

Part of the problem was that support for players like Keeler, Young, and Ed Delahanty, all of whom straddled the 1900 date, was diluted because they received votes in each of the two categories. And despite Ford Frick's pleas to writers that they not vote for an all-star team, it was clear that some did, with current players like Charley Gehringer, Lefty Grove, Dizzy Dean, and Gabby Hartnett receiving votes and further diluting the support for old-timers. That promoted a new rule specifying that only those players retired for at least five years would be eligible.

From the start, a straight vote had the feel of a free-for-all, with writers and officials unable to agree, as Bill James would point out, not only "which players, as we have now, but what type of players" should be elected to the Hall. Making the system particularly difficult was the lack, in 1936, of a scholarly history of the game, or of the kind of easily available statistics as we have these days. It prompted some wildly divergent ideas on who was deserving of enshrinement: Landis advocated the election of Eddie Grant, a Harvard-grad-turned Giant-infielder who was best known as the first baseball player to die from combat in World War I. Grant was eulogized as a hero after his death, and writers would erect a monument in centerfield of the Polo Grounds in his honor, but he was only a three-year starter, with Landis urging his election, not for his modest skills on the ball field, but for the heroic image it would provide.

The writers never elected Grant. At the same time, they had some odd favorites of themselves. In 1937, for instance, they gave two votes to Marty Bergen, an 1890s-era Braves utility catcher whose claim to fame was—no joke—murdering his wife and two children, and then killing himself. It was one writer's idea of a joke.

Throwaway votes aside, the writers faced a challenge without many of the statistics that color baseball today. Beyond big-city newspaper morgues, there weren't many ways of investigating or knowing much about the careers of former players Buck Ewing, Cap Anson, or Wee Willie Keeler, none of whom had picked up a bat in decades. That's difficult to fathom in this era of statistical over-load in which ESPN broadcasts sports twenty-four hours a day and the Elias Sports Bureau presents every conceivable number about players. These days, *The Baseball Encyclopedia*, first published in 1968, offers the lifetime records of every player who ever suited up in a big-league uniform, down to Eddie Gaedel, a midget with one at-bat for the '51 Browns. Meantime, baseball books often occupy a whole section of bookstores, and baseball research is the providence of devoted members of the Society for American Baseball Research. Not so in 1936 and '37 when radio was in its infancy, television hadn't been born, and there was no such thing as bringing the past alive through microfilm—it hadn't yet been invented.

Things were somewhat more definite with the old-timers com-mittee, the group charged in stocking the Hall with pre-1900 players and officials. When the initial committee of five didn't elect a single person in 1936, baseball officials reworked it into one made up of themselves. So concurrent to the vote of the regular baseball writers, this new "Centennial Commission" was comprised of Landis, Frick, John Heydler, and Will Harridge as its major-league representatives, and William Bramham and George Trautman, president and chairman of the National Association of Professional Baseball Leagues, to represent the minor leagues. With its mission of electing the five most important "builders of baseball," the committee wasted little time in choosing George Wright, shortstop and manager of the 1869 Cincinnati Reds; Mills Commission member and the first National League president, Morgan Bulkeley; American League founder Ban Johnson; as well as John McGraw and Connie Mack.

For Cleland, the publicity windfall, even the criticism, was a godsend. After all, people weren't criticizing the concept of the Hall of Fame, but rather the process and who was being omitted, which only fueled the interest. In January 1937, when the second round of voting neglected a whole new round of deserving names, howls of protest were lodged far and wide, resulting in a spate of new articles. In the *New York American*, Bill Slocum wondered why greats like Keeler, Ed Delahanty, and John McGraw were omitted. The '37 balloting process was better in some regards—writers could now only cast votes for players retired five years—but they voted for a total of 111 different players, further diluting the numbers. The process had become so unwieldy that Dan Daniel in the *Sporting News* took a good-natured jab at others who should be considered: Why not, he suggested, elect the originator of spring training since he'd created a pleasant way for the writers to visit Florida? And what about inventors of the hot dog and the peanut? On a more serious note, Daniel also lobbied for the inclusion of umpires on the ballot; they would make it eventually, starting in 1952, with the election of Bill Klem.

Meantime, news of each person elected and the deluge of even the most critical of columns, especially during voting time in the dead of winter, fueled the interest. Interest was more intense than anyone could have imagined, and kept the Hall of Fame in the news constantly throughout 1937 and '38, such that today, along with trade talks, it remains *the* hot-stove topic. As the *Sporting News* urged longtime fans, those with "first-hand knowledge of the players," to send their lists of deserving old-timers to Cooperstown, Cleland received a stream of letters from fans, most of whom seemed to have a personal connection to the players they favored. Among them was Horace J. Bradley of Ephrata, Pennsylvania, who wrote Cleland to lobby for the inclusion of more premodern players, including his father, George Washington Bradley, who had pitched the National League's first no-hit, no-run game, in 1876 for St. Louis. Bradley had a successful career—winning 139 games in eight big-league seasons—but never was elected.

◆   ◆   ◆

Alexander Cleland was wise not to involve himself too deeply in the arguments that raged about who belonged in the Hall of Fame. He had too many other things to do anyway, from stirring up publicity to overseeing construction of the building and collecting artifacts.

Though Cleland was continuing to find a lot of valuable donations, he was having particular trouble in securing items from the one group who could help the most: old players. Told that the eighty-nine-year-old George Wright was living in Boston, Cleland wrote to him, only to find that the famous player still had some old equipment and uniforms, but was reluctant to send them anywhere since he'd loaned things in the past that had never been returned. But realizing the Cooperstown museum was different, he promised some items. Wright never sent a thing, even after he had been elected to the Hall in 1937.

Asking Albert Spalding's son, Keith, for help in acquiring some drawings that included one hundred full-page engravings from Spalding's seminal book on baseball history, *America's National Game*, Cleland had to settle for photocopies. The drawings had been donated to the New York Public Library, where officials were reluctant to break up the original collection.

Thinking he had a bead on a uniform from the late-1880s-era great Roger Connor, Cleland contacted a series of people who had known the former Giants outfielder. The trail started with a brother of Connor's old teammate Joe Dunbar to Connor's daughter and a Connecticut sports promoter who apparently had received all of Connor's equipment. But the trail was cold, completely cold, and despite repeated assurances, Cleland ended up empty-handed.

Cleland soldiered on anyway, creating a pamphlet describing Cooperstown's efforts to create the Hall of Fame in hopes that it would ease the task of salesmanship. Meantime, through Frank Graham, baseball writer for the *New York Sun*, he made another valuable connection: sportswriter Bill Brandt, manager of the National League Service Bureau, who was genuinely excited by the idea of a Hall of Fame and pledged to write some stories about it. Good to his word, Brandt became a one-man publicity machine, turning out releases on each new find and more general pieces about Cooperstown that newspapers were eager to run. Brandt covered every conceivable angle of the Hall of Fame progress, from donations to detailed accounts of Cooperstown's role in baseball history, and plans for the Centennial celebration in three years.

Arguably, Brandt's efforts amounted to the official birth of baseball mythology. Knowing full well that Cooperstown's role in the start of baseball was murky, he plunged ahead anyway, detailing in the May 21, 1936 *Sporting News*, not just news of the planned Centennial and Cooperstown's supposed role in the origins of the game, but where Cooperstown was and how to get there. With every article, interest increased and the little town became synonymous with baseball history. "The main road passes by the stone-posted gateway of Doubleday Field in Cooperstown, NY," Brandt's piece begins. "It's a modern road of concrete broad-gauged, ribbing far over the hills in either direction. . . . Outside of town, the road becomes U.S. 28. . . ."

Brandt spun a similar piece for the 1936 *Spalding Baseball Guide*, writing that the "nationwide interest in the selection of baseball immortals for the Cooperstown Hall of Fame gives promise of making the Centennial celebration of baseball's birth-year an important event in the 1939 sports year."

Jumping in was Cooperstown state senator Walter Stokes who suggested that tourists planning a visit in 1939 to the World's Fair in New York City squeeze in a trip to Cooperstown as well. "Ancient Egypt had its sport of kings, Rome its chariot races," Stokes said in late May. "These depended largely upon sacrifice of human life for success. America has its baseball—the greatest, cleanest and best of sports that instead of sacrifice glorifies manhood. . . ." Whew. At least Stokes's verbosity went somewhere; he joined a New York State delegation charged with building publicity for the Centennial.

Meantime, Brandt's efforts were starting to yield results. In August, Benjamin Shibe, whose family owned the A's, donated to the Hall a series of baseballs manufactured between 1866 and 1876 that had been exhibited at Centennial Exposition in Philadelphia. In September, Christy Mathewson's widow, Jane, donated her late husband's favorite mitt that was immediately put on display. Meantime, another widow, John McGraw's wife, Blanche, sent in a small statue of the great Giants manager that he had loaned St. Bonaventure College, which her husband had attended for a year. And from places all over the country came a rich assortment of vintage baseball odds and ends: old photos, baseballs, and a bat used by the Penobscot Indian Louis Sockalexis whose heroics as a member of the 1897 Cleveland Spiders led a change in the team's nickname to "Indians."

Stephen Clark himself kept rummaging around and came up with other items to donate: a print of an early Cooperstown team, a signed Babe Ruth ball, a bust of Christy Mathewson, and a vintage novelty bank that was a likeness of an underhanded pitcher. From fans came scorecards from Johnny Vander Meer's consecutive no-hitters; and framed photos of Spalding's 1889 Round-the-World tour and 1930 Boston Braves' Old-Timers' day; as well as a display of World Series press pins. And from seventy-six-year-old turn-of-the-century big leaguer Joe Gunson came a vintage catcher's mitt, which looked more like a thin leather cushion about the size of a Frisbee; with it, Gunson had enclosed a bunch of newspaper articles and affidavits from former players claiming that he had developed and worn the world's first catcher's mitt.

Sportswriter Fred Lieb's contribution was another baseball—this one used in 1931 by a big-league all-star team in Japan. Helen DeBost of New York contributed a ball used by her father in an 1858 game between teams from Brooklyn and Manhattan. And from John Hooper of New York came a painting of his father, the actor De Wolf Hooper, famous for his rendition of the poem "Casey at the Bat."

Meantime, the Hall continued to zero in on the early Hall of Famers themselves for artifacts, but to Cleland's considerable disappointment, was coming up empty-handed. Throughout 1936 and into '37, Cleland fired off letters to the inaugural electees, whose involvement he considered crucial to the overall success of the Hall. He twice wrote Walter Johnson at his farm in Maryland, but the Big Train, perhaps distracted by his rising political interests, did not respond. Nor did Napoleon Lajoie, Ty Cobb, Tris Speaker, Babe

Ruth, or Honus Wagner, who promised to send a few items when he got around to it. Nothing arrived.

Finally, an immortal responded: It was Cy Young, who, in early 1937, wrote to say he had a number of items on his Ohio farm that he was willing to donate, from a ball he used in 1908 in his five hundredth win to his last uniform, from 1911, and a collection of honorary cups. Young included a cautionary note in his letter to Cleland: It might take a while to assemble and mail the items to Cooperstown. Cleland, who figured that obtaining some items related to the careers of these first few Hall of Famers was critical to the museum's overall success, was relieved, particularly because he had started work on the player plaques that would hang in the Hall. He wrote back with enthusiasm, asking that Young try to send the items by May. But May came and went, and there was no further word from Young.

Despite the continuing publicity, plans for the Hall seemed in a rut. So in the spring of 1937 with the project stalled, Cleland decided to take a trip—a long car journey in which he'd visit as many of the Hall of Famers as possible, hoping to secure a few priceless items from the immortals themselves. Nothing that a little face time couldn't solve.

◆　◆　◆

Through most of their fifty-two years, the St. Louis Browns were year-in and year-out baseball's worst team—so bad they were almost lovable. Today, they're remembered as the only team with a midget (the 3'7" batsman Eddie Gaedel in 1951); a one-armed outfielder (Pete Gray in '45); and a team that always played second fiddle to the Cardinals, their crosstown National League rivals. In St. Louis, the Browns were so forgettable that in 1935, the team drew just over 80,000 *for the whole season*, one in which they didn't even finish last.

Only in the latter stages of World War II, in 1944, when the many top big leaguers were in the service did the Browns take an American League pennant, losing ironically in the World Series to the Cardinals. And only because the Browns were lucky enough to be awarded George Sisler in a contract dispute were they spared from being truly horrendous. Just think how desolate things would have been for the team had baseball awarded Sisler to the Pirates, who had signed him back in 1915, but did so without the consent of his parents as required, which voided his contract. With the league then sending Sisler to the Browns, Pittsburgh owner Barney Dreyfuss became so enraged that he never again spoke to his friend Garry Hermann of the National League Commission.

Stepping to the microphone as the sixth living Hall of Famer to be introduced in Cooperstown, the forty-six-year-old Sisler, looking dapper in a cream-colored suit, kept it short, a little bland and self-deprecating—and choosing not to mention the fact that he was skipping the day's graduation of his son, George, from Colgate, to be there. "I'm one of the youngsters of this Hall of Fame," he said, "but it is certainly nice to be back here and to greet all of you gentlemen. I think this is a great thing for baseball to commemorate the fine records of all these great men who had played baseball. I'm certainly glad to do my little part in helping this great day."

Those few remarks revealed a great deal about Sisler. In a game of outsized personalities and big egos, he was the rare star who didn't care about flaunting his remarkable gifts. Reminiscing in retirement to St. Louis baseball writer Bob Broeg about rebounding from an eye infection that sidelined him for 1923 to hit .305 and collect 194 hits in '24, Sisler sniffed and said, "I didn't consider that real good hitting."

Not when you hit .420 in 1922—which wasn't even his best season. By his own judgment, Sisler had compiled the best of his fifteen big-league seasons two years earlier, in 1920, when he played every inning of every game; he had 257 hits, not broken for eighty-four years; and batted .407. He had forty-six doubles, eighteen triples, and nineteen home runs—a distant second to Ruth's fifty-four. All that from a man who wasn't particularly big at 5'11" and 170 pounds, making him positively dwarfish, sandwiched between Lajoie and Johnson, at picture time.

Sisler's gift was speed, versatility, surprising upper-body strength, and baseball instincts, giving him a resemblance to modern-era Hall of Famers like George Brett or Paul Molitor. On the last day of 1920, against the White Sox, Sisler gave a clinic—banging out three hits, scoring two runs, and stealing three bases, including home. He even pitched the last inning, striking out two. At least that wasn't so far-fetched: Like Ruth, Sisler had started in the major leagues as a left-handed pitcher. He'd done so after compiling a 50–0 record—not a misprint—at the University of Michigan. Then, in his first big-league outing, in 1915, against the Senators, he outdueled Walter Johnson, his hero. "For a minute, I thought maybe I'd go over and shake his hand, and tell him that I'm sorry I beat him," Sisler said of Johnson. "But I guess that was just the silly idea of a young kid who had just come face-to-face with his idol and beaten him."

Using a choked-up grip on a heavy, forty-two-ounce hickory bat, Sisler was too good to play every four days. So later in the season, he became a full-time, left-handed-hitting first baseman—batting .281 in eighty-one games, and following up in 1916 with a .305 average, his first of nine straight years above .300. At bat, on the bases, and in the field, he was a player without flaws—and along with Larry Lajoie and in later years, Ernie Banks, he was perhaps the best player never to make it to the World Series. Sisler had speed and led the National

League four times in stolen bases, and could hit with power just as readily as he could beat out a drag bunt, while at first, he led the league six times in assists. His college coach and mentor, Branch Rickey, said that one day when Sisler fielded a ball only to find the pitcher wasn't covering the base, he instinctively leapt forward and caught his own throw for the out.

Sisler compiled a .340 lifetime batting average, and only injuries kept him from amassing three thousand hits—he finished with 2,811. But he never took his skills for granted; the long train trips east afforded Sisler plenty of time to think about the game and, similar to Cobb, become a student of hitting in particular and of what it took to succeed. "What I have learned about batting, nobody taught me," he told F. C. Lane in the 1925 book *Hitting*. "I had to dig it out for myself."

Indeed, Sisler could be verbose in holding forth on baseball, which he considered far preferable to talking about himself. "The secret of batting may be in the eye, but it's also in proper coordination," he told Lane. "A man's shoulders and arms must work together with his eye. The element of time is very essential." Just as many said of Ruth, Sisler considered his early career as a pitcher as another advantage. "I used to stand on the mound myself, study the batter, and wonder how I could fool him. Now, when I am at the plate, I can more easily place myself in the pitcher's position and figure what is passing through his mind."

Sisler stood out for other reasons. Reverential and formal to elders, Sisler always called Rickey "coach" even after Branch had taken over as Browns manager. In contrast to most of his teammates, Sisler hadn't just coasted through college, but graduated with a degree in mechanical engineering, earning him the early derisive nickname, "college boy."

At a time when drinking comprised a big part of a player's entertainment, Sisler refrained; he didn't smoke, either. Invited by W. C. Fields to his whiskey-stacked dressing room at the Majestic Theater in Boston, Sisler was lauded by the famous comedian. "You fascinate me, George," he said in his famous nasal tenor. "I've seen you many times and have admired your artistry very much. Uh, help yourself to the snake-bite cure."

"No thanks," replied Sisler, politely. "I don't drink."

Disappointment flooded Fields's face. Helping himself to a beaker of rye, he sighed and said thoughtfully: "Oh well, not even the perfect ballplayer can have everything."

His teammates tested Sisler early in his career, but discovered a surprisingly hard edge to a quiet man. When Browns pitcher Bob Groom perceived the young, recently converted first baseman as having some fielding troubles, he exploded at Sisler in the dugout.

"Listen, you f——ing college boy," Groom yelled at the rookie. "You run harder for those f——ing balls. Where the hell do you think you are, at a f——ing tea party?"

Sisler's face went white. No one had ever addressed him like that. They never would again, either: Staring at Groom for an instant, Sisler reared back and decked him with a left hook.

An eye injury cut Sisler's career, making it considerably shorter than the other Cooperstown immortals. He was seventeen and a senior at Central High School in Akron when he signed with the town's Ohio-Pennsylvania League team, not telling his parents because, as Sisler put it, "they'd be sore if they knew I wanted to be a ballplayer."

Sold from Akron to Columbus and then to the Pirates, Sisler was asked to play in Pittsburgh when he graduated from high school. But when his father found out that he had signed without his approval, the contact was nullified. The ensuing controversy, the first of many deadball-era player allocations, was one of the prime reasons baseball magnates would scrap the three-man National commission and eventually transfer power to the commissioner.

So Sisler went to college, shaving perhaps three years off his big-league career. The eye infection felled him in '23, causing double vision until the end of his career. Sisler still excelled—hitting a hefty .345 in 1925, and serving as player-manager. He held on for three more years until the Browns sent him to the Senators, where he played twenty games and was unloaded to the Braves and then a couple of minor league teams before retiring at the age of thirty-nine. With three sons and a daughter at home, Sisler returned to St. Louis to run a printing company.

Yet, Sisler's extraordinary career rates barely a blip on the baseball radar screen of today. He didn't even make baseball's All-Century Team, which includes two first basemen—Lou Gehrig and Mark McGwire. There are several reasons, starting with his abbreviated career and playing in St. Louis, which for years was baseball's furthest outpost. But those who played against him knew better: Cobb, in his autobiography, rated Sisler as his first baseman of choice, ahead of Gehrig, Jimmie Foxx, and Bill Terry.

To the end, Sisler himself remained uninterested in the attention, preferring to talk about the art of hitting.

◆　　◆　　◆

In his quest for Hall of Fame items, Alexander Cleland planned to drive from New York City south to Washington, D.C., and then on to Maryland and west to Pennsylvania and Ohio. The plan was to visit people whom he hoped would make contributions to the museum: John Foster, editor of *The Spalding Guide*, in Washington, D.C.; Walter Johnson at the farm in Germantown, Maryland; Honus Wagner, outside Pittsburgh; and Cy Young on his farm in central Ohio. A quick jaunt north to Cleveland to see both Tris Speaker and Larry Lajoie was put on hold with Tris's slow recovery from a skull fracture suffered in a fall.

The America that beckoned Alexander Cleland was more difficult to traverse in 1937.

America's first continuous coast-to-coast highway, the Lincoln Highway, had been completed a dozen years before, but limited cars to a 35-mph speed limit and trucks to 10.

On the other hand, the country was starting to emerge from nearly a decade of deep economic turmoil symbolized by the colossal World's Fair construction project underway in Flushing Meadows, Queens. The Fair was the nation's biggest reclamation project of its time—a 1,216 1/2-acre global village, including two artificial lakes on the site of a former dumping ground for ash—a man-made mountain of ash, up to ninety feet high, and the very same "valley of ashes" immortalized by F. Scott Fitzgerald in *The Great Gatsby*. The Fair, which President Roosevelt was set to open just weeks prior to the festivities in Cooperstown, would draw tens of millions of visitors to New York, and link the Grand Central Parkway to another massive project, the Triborough Bridge; in the meantime, it provided thousands of much-needed jobs and served as a glowing symbol of American ingenuity at a time when the country needed a jolt of good news.

That Roosevelt would inaugurate the Fair was entirely appropriate. He was the visionary whose leadership had steered America through the worst of the Depression with enormous New Deal job programs that ushered in modern government and an extraordinary tapestry of new highways, bridges, and tunnels. In New York City, those projects ranged from the opening of the George Washington Bridge in 1931 to the city's first airport, North Beach—now LaGuardia—and a lot in between like the Triborough, the Bronx-Whitestone Expressway, the Lincoln Tunnel, the Gowanus Expressway, and the Belt and Henry Hudson parkways.

New York's growth was excessive, even for the New Deal, thanks in part to an energetic bulldog—its parks commissioner, Robert Moses. On the other hand, it symbolized the importance of New York of the time as America's most important, vital city, a place of bright lights, burning ambition, and sophistication that ran across the country and seemed mighty appealing to the folks back in Oshkosh.

Baseball was an integral part of New York City's complicated tapestry. In numbers alone, the city that Cleland left on his car trip dwarfed anything else in the country, starting with its three big-league teams, the Yankees, Giants, and Brooklyn Dodgers, at least one of which seemed to be in the World Series every fall. New York had two glorious train stations, Pennsylvania and Grand Central; three subway lines; and five crowded boroughs with 12.5 million people, more than any other city in the country. It had eight major daily newspapers, nearly 45,000 factories, and 81,657 teachers. New York was the country's center of finance, manufacturing, publishing, education, and entertainment—and dotted by cultural icons from the Great White Way of Broadway to Tin Pan Alley, Forty-second Street, the elegant Stork Club, the towering Empire State Building (the world's tallest), and the African American cultural homeland of Harlem.

But if anything tuned Americans into the glamor, glitz, and energy of New York, it was radio, which was always on, somewhere, in the late 1930s, from living rooms to department stores, bars, and cross-town cabs. One '30s-era visitor to New York, as quoted in David Gelernter's book *1939: The Lost World of the Fair*, said that radio "furnishes a jazz undertone to the rumble of the city." Yes, but "he never remembers to switch off the radio," said his companion. Baseball owners, fearing at first that broadcasts of the game would cut attendance, had resisted radio until they realized they were wrong, dead wrong. Just the opposite was true, and radio broadcasts in fact swelled the interest—taking the baseball action from the biggest stadiums into the most remote hamlets.

Tune in to radio on a typical Sunday night in New York in 1937, and you could catch the comedy of Jack Benny at 7 and Edgar Bergen at 8, and Walter Winchell's gossip at 9:30, most of it generated locally and beamed across the country. Radio of the era presented not just a steady stream of comedy, gossip, and dance bands, but news of the impending crisis abroad, the president's inspiring fireside chats, and baseball. Dodger radio announcer Red Barber, who delivered games from atop Ebbets Field in what he called the "catbird seat," said a person could walk the streets of Brooklyn during a broadcast and know from all the radios tuned in to the game exactly what was happening.

This virtual broadcast explosion—television would arrive in 1939—fueled the interest in public culture. Magazines, most of them New York-based, had caught on, and readers avidly devoured familiar publications such as *Time* and *Life* as well as the late and not-so-great *Click* and *See*. Advertising was plastered just about anywhere, and hawking everything from Planter's Peanuts ("A Bag a Day for More Pep") to cigarettes ("Camels Never Get On Your Nerves").

Jazz was hitting its heyday, underscored by the elegant rhythms of

George Gershwin, who would tragically die in 1937 of a cerebral hemorrhage at only thirty-nine, and others like Billie Holliday and Ella Fitzgerald. Jazz attracted the era's top young musicians, regardless of race; consider the enormity of a single 1937 New York jam session, where Artie Shaw on clarinet, Chick Webb on traps, and Duke Ellington on piano improvised for ten minutes on Gershwin's "I Got Rhythm."

Hollywood as well was starting to emerge from the gloom of the Depression with a series of blockbuster epics of surprising depth that gave rise to some new stars of their own. Spencer Tracy took his first Oscar in 1937 for Best Actor for his performance as Manuel in *Captains Courageous*, a simple Portuguese fisherman who mentors a bratty English boy by teaching him lessons in hard work and honesty; Tracy would win again in '38 for his memorable performance as Father Flanagan in *Boys Town*. Meantime, Luise Rainer would take the second of her back-to-back Best Actress Oscars in '37 for her performance as the strong and silent O-Lan, a self-sacrificing Chinese peasant farm wife in *The Good Earth*. The Oscar for the year's best film went to *The Life of Emile Zola*, a beautifully well-crafted screen biography of the crusading nineteenth-century French literary novelist who fought to defend army officer Captain Alfred Dreyfus from an unjust, anti-Semitic accusation of treason and exile to the infamous French penal colony, Devil's Island.

In sports, baseball ruled the roost in 1937, followed in interest by boxing, horse racing, and college football. Neither pro football nor basketball drew anything resembling a national audience, while interest in hockey and its six-team National Hockey League was strictly regional, relegated mostly to the Northeast and Canada. Think of an athlete from the era, and most likely, the name is a baseball player: Two extraordinary young talents, Joe DiMaggio and Bob

Feller, had debuted the previous year, and were already making their mark. DiMaggio, the son of a San Francisco fisherman, had started with a bang—getting three hits, including a triple, in his first start— and led the Yanks to a six-game 1936 World Series demolishing of the Giants. Feller's first start had been just as astonishing, with the seventeen-year-old right-handed fireballer striking out fifteen St. Louis Browns in a 4–1 victory. That was one less than the American League record, which he'd get only a month later.

◆   ◆   ◆

Alexander Cleland's doggedness was starting to pay off. Visiting Walter Johnson in Maryland, he secured a pledge from the Big Train to sort through some old trunks of equipment and see what he might find for the Hall of Fame. Letters to some of the other new Hall of Famers, including Young, Lajoie, and Cobb, paid dividends as well; all three promised items to Cooperstown.

Lajoie responded by late summer with a note of thanks on his election to the Hall and a short time later, with both the uniform and the bat from his three-thousandth hit. Cobb came through after several letters, explaining that he had already given away most of the suitable items to souvenir sellers, while complaining with some jus- tification that he had neither received notification of his election nor any details about the museum in general.

Cleland wrote back, sending Cobb a promotional Hall of Fame booklet, intended as a mea culpa of sorts that the Hall had not fol- lowed up his letter with an official letter. Promising to invite Cobb to the inauguration of the baseball museum, he asked again for any items that Cobb could think to send, promising they would go on immediate display for a whole generation of young fans who had

On June 12, 1939, in Cooperstown: An autograph and another story from Honus Wagner.

All the way down Main Street to the flagpole in the center of town and beyond,
they gathered for baseball's great day.

June 12, 1939: All roads
lead to Cooperstown.

LET THE GAMES BEGIN: Wagner (left) and Eddie Collins (right)
choose sides for the Centennial All-Star Game the old-fashioned
way, by sliding their fists up the bat handle. Last man able to
make a fist picks first.

The Centennial Stamp is rolled out at the Cooperstown post office by Postmaster General Jim
Farley (left) and Commissioner Kenesaw Mountain Landis (right).

Many in the crowd estimated at more than 10,000 seemed to be men in hats.

THE BABE AT BAT: A hefty swing … and a pop-up at the Centennial All-Star Game.

Cy Young, a bit paunchy at
thirty-eight
with the 1905 Red Sox.

IN THEIR PRIME: The Babe, circa 1927.

Connie Mack, who managed for more than
fifty years, always inpeccably dressed.

Alexander Cartwright, late in life. The hat is a gift of the fire department in Honolulu, where he had moved from New York.

Eddie Collins of the White Sox.

THE GREAT GEORGE SISLER OF THE ST. LOUIS BROWNS: "He could do everything," Ty Cobb said of him.

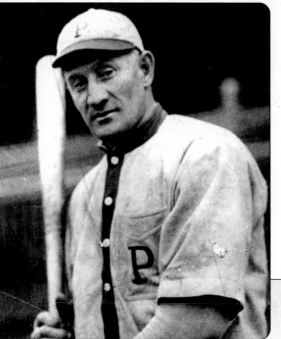

Pittsburgh's
Honus Wagner.

GENERAL ABNER DOUBLEDAY:
Posing for the artist, he is most likely not
thinking about baseball.

GROVER CLEVELAND ALEXANDER: With the Phillies, he won an astounding
ninety-four games in three years, despite the size of his mitt.

THE VISIONARY: Stephen Clark.

THE TYCOON: Albert Spalding.

So beloved in Cleveland was Napoleon "Larry" Lajoie that the Indians for a time were known as the "Naps."

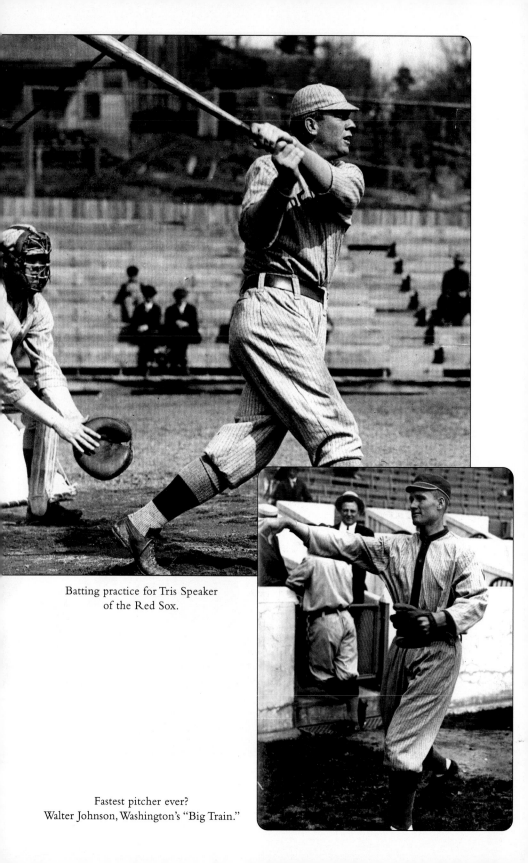

Batting practice for Tris Speaker
of the Red Sox.

Fastest pitcher ever?
Walter Johnson, Washington's "Big Train."

never seen him play. His plea to the old player's vanity worked; a month or so later, Cobb sent a large package containing a sweater, shirt, pants, and stockings from his Tiger days, and a pair of shoes he'd worn with the A's. Nearly two years later, in April 1939, just weeks before the museum dedication, Cobb sent another item—a bat he had misplaced in the process of moving to California from Georgia. True to his word, Cleland wasted no time in placing it on display.

Cobb's contribution was important in another unexpected way. As the centerpiece to the Hall of Fame, Cleland had tasked baseball writer Harry Edwards with the preparation of bronze plaques that would feature a player's likeness along with his years in the league, positions played, statistics, and a six-line synopsis of his career. But when Cobb saw the proposed write-ups, he found several errors, namely the number of hits he was credited with—4,025 as opposed to the actual 4,191—and his year of entry into major league baseball, which the plaque said was 1904 when in fact it had been a year later. Embarrassed, baseball officials quickly made corrections—vowing as well to double-check the other plaques.

◆　◆　◆

By the summer of 1937, it was clear that an upstairs room of the local Village Club was no longer adequate to support the growing number of baseball artifacts. Cleland and Stephen Clark could afford to think of a number of options: Big-league baseball officials' promise of $100,000 to tie in the Centennial with the Hall of Fame and museum, in fact, was approved in December, along with the appointment of a representative to oversee plans for the celebration.

For help, Clark and Cleland turned to another Cooperstown native who had made it big in New York: Frank Whiting, an architect who had helped design the Singer Building in Manhattan. In July, his plan for a new museum, to become a true warehouse for the protection of baseball treasures for all time, was unveiled in *The Otsego Farmer*. Whiting's design was elegant and in the classical tradition—a colonial two-story building flanked by four majestic pillars and four white marble steps surrounded by wrought-iron railings and featuring a carved emblem in stone above the main door that would include a replica of the Doubleday baseball. The building's walls would be red brick made from James River Colonial brick, similar in color to that of the buildings in Williamsburg, Virginia, integrated with stone and topped off by a slate roof. Five square-shaped windows stretched across the front of the second story from which a big baseball flag would be hung during the Cavalcade.

To be built at 25 Main Street on the site of the old Leo Block, and connected to Clark Gymnasium, some two blocks south of Doubleday Field, the building's understated design had the look of a library—and was very much in keeping with Clark's vision to blend into the overall appearance of the town. Inside the building, Whiting had designed a spacious 1,200-square-foot central room on the first floor where plaques of the Hall of Famers would be displayed and the walls lined with portraits and photos. He even added a fireplace, above which would go an oil painting of Abner Doubleday, and on the mantelpiece, the Doubleday ball encased in glass—giving the museum a comfortable, homey feel. Most of the donated books would be headed to the library, planned for the second floor.

Overall, the oversized windows would bathe the room in light, delighting visitors, but creating a conservator's nightmare with direct sunlight focused directly on the growing number of artifacts. It's a far cry from today's renovated, three-story museum, where the 2.6

million items are housed in climate-controlled areas and maintained by professional staff using state-of-the-art archival techniques.

Organizers made a particular point to stress that the museum would be fireproof, a critical point for many considering donations of their priceless baseball mementos and wanting assurance that the items would be safe. Its connection to the gym meant the two facilities could share the heating plant and help cut fuel costs, an important consideration during Cooperstown winters. The design added offices for Cleland and William Beattie, the gym director now serving as museum curator.

Around the country, news that the Hall of a Fame and Museum would be getting its own elegant building was a sure sign that Cleland's publicity machine was gathering momentum. Artifacts and letters continued to pour in from everywhere, as Cleland heard from everyone from publicists to cabinet manufacturers—most legitimate and some not—anxious to get involved. When a man from Albany wrote to offer a uniform from the great Johnny "Iver," Cleland knew that couldn't be right. He wrote back immediately to point out that the letter writer was almost certainly referring to Johnny "Evers," the great Cubs second baseman of a generation earlier and a native of nearby Troy, New York. Others whose business was public relations and promotions, like John Clark of New York City, a manufacturer of exhibition cases, were taken more seriously. Clark's company, H. F. Beers, got the contract. So did E. H. Leon of the Robinson Clay Product Co. for a series of ashtrays adorned with a black-and-white print of a design reading "Baseball Centennial." Meanwhile, Cooperstown baseball enthusiasts were able to convince the Standard Oil Co. to feature their town in the company's popular New York State roadmaps as the birthplace of baseball.

Meanwhile, the publicity was showing no sign of letting up. In

January 1938, *Time* magazine described the celebration plans and how baseball had supposedly started in Cooperstown, where the civic pride of the citizens had been stirred. And that spring came word from the World's Fair, also planned for a '39 opening, that a sports float had been part of an entry in a New York City parade, although Fair officials seemed to be unaware of when the baseball festivities were due to kick off.

Time magazine's coverage was another example of how Cooperstown's plan had moved from a small-town endeavor of civic boosters to the big time. With requests continuing to pour in for Hall of Fame tie-ins to commemorative bats and balls, booklets, and baseball histories, Cooperstown officials secured a copyright on usage of the term, "Birthplace of Baseball." Cooperstown residents themselves pitched in; when a local bowling team headed off to a tournament in New York, they went wearing shirts emblazoned with the insignia, "Birthplace of Baseball."

The January 1938 decision of baseball writers to elect Grover Cleveland Alexander to the Hall of Fame was another publicity bonanza in the middle of winter. Preceded by the quieter Hall of Fame selection announced the month before at the winter baseball meetings in Chicago of five more builders—John McGraw and Connie Mack, along with American League founder Ban Johnson; the first president of the National League and Mills Committee member Morgan Bulkeley; and the star of the 1869 Reds, baseball's first pro team, George Wright—that news was buried somewhat by the Associated Press report that the Red Sox had purchased a "husky" nineteen-year-old recruit named Ted Williams, who, after only two years in professional baseball, "had made rapid strides."

By midsummer 1938, with Centennial plans all of one year off, baseball officials turned to more immediate concerns: the upgrading of Doubleday Field, where a postceremony game of current big-league all-stars was being planned. With each team due to send two of its best players for the game, Frick turned to *his* best: longtime Polo Grounds groundskeeper Henry Fabian. An intimate of John McGraw, Christy Mathewson, and Damon Runyon—who called him "Hennerie"—Fabian, at seventy-three, was the Babe Ruth of grounds—a recognized expert on how best to care for ball fields, a onetime pro ballplayer with a quarter-century of experience already under his belt. Among Fabian's challenges was expanding the field—left field was only 248 feet with right field only a foot longer, making the game more than adequate for local games, but unsuitable for the big leaguers.

Accompanied to Doubleday Field by a group of local village trustees, Fabian declared himself well satisfied with the condition of the field for big-league use, and urged that the all-dirt or "skinned" infield be sodded to simulate the big-league fields, all of which were now constructed with grass. Back for a meeting with the officials at the Cooper Inn, he then asked that the renovation project start soon so he could return in September to review the work.

To take care of the improvements, officials turned to the Works Progress Administration or WPA, one of President Roosevelt's signature creations to provide economic relief during the Depression. The WPA supplied twenty-eight workers who not only added the infield grass to the field and resodded the rest, but also tore down the existing bleachers, and in its place, added a crescent-shaped, steel-covered grandstand with a capacity for eight hundred, and bleachers extending down both lines. It was a good deal all the way around—with the New York WPA pitching in the lion's share of the project, more than $23,000. Cooperstown's bill for the cost of materials and equipment rentals was $17,300.

By the fall of '38, big-league baseball had jumped on the band-wagon full-scale, a fact that stole a bit of thunder from what Coop-erstown officials were doing, but certainly served the cause. Officially, the group now running the organization was the grandly named National Baseball Centennial Commission, comprised of Judge Landis, Frick, John Heydler, and W. A. Harridge. For the most part, it was an opportunity for big names to grab some headlines: At its first meeting in October 1938 in Chicago at the Hotel Roosevelt, the group did little but to create another layer of bureaucracy, an executive committee comprised of more baseball officials as well as military heavyweights like General John Pershing as well as top gen-erals for the marine corps, navy, and army.

With the exception of Frick, most of those names were there as window dressing—Cleland wouldn't be asked to join until December. Leave it to two little-known names at the bottom of the list to wield the committee's real power.

◆ ◆ ◆

Baseball mattered in 1939 in a way it simply doesn't today. In a sports landscape where football, basketball, hockey, and other sports were either overly regional or still too ramshackle, baseball was king. Whole sports pages were given to how Lefty Grove was pitching or how the Yankees were faring, unmatched in attention of the nation except for the occasional Army-Navy college football game or U.S. Open tennis match. What American boy in the 1930 didn't want to hit for power like Jimmie Foxx or Joe DiMaggio? Adding to the excitement was baseball on radio, which brought both the action from the big stadiums and a new generation of young stars, like Williams in Boston and the Cleveland Indians spectacular twenty-year-old fireballer Bob Feller, already in his fourth big-league season, into the most remote hamlets.

Looking for their fourth pennant in a row, the Yankees had opened the season back on April 20 in predictable form—with Red Ruffing shutting down the Red Sox 2–0 on seven hits including a double from Williams, now twenty-one, and the team's rookie right-fielder. The '30s had pretty much belonged to the Yankees—the team had rolled to World Series triumphs four of the previous seven years—thanks to the steady pitching of veterans like Ruffing and Lefty Gomez; an infield anchored by catcher Bill Dickey and first baseman Lou Gehrig; and, in 1936, the emergence of DiMaggio.

By '39, DiMaggio had already powered the Yankees to Series titles in each of his first three seasons. He had hit .323 his rookie season, and then put together a season for the ages in '37, batting .346 with an America League-leading forty-six home runs, no small feat in the cavernous expanse of Yankee Stadium. DiMaggio fielded flawlessly, and despite a periodic knee injury, was seldom caught off-base. His game was virtually flawless, and despite shunning the bright lights of New York, he had become the soul of the Yankee dynasty and an inspiration to Italian immigrants. Even an unfortunate profile in the May 1 issue of *Life*—DiMaggio "speaks English without an accent" and "never reeks of garlic," the magazine reported in a piece that underscored many of the deep-seated ethnic stereotypes of the day—couldn't derail his popularity. The tone was typical for the era; in 1937, Dan Parker in the *Daily News* wrote that the young star was strong and agile even "before taking aboard his cargo of pasta fagiole."

For all these young stars, there was concern that another, more established bright light was struggling. Yankee captain Lou Gehrig, the man they called "The Iron Horse" because he hadn't missed a game for fifteen years, had dropped off at an alarming degree. The decline for the thirty-six-year-old Gehrig had started the year before when he had batted .295, his first sub-.300 season in thirteen years, and hit *only* twenty-nine home runs, his first sub-thirty year in more than a decade. Opening Day in '39 was another sign that something was dreadfully wrong—in Gehrig's 2,124th straight game, he had no hits and twice hit into double plays. Gehrig's fielding was further confirmation; his reflexes appeared to be shot and he had trouble even getting to the first-base bag for throws. In the clubhouse, friendly joshing about his mistakes had quickly given way to embarrassed silence.

On April 29 against the Senators, Gehrig mustered a single in three at-bats against left-hander Ken Chase in a 3–1 Yankee loss. Then on Sunday, the day President Roosevelt went to Queens to open the New York World's Fair, Gehrig went hitless in four at-bats against the Senators in another loss, this time 3–2. Hitting a miserable .143 with four singles and one RBI in twenty-eight at-bats, Gehrig was benched two days later in Detroit, ending his consecutive-game streak at 2,130 games. Players and fans alike were stunned. Gehrig himself wept, but the quiet, dignified man with a good word for everyone slapped his replacement, Babe Dahlgren, on the back, telling him to "get out there and knock in some runs."

Yankee manager Joe McCarthy had a practical explanation for benching this baseball icon. "I was afraid of his getting hit with a pitched ball," he said. "He wouldn't have been able to get out of the way. That's how bad it was." The ever-gracious Gehrig agreed. "I'm not doing the club any good," he said.

The incident personified what had already become a baseball season crowded with drama, of which the Baseball Centennial was a crucial part. Just a few weeks later, on May 17, in the improbable setting of a Columbia-Princeton game at Baker Field on the northern fringe of Manhattan, televised baseball made its debut. At the time, "radio camera," as it was called, was spanking new, having made a sizable stir just days before with President Franklin Roosevelt's speech at the World's Fair, the first event to be televised. To broadcast the Columbia game, NBC used a lone camera and a $150,000 mobile van behind first base that bounced the signal to a transmitter atop the Empire State Building, from where the game was beamed to viewers in a fifty-mile radius. Veteran announcer Bill Stern described the action of the second game of a doubleheader, won by Princeton 2–1 in ten innings, to a few hundred viewers at most.

The broadcast wasn't memorable. The single camera gave off a constant image of fuzzy white for the ball and couldn't squeeze more than three players at a time on the screen. For the most part the camera followed the pitcher's windup—quickly swiveling to the plate and the batter, and even the base runner. "Too often when the speck-like ball was struck," sniffed Orrin Dunlap in the *Times*, "it ne'er was found, like a white pinpoint it sailed off the screen." But even Dunlap realized the potential reach of the new medium: "This photographic art is too young to expect it to 'paint' electrically . . . a panoramic view," he wrote, "although there is little doubt that the future will bring the complete picture."

He was right, and it would be NBC again, through its local station W2XBS, that introduced television to the big leagues—on August 29 in Brooklyn, where at Ebbets Field, "two prying electric 'eyes,'" as the *Times* was by then calling it, broadcast the Dodgers-Reds doubleheader. Dunlap had urged NBC to use several cameras to help viewers follow the action: NBC listened, and for the Dodger game used two cameras—one near the third-base dugout for close-ups of the batters and the other in a second tier behind home offering an expansive view of the field.

The event was a critical success—sort of. "At times, it was possible to catch a fleeting glimpse of the ball," a critic wrote. As in the Columbia game, the signal was relayed to the Empire State Building transmitter to viewers within fifty miles. Only three commercials were shown—for Ivory Soap, Mobil Oil, and Wheaties. The game's broadcaster: Red Barber, the regular Dodger radioman, who ad-libbed throughout and squeezed in interviews with the teams' managers, Leo Durocher of the Dodgers and Bill McKechnie of the Reds, and Dodger slugger Dolph Camilli.

◆   ◆   ◆

Describing Dodger games for his radio audience from the press box high atop Ebbets Field, Red Barber was at the forefront of a 1930s revolution in baseball broadcasting that came full circle in Cooperstown. Barber called his perch the "catbird seat," and managers who stormed the field in protesting a call were stirring up "rhubarb in the pea patch." Chances are that many of his listeners over WOR Radio had never set eyes on a Southerner—Barber was from Mississippi—but his sonorous, syrupy cadence, and gentle delivery was an instant hit in the polyglot community of Brooklyn. "Red's appeal soared because people sensitive about the image of 'dees' and 'dems,'" Bob Costas told writer Curt Smith, "were pleased that this erudite man represented them." It is said that on a pleasant summer night in Brooklyn, you could walk the streets, and follow every Dodger play, thanks to Barber's pleasant voice booming through a thousand open windows.

Appropriately, the country's first radio station, Pittsburgh's KDKA, had launched baseball broadcasting—on August 5, 1920, at Forbes Field in Pittsburgh. There, a twenty-six-year-old foreman at Westinghouse

Co. named Harold Arlin filled a ground-level box seat, his equipment flanking the screen behind home plate, and spoke into a converted telephone as he described an 8–5 Pirates drubbing of the Phillies. At the 1921 World Series, between the Yankees and Giants, famed sportswriter Grantland Rice donned a set of earphones and broadcast game one from the Polo Grounds to listeners on a network of three stations—KDKA, WJZ in Newark, and WBZ of Springfield, Massachusetts.

Television still had a ways to go for viewers. But radio was quickly coming to mean as much in the country as television does now. A year—and $60 million worth of radios—later, it had become a way of life. By the early '30s, radio was as much a part of the household landscape as the kitchen faucet. At first, baseball officialdom was apprehensive—thinking that broadcasting games would hurt attendance—but within a few years, they realized that the effect was just the opposite. From 1933 to 1939, the American League's income from radio revenues increased more than forty times to $420,000.

Officials of the three New York teams thought they had the most to lose from radio, and in the 1920s, slapped a five-year ban on broadcasts of their games, a curious decision given their city was the country's media capital. Leave it then to Midwestern teams to lead the way: In 1925, the Chicago Cubs became the first big-league club to offer baseball on a regular basis, sending horse-racing sportscaster Jack Drees to the WIND studio each evening at 7 to reenact the day's game. Three years later, Ty Tyson became the radio voice of the Tigers, broadcasting games directly from Detroit's Navin Field. That was about the time the smooth but fast-talking Tom Manning was named as radio voice of the Indians on Cleveland station WTAM—an affiliation lasting until 1931 when the team moved to WHK, and he was dumped in favor of a former Indians left fielder, the popular Jack Graney, the first former big leaguer to occupy the booth.

But Manning was a broadcaster too talented to ignore. A booming voice helped; growing up in Cleveland, Manning achieved a smidgen of local fame as the newsboy with "the loudest voice," an unusual talent he parlayed in the early '20s to a position as the Indians public address announcer. Armed with only a megaphone, he would stand behind home plate at League Park and bellow out the starting lineups. Radio made him a fixture throughout Ohio, a career he augmented with his outgoing, gregarious personality, which came across on the air and, like Tyson and Barber, helped him take base-ball into homes, gas stations, general stores, and just about every-where else the broadcasts could be heard. After the Indians fired him in 1931, Manning never went back to regular baseball broadcasting, but he'd gone national by then anyway—to NBC, which tapped him for heavyweight title fights and the World Series. A particular favorite of another Midwesterner, Judge Landis, Manning continued to live in Cleveland, content to venture off when asked, as he would be on June 12, 1939, in Cooperstown.

By then, New York clubs had grown wise to the advantages of broadcasting. Larry MacPhail, who took over the Dodgers in 1939 after running the Cincinnati Reds, was the first of the New York executives to grow wise to radio, bringing Barber, who had been the Reds broadcaster for three years, with him to Brooklyn. With Barber describing the action and the Dodgers themselves much improved under Leo Durocher, Ebbets Field attendance soared more than 300,000 in '39, with the team outdrawing both the Yankees, by 100,000, and the Giants, by a mammoth quarter-million. Now that got the attention of the others, and before the season was finished, all three New York big-league teams were broadcasting their games—the Giants with Arch McDonald, brought by way of Tennessee from Washington, where he had been voice of the Senators, and the Yankees with yet another young Southerner, the twenty-six-year-old Mel Allen, whose rise had been nothing short of meteoric.

Who would ever had thought that Southerners would dominate baseball broadcasting in sophisticated New York? Like Barber, McDonald had an accent thick as butter and his own homespun sayings and shameless rooting for "our boys" that matched the rhythms of baseball. Hired by the Senators in 1934, McDonald talked about "ducks on the ponds"—his expression for Washington base runners—and pitches thrown "right down Broadway"—fat pitches over the middle of the plate. "There she goes, Mrs. Murphy!" he would yell in the rare occasion of a Senators home run. And for really exciting events—a clean double play, a ball smacked into the gap, and, gasp, a rare Senators win—McDonald pulled out all the stops: "They did it again," he'd say in quoting an old country ballad, "they cut down the old pine tree." McDonald became known as "The Old Tree," a fitting moniker for a man who'd worked, prior to his baseball career, as a peanut vendor, a boxing referee, a crop hand, and a patent-medicine salesman. "He was a huckster, a hustler, and his broadcasts, a midway," wrote Curt Smith in his 1987 book *Voices of the Game.* So who *was* Mrs. Murphy anyway? Years after McDonald's death, Smith tracked down his son Arch Jr. to ask the pressing question: "Beats the hell out of me," he said. "[It came] out of thin air, I think."

Along the way, McDonald became the first acknowledged master of another job requirement of early baseball broadcasters—re-creating the road game. At a time when stations considered it an extravagance to pay for broadcasters to accompany their team on the road, McDonald staged Senators away games in the second-floor window of People's Drugstore on G Street, three blocks from the White House, relying on the summary from a couple of Western Union operators. The broadcasts came with embellishments like canned crowd noise, bells and whistles, and in McDonald's case, a gong that he'd bang for anything that struck his fancy. Ticker breakdowns were so common that McDonald often had to improvise and just talk while the operators patched things up. His broadcasts became a happening in Washington, so popular that the radio station moved his studio to the drugstore's basement and erected bleachers for fans to attend and just listen.

So it was to McDonald, Manning, and Mel Allen, just two years removed from tiny Johns, Alabama, that baseball officials turned to broadcast Cavalcade events.

Still younger than most of the players he covered and admittedly more of a fan than a journalist, Allen had already developed a distinctive style. "How about that?" Allen would say simply after a sparkling play in the field or a big home run in what became *his* signature call. He set the scene, talked about the weather, seldom criticized anyone, and broadcast Yankee games, he said, in a "partisan" but not a "prejudicial" manner. Allen gave nicknames to the players: DiMaggio became "the Yankee Clipper," Gehrig, "Larrupin' Lou," and the deft 5'6" shortstop Phil Rizzuto, "the Scooter." He became not just the first notable Yankee "voice," but "The Voice," the best announcer on the planet for the best team on the planet, a man born to do what he did. "Talk about being in the right place at the right time," Allen would say a generation later, never taking success for granted. "I was so damned fortunate."

At the Cooperstown festivities, which NBC was broadcasting nationally in a special hour-long presentation, Manning was set to handle the player introductions, with Allen and McDonald set up

out at Doubleday Field to broadcast the all-star game. Both assign-
ments had their challenges; Allen still wasn't sure how many innings
the game would be, nor what big-league all-stars were on what team.
Meanwhile, back on stage, the introductions and speeches of the
baseball immortals were moving so quickly with little or no time in
between that even the fast-talking Manning had to push to describe
the events.

CHAPTER 6

"The Point Is to Get Baseball into the Other Pages as Well as the Sports Page"

This is about the proudest day of my life," said the day's next speaker, Eddie Collins. "To be able to rub elbows with the players here today, why I feel that I'd be happy to be the batboy for such a team as this. It's certainly a happy moment for me, and I'm certainly grateful to the baseball writers who have made it possible for me to be in this Hall of Fame."

The statement was apt: Collins *did* resemble a batboy. That he was dressed in a slick double-breasted suit and white-tinged shoes—the nattiest of those honored—didn't hide what dominated his features, his sleepy eyes, prominent jug ears, and 5'9" in height, which made him appear far younger than his fifty-two years. He looked more like an aging stock boy than one of baseball's greatest stars—perhaps part of what drove him as a ballplayer. A lifetime .333 hitter, Collins was a daring base runner, so fast he twice stole six bases in a game, and a man infused with so much self-confidence that he had earned a nickname: "Cocky."

Collins wasn't kidding at his pride in being included in this inaugural group of Hall of Famers—he rated Cobb, Sisler, Wagner, and Ruth as the greatest players he had seen. But he couldn't resist a touch of that old bravado, adding that he'd have received even more recognition if his career hadn't run smack dab up against Cobb, whom ironically he ended up with as a teammate for the '28 A's, along with Tris Speaker. Brusque, direct, impatient, and smart, qualities that served him effectively in his current role as Red Sox general manager, Collins was so fierce a competitor that as a member of the '19 White Sox, he became so distraught and infuriated that his teammates had conspired to throw the World Series that he found it difficult years later even to talk about the fix. For the most part, all questions from reporters about what he thought of his corrupt teammates were verboten. The few times Collins spoke about the 1919 Series, he reserved not a shred of compassion for Sox third baseman Buck Weaver whose only crime had been not ratting on his teammates.

The White Sox conspirators didn't like Collins much themselves, a theme explored by John Sayles in his film of the Eliot Asinof book *Eight Men Out*. Despite their ability to win just about anytime they felt like it, the '19 Sox had been a team riddled with dissension: Neither first baseman Chick Gandil or shortstop Swede Risberg, both banned in the fix, would even talk to Collins, the team captain. Feelings grew so testy that Collins had few teammates even willing to throw him the ball during practice, unless it was catcher Ray Schalk. A deep regional and economic chasm divided those Sox—two of the team's premier players, the illiterate Shoeless Joe Jackson and Left Williams were Southerners and stuck together, and were joined by Gandil and Risberg, both from rural California, and the easygoing, barely-educated Happy Felsch, the centerfielder; all would be implicated in the Series fix. To them, Collins was simply the "college boy," so named because he'd graduated from Columbia University, and, so they claimed, was smug, aloof, and arrogant. They scorned Collins as a square, a man who preferred gum to chewing tobacco; at the plate, Collins would remove the gum from his mouth and stick it on the button atop his cap, but popped the gum back into his mouth for two-strike counts. They mocked him as a family man—Collins was happily married to Mabel and the father of two sons—at a time when many ballplayers preferred a more randy lifestyle. And they resented Collins because he was crafty and hard enough to insist that his hefty $14,500 salary be written into his contract when the Sox bought him from the A's in '15. The amount was more than double the amount earned by any of his teammates.

Numbers were the barometer of Collins's career, revealing his true greatness. Although he batted only .226 in the '19 Series—lower than several of the Sox conspirators—his composite average in six World Series, four as a member of Connie Mack's famed "$100,000 Infield," was .328. Collins played twenty-five years, longer than any of the other inaugural Hall of Famers—compiling 3,310 base hits, 744 stolen bases, and achieving such steadiness at second that he rarely made an error. His steadiness made it easy—and Eddie Collins was the star who rarely got the credit he deserved.

Few moments define that paradox as well as game six of the '17 Series against the Giants when Collins's daring and savvy practically willed the win—and the Series—for the White Sox. With Collins dancing off third base and Joe Jackson on first, Happy Felsch hit a bouncer back to pitcher Rube Benton. Traditional thinking would dictate that Collins head safely back to third, so Benton could nab Felsch at first. But not Collins, who sensed an opportunity: By pretending to run home, he'd draw a throw to keep the pitcher from going to first and possibly starting a rally-ending double play. So Collins faked a break for home, forcing Benton to throw to catcher Bill Rariden. Then, heading back to third, he gave Jackson precious seconds to steam around the bases, before breaking for the plate—recognizing in a heartbeat that neither Benton nor Giants first baseman Walter Holke had bothered to back up Rariden. Drawing the attentions of the catcher and Giants third baseman Heinie Zimmerman into a rundown, he lured Rariden up the line and a throw to third, before breaking quickly to the plate, which was clear of any Giants. Zimmerman chased Collins all the way across the plate as Eddie scored with a run that helped provide the 4–2 margin of victory and clinch the Series for the Sox.

But as was most often the case with Collins, he didn't get the credit as much as Zimmerman got stuck as the goat. Giants manager John McGraw absolved his third baseman, pointing out that Holke should have been at the plate to back up the catcher. But the writers were merciless: "Thirty-four thousand fans [at the Polo Grounds] lay back in their seats, and gasped, like landed trout, in astonishment," wrote Damon Runyon in the *New York Tribune*. "The balloting for Chief Goat of the Series ended right there. Poor Heinie Zim was unanimously elected." Said Zimmerman, mounting a weak defense: "Who the hell was I supposed to throw the ball to? [Umpire Bill] Klem?"

The play was vintage Collins, a moment that didn't make the box score, but showed his superior baseball instincts. As with Cobb, Collins's gift was combining those skills with raw baseball intelligence, the kind of intangibles that he used to read pitchers, steal bases, squeeze runs—and drive his teammates to success. Like Cobb, Collins played baseball in the deadball era better than just about anyone, which meant using little power, but a lot of bat control. Indeed, he used his left-handed choke-grip to spray the ball to all fields, hit behind the runner, and drag bunt to near-perfection, all of which without hardly ever missing a game to injury. "I could have been a doctor, lawyer, or teacher," Collins said with characteristic cockiness. "And I'm sure I could have done well in industry or finance. But I became a professional baseball player and loved it."

He hadn't even been Collins early in his career. He'd been "Sullivan," a pseudonym he used to play semipro ball and preserve his eligibility before his senior year at Columbia. Born near the New York town of Kingston, Collins was raised mostly in the suburban New York City village of Tarrytown, and, at sixteen, enrolled at Columbia, where he became the football team's 140-pound varsity quarterback, and captained the baseball team. Connie Mack spotted Collins—make that Sullivan—in the summer of 1906, and offered him a contract. By then, Collins was nineteen, had put on a few pounds, and was quickly thrown into his first big-league game that September against the Hall of Fame master-spitballer Ed Walsh of the White Sox. Still playing as Sullivan—Mack was hoping the college officials wouldn't discover his prospect—he singled in his first at-bat, handled six chances at shortstop flawlessly, and officially became a big leaguer.

But when Columbia officials discovered "Sullivan" and "Collins" were the same person, he was denied eligibility—ironically not because he'd played for the A's, but because earlier that summer, he had played under his own name in a semipro league. He returned to Columbia anyway and graduated, in 1907. Unable to play college ball,

Collins coached the team instead, and didn't seem to mind—calling it "the first time in any school that an undergraduate was paid to coach."

Not that Collins was beating away the scouts; the A's had been the only team to offer him a contract after scout Billy Lush had seen him and written to Mack. Collins's slight stature—eventually, he filled out to 175 pounds on a 5'9" frame—was hardly enough to scare anyone. John McGraw could have had him for his hometown Giants—playing for Columbia in an exhibition game against the New Yorkers, Collins once doubled off the great Iron Man Joe McGinnity. But as Collins later put it, "McGraw probably thought . . . McGinnity threw it in there for one of the college kids."

By 1908, Collins was back in Philadelphia, and a year later had become a big-league star, batting .346. Admitting that Collins was no shortstop, and wanting his bat in the lineup, Mack made him a second baseman by moving Danny Murphy to the outfield. It was the crowning move to Mack's "$100,000 Infield"—the talk of baseball in those deadball days and the anchor of the first A's dynasty. Anchored by Stuffy McInnis at first, Collins at second, shortstop Jack Barry, and third baseman Frank "Home Run" Baker, Mack's A's became the class of baseball—beating the Cubs in 1910 in five games for its first world title, and then taking two more Series in the next five years. Collins called the second game of the '10 Series, one in which he collected three hits and the A's knocked Three-Finger Brown from the box en route to a 9–3 win, his greatest thrill in baseball.

But for all the care Mack took in building his powerhouse team, he dismantled the A's after '14, the year the Boston Braves climbed from last after the Fourth of July, to first, and swept his Philadelphians in the World Series. After the Series and throughout the next season, Mack peddled off his stars, including Collins, for a then-record sum of $50,000 to the White Sox.

Collins was the regular second baseman for the Sox for a dozen years, serving as player-manager in 1925 and '26, his final two seasons in Chicago. His old catcher, Ray Schalk, replaced him, shortly before Mack called, this time offering him a contract to resume as A's second baseman. So the thirty-nine-year-old Collins returned to Philadelphia and captained the team—playing part-time. He retired in 1930.

Long after his playing days, Collins never found it any easier to talk about the crushing disappointment of the 1919 World Series fix, mainly because he considered that White Sox team to have been the best team ever—better than even his great A's of "$100,000 Infield" days, John McGraw's Giants, or Ruth's Yankees. "It was one hell of a ball club," he said. "When they wanted to win, they won, and when they wanted to lose, they lost, but usually it was a struggle. If there was ever a greater ball team than [manager] Kid Gleason's White Sox, I didn't get to see it."

Still coaching for the A's in 1933, Collins learned that a young man named Tom Yawkey, whose father had been a part owner of the Tigers, was planning to purchase the woeful Red Sox, whose best season in the last decade had been sixth. Collins and Yawkey had been friends back in Tarrytown, New York, in the Irving School, and the new owner wanted his old classmate to join him in Boston as Red Sox vice president, treasurer, and general manager. Collins hesitated out of loyalty to Mack, whom he considered his mentor and guide. But the old man urged him to take the Boston offer: "You figure prominently in our future plans," Mack said, "but this is an opportunity you can't afford to pass up."

So Collins was charged with remaking the Red Sox, a tall order since they hadn't won a World Series since 1918, and had fallen on hard times since former owner Harry Frazee, the New York theatrical magnate, had sold off many of his frontline players, most of whom, like Babe Ruth, Waite Hoyt, and Herb Pennock, seemed to end up as stars for the Yankees.

Collins was given a liberal reign to remake the Red Sox in his way. Spending a great deal of Yawkey's money—writers dubbed the team the "Gold Sox"—he focused on building a powerful farm system and producing a winner. Collins tinkered away— bringing in Bucky Harris and then Joe Cronin as manager, and shrewdly plucking from the A's his old teammate, the slugger Jimmie Foxx, who posted some powerful numbers. The Red Sox made a go of it, clawing into second place by 1938, lagging behind only the Yankees.

Collins's gift as a baseball executive was sizing up talent, most notably the "husky" nineteen-year-old Ted Williams. On a 1937 trip to San Diego to scout Bobby Doerr, Collins discovered Williams, just graduated from Hoover High, while watching San Diego Padres batting practice. Not even knowing Williams's name, Collins locked in on that batting stroke, and recognized greatness. Says baseball historian Donald Honig of the epic moment: "Eddie has played with Jackson and Ruth; he knew the swing, knew what it meant." Williams batted .327 in his first season in Boston. Not bad for a rookie, Eddie Collins was probably thinking to himself.

♦   ♦   ♦

Steve Hannagan and Al Stoughton were pushing all the right buttons at the beginning of 1939. These veteran public relations executives, both named to the Centennial Commission almost as an afterthought next to all the notable soldiers, had unleashed the game's first successful national public relations campaign. Dripping with small-town goodness, and wrapped in red, white, and blue, their campaign blended a noble nod to baseball's past with a heavy reliance on the myth that yes, Abner Doubleday really had started it all.

"Entirely too much is taken for granted in newspapers today," Stoughton wrote in a nod to the philosophy of this dynamic PR duo. "I, for one, consider the public as folks who want to be educated and not considered as little groups of experts. Ask a dozen men what they read in the papers and three will tell you—'this page or that, but not the whole paper.' The point [is] to get baseball into other pages as well as the sports page."

Thanks to Hannagan and Stoughton, America was starting to focus on the story of Cooperstown in early 1939. In an era when print media was still the most reliable form of promotion, articles about baseball's birth and the upcoming Centennial celebration could be found just about anywhere and everywhere. "Baseball's first 100 years make a glamorous story," wrote Ford Frick in a January 1939 piece distributed around the country. "The boys scampering around the village green of Cooperstown, in upstate New York, learning principles in mechanics and rules that brought order and meaning to their helter-skelter exertions. Abner Doubleday devised the rules entirely to help the local youngsters get more enjoyment out of their play."

It hardly mattered that Frick hadn't written the piece, and was vacationing in Italy when it hit the newspapers. The real author: not the National League president, but Stoughton, whose ghosted article underscored the well-coordinated, multidimensional print and promotional campaign. In January alone, Sid Mercer of the *New York Journal-American* ran a thirteen-part series on baseball history, saying all the right things, including his assertion that there was "little doubt . . . that Cooperstown, N.Y. is where the seed was planted in 1839 by Abner Doubleday, a schoolboy with a flair for organization." Other papers such as the *Union* in Springfield, Massachusetts, and the *Albany Times-Union* ran similar series with similar claims, as did *The Christian Science Monitor*, and trade magazines such as *Hardware Age, Buick Magazine*, and *Photo*. Even *Newsweek* devoted its June 19 cover story to the festivities—buying the legend wholesale and making Doubleday its cover boy—more than forty years after his death— with the solid assertion that he had "fathered baseball 100 years ago." The *Newsweek* coverage was a pleasant summer break from the usual drumbeat of serious news: Grabbing the following week's cover would be another military man, Japanese war minister Seishiro Itangaki.

Hannagan and Stoughton were the right men for the job. The forty-year-old Hannagan was a flamboyant PR veteran with a twinkle in his eye, a healthy dose of hucksterism, and the ability to think big while never forgetting the folks back home. A Lafayette, Indiana, native, Hannagan was his hometown's correspondent for the *Indianapolis Star* by the age of fourteen. A young man in a hurry, he lasted two years at Purdue before leaving to write sports for the *Star*, and then moved to New York as a columnist for the Newspaper Enterprise Association and United Features Syndicate. At twenty- five, Hannagan opened a publicity office and soon was serving an eclectic collection of clients from the Indianapolis Motor Speedway, Detroit pro football, speedboat racing, and exotic vacation spots from Miami Beach to Sun Valley, Idaho.

Hannagan worked hard, arriving at his office at 8:45 A.M. every day on the button. He mixed considerable charm, a refreshing dose of integrity, and a clear understanding of a reporter's needs by flooding small newspapers with the prerequisite photos of Miami Beach beauties, but also with news and pictures of the folks from back home visiting his resorts, knowing full well they would usu- ally be printed. He insisted that his staff have newspaper experience themselves, and warned them constantly that "the truth will never hurt you as much as a reporter's suspicion." And if the news was bad, well, Hannagan wouldn't hide it; when, in 1930, the editor at a magazine wired him for a summary of how the season was going at Miami Beach, he gave them a detailed summary showing that it had badly slumped: "Cancel that story," the editor barked. "Let's do one instead about an honest press agent."

The thirty-five-year-old Stoughton brought to his new job with the Hall acute baseball knowledge, public-speaking ability, and a valuable connection. As the nephew of Christy Mathewson—the great pitcher's wife's sister was Stoughton's aunt—he was the organizer and secretary of Mathewson's Memorial Corporation, and, like the great pitcher, was a Bucknell graduate. A former newspaper reporter, Stoughton had spent most of his professional life back at Bucknell as the university's alumni secretary and publicity director, and then joined the New York City YMCA as a publicist. In May 1936, he asked Hannagan for a position on the Cooperstown committee by citing his public-speaking abilities, contacts with baseball people, and ability to "use the right fork, wear the right tie, and order a meal or a drink—in most any company."

Teamed with Hannagan, Stoughton was a dynamo—spitting out a flurry of ideas for Cooperstown publicity and tie-ins, many of which were adopted. He urged Postmaster General Jim Farley to get involved with the creation and distribution of a special Centennial baseball stamp and that a series of commemorative games be played at estates of the wealthy. Stoughton was the mastermind of the Baseball Centennial publicity and newsreel packages, and the eventual decision to create a Hollywood documentary on baseball history. Perhaps most important of all, he was the man behind the commission's decision to stand behind the legend that the game's long and storied history had all started, ahem, with Abner Doubleday. "The tie with history is a gold mine of ramifications into many fields," Stoughton wrote. "The whole story of baseball is one of personalities—living, fighting hard [and] playing. . . . [They were] colorful men of action who had to catch the imagination of the mob—above the job of playing a good game that people paid to watch."

Working with organized baseball, Hannagan and Stoughton developed a plan that in essence was the birth of baseball nostalgia—heavy on local tie-ins to parades, dedications of local memorials to baseball legends, and the branding of a series of "Centennial" baseball diamonds. They foresaw the creation of games between service clubs (Rotary vs. Lions), businesses (newspapers vs. banks), military branches, airport employees (air vs. ground crews), and post offices (clerks vs. carriers). They contacted the producers of the popular "March of Time" newsreels, asking that they be sure to cover the upcoming festivities on June 12. Hannagan had already contacted Sam Goldwyn in Hollywood about developing a show on baseball history to which the mogul had reacted favorably—asking for an outline of what he intended to feature.

Postmaster General Farley became an enthused supporter of the Centennial baseball stamp, and even got his boss, president Roosevelt, to back him up. Not much of a baseball fan, the president was a lifelong stamp collector who enjoyed relieving the most trying times of his administration by losing himself in his stamp collection.

With a judicious nod to former National League president John Heydler, the PR men reached out to the minor leagues and colleges by setting up a series of games to promote both Cooperstown and Hall of Fame day, now being called the "Cavalcade of Baseball." Kicking things off would be a high school game on May 6 at Doubleday Field, to be followed later that month by college games featuring West Point, Colgate, and Bucknell. The May 27 Bucknell vs. St. Lawrence game would feature the unveiling of Mathewson's bust at the Hall of Fame by his widow, Jane. The games and events would last all summer, designed to showcase Cooperstown as a charming tourist spot.

Those visiting the town could purchase the handsome red, white, and blue "official program" that Hannagan and Stoughton produced, a deft mix of proclamations, baseball history, and small-town boosters designed to promote tourism. The program featured loads of information on Honus Wagner and Babe Ruth as well as local landmarks cited in the novels of James Fenimore Cooper and where to bank. (The Second National Bank of Cooperstown at the entrance of Doubleday Field "is a guarantee against being 'struck out,'" an ad reads.) Later that summer, Cooperstown would host a country music festival, a boy-scout jamboree, special days for the American Legion and firemen, and lots of high school and minor-league games in between. In a nod to Alexander Cartwright and his family, there would be a day in his honor, and yet another opportunity for Cooperstown mayor Rowan Spraker to grab some attention—a July 4 "Mayor's Day."

Hannagan and Stoughton were already assured of the attention of baseball fans, so they shifted their focus to a more general demographic —the novice or casual fan who rarely perused the sports section. To capture their attention, the public relations men resorted to a tried-and-true strategy—making the Centennial a walking, talking billboard for America, all at a time when people were more idealistic. So baseball went patriotic—with the game's greatest contribution, the organizers said, its "building of a national spirit of fair play." Baseball, added Stoughton, was "one of the greatest single contributors to the making of what is known as 'The American Spirit.'" And if that wasn't sappy enough, the game's greatest contribution was that "the building of American ideals and character could be carried onto every walk of life" during the celebration.

To help spread the word, the organizers assembled neatly packaged collections of publicity materials for editors, civic leaders, and chambers of commerce throughout the country. Included were articles for local papers, prepared speeches, ideas on how to run baseball clinics—and more patriotism. "Abraham Lincoln was a ballplayer, and a good one," wrote Stoughton in a suggested address. "When Mr. Lincoln was down at Springfield, Illinois, and the committee came down from Chicago to tell him that he had been nominated for the presidency of the United States, they found him on the baseball diamond. Mr. Lincoln sent word that the gentlemen would simply have to wait until he got his turn at bat."

There is no record on how many civic leaders actually included such nonsense in their talks. But it didn't matter, for Hannagan and Stoughton had people thinking that not supporting baseball would be, well, downright un-American. Central to the campaign as well was that Abner Doubleday, then a "West Point Cadet and a stripling lad of 20," as Stoughton put it, "was merely trying to simplify the existing game of town ball when he devised the first baseball diamond." Conveniently overlooked was some recent research performed by a West Point public relations officer who wandered into the military academy's archives to find an obituary of the late general in which a classmate and longtime friend had described Doubleday as "a man who did not care for or go into any outdoor sports."

That most everyone chose to overlook the Abner Doubleday myth was a nod to how skillfully Hannagan and Stoughton were manning their flashy "Cavalcade" Campaign. But down in New York City, some cranky newspaper editors knew better. Whatever happened, they asked, to Alexander Cartwright, the game's real father?

✕ CHAPTER 7 ✕

An "Embarrassing Revelation" for Baseball

There was nothing flashy about the next baseball immortal to be introduced. Shuffling to the lectern to thunderous applause from spectators familiar with his decades-long battle with alcoholism, Grover Cleveland Alexander wasn't the type to dress nattily or work up a good quote. On the mound, he delivered his rocket of a fastball with barely a windup, and worked quickly as if he had somewhere he needed to be. As a member of the 1916 Phillies, "Old Pete," as he was universally known with affection and a nod to his often haggard appearance, once beat the Reds in the first game of a doubleheader only to be asked to pitch the second game—and make it snappy. Late for a train, Alex was told the game had better end in an hour. "Get it over fast," his manager, Pat

Moran, said. So Alexander did—shutting out the Reds in fifty-eight minutes.

The fifty-two-year-old Alexander looked twenty years older. His hair was perpetually mussed up and he moved with a slow shuffle. Though Alex was dressed in a vested suit, he appeared distracted, and kept his hands scrunched deep in his pockets much of his time in Cooperstown. So it went for a man afflicted with the ravages of alcoholism, rarely what it was called back then, but a disease that scarred Alexander deeply—ruining both his marriage and his savings. Because of alcoholism, Alex had to scrape for work that traded on his famous name and ranged from a series of jobs in the Midwest and one in New York City, where he had recently finished a stint in Times Square as an attraction at a freak show, the old St. Hubert's Flea Circus on Forty-second Street just off Broadway. In January, a year since he'd been elected to the Hall of Fame, Old Pete had been sitting among the bearded ladies, albinos, and snake women of this antiquated attraction of a freak show waiting to deliver a baseball clinic featuring his pitching techniques. Deeply grateful at his election to the Hall, Old Pete would nonetheless regret that the honor would not help his wallet: "They gave me a tablet," he'd say later, "but I can't eat any tablet."

Baseball officials had wondered privately whether Alexander would even be able to get on the train to Cooperstown. Well liked and always a gentleman, his election had inspired a steady stream of articles that chronicled his rambling, itinerant life. Indeed, Alexander's file at the National Baseball Hall of Fame Library is thicker than most, a testament to the wide interest reporters took in him long after his storied career.

But Alexander had made it to Cooperstown, and risen to the occasion with his usual graciousness. He was the day's most intriguing Hall of Fame honoree, a man many were anxious to see and hear because there had been only spotty news of him for years. "I had many a thrill in my baseball career and many a treat, but I consider this the greatest treat, and one of the greatest thrills I have had in my long career in baseball," Pete said in a surprisingly soft and sonorous voice that many in the crowd had to strain to hear. "I'm proud to be a member with these gentlemen here. In my dreams, I often think about what I could do with a team like this. I'd have no mistakes to be worrying about. And when they hit those line drives, I'd have no trouble wondering who was going to get them. I do wish to say it's a mighty proud moment in my life to be here."

It was the Cavalcade of Baseball's quietest delivery, but the moment was electrifying. Alexander had been a virtual no-show to big-league games since retiring nearly a decade ago—he'd worked in an airplane factory and barnstormed as manager of a semipro team, the House of David, where, curiously, he fit in well with the team's players, all of whom had deep religious convictions and long-flowing beards. His marriage to Aimee Arrants had broken up back in '29, when she had stated in court that Alexander had tried sobering up six times at a sanitarium—"taking the cure," it was then called—but had always reverted to destructive habits. Alexander had sought a job as a big-league pitching coach, but no team had taken a chance, with the $250,000 that he was thought to have earned in baseball long since gone. But here he was in Cooperstown, having delivered a few words with passion and eloquence. As Old Pete turned from the lectern to find his seat, Walter Johnson instinctively wrapped his massive arms around him.

It was Alexander's sturdy thunderbolt of a right arm that got him to Cooperstown. Old Pete completed his career with an astounding 373 wins, a mark matched by Mathewson and exceeded by only

Cy Young and Walter Johnson. His seeming indifference to pressure was another reason—few baseball situations fazed Alexander, whose most famous moment, among the most dramatic of all sports stories, had come in game seven of the 1926 World Series with the upstart Cardinals seeking to upset the mighty Yankees. The thirty-nine-year-old Pete, who had been sold for a song by the Cubs at midseason following his suspension for a drinking binge, had already won the second and sixth games, and figured his time was done.

But in the seventh inning, Jesse Haines filled the bases with two out, and manager Rogers Hornsby summoned Alexander from the bullpen. Looking into Alexander's eyes, the manager noticed they were clear, and handed him the ball. "Pete," said third baseman Les Bell, "there are three men on base."

Alexander looked around, and grinned. "Damned if you're not right," he drawled. "I reckon I better strike him out."

"Him" was the powerful Tony Lazzeri. On the 1–1 pitch, Alexander delivered an inside fastball that Lazzeri whistled down the left-field line and curved foul at the last moment. "A few feet more," Pete said later, "and he'd have been a hero and I'd have been a bum." A pitch later, Alexander struck him out, ending the Yankee threat.

Alexander's clutch pitching had preserved the win, and the Cardinals' first-ever Series victory; he pitched the game's last two innings and got the save as well. The Lazzeri strikeout was an extraordinary moment, fueled in part by the legend that Pete had been drunk from the big celebration after his complete game 10–2 win in game six. Not true, swore Alexander, who said he went back to the hotel that night and stayed sober, "although there were plenty of other nights when I wasn't." Most responsible for the story was Damon Runyon whose florid game summary had Alexander called in to pitch, not from the bullpen, but from a barstool at Billy LaHiff's tavern in

Manhattan, which was quite logistically impossible considering he'd have to have hopped in a cab for the five-mile ride to Yankee Stadium in the Bronx. Fueling the legend was Hornsby, who, in the jubilation of the winning clubhouse, blurted out, "Alex can pitch better drunk than any other pitcher sober."

Born to a farming family of thirteen children, twelve of them boys, in Elba, Nebraska, Alexander described his youth as "more or less a matter of long days of work and short nights of sleep." Manning a plow gave him strong legs and sinewy thighs, which, Alexander maintained, created an untold advantage on the mound: "A pitcher may still have a great arm," he said, "but if his legs don't hold up under him, he's a dead duck." Farmwork also gave him upper-body strength, but not bulk—and Pete always retained a lithe bearing, never carrying more than 185 pounds on his modest 6'1" frame. For fun, he and his eleven brothers, a team unto themselves, played pickup baseball. And they hunted with Pete, actually rounding up dinner by felling unfortunate chickens and turkeys with rocks— a practice he claimed gave him superb control.

Pete's father, William, had hoped the son he named after the president would study law. But Grover Cleveland Alexander joined the telephone company as a lineman instead, pitching on weekends for independent and semipro teams around Nebraska. In 1909, Alex turned pro, going 15–8 for Galesburg of the Illinois-Missouri League. Sold to Indianapolis, he was soon unloaded to Syracuse of the old New York State League as a "lame duck" after hurting his arm in a hunting accident, when a rival manager, Patsy O'Rourke of Albany, spotted him.

"Is he good?" asked Phillies president Horace Fogel.

"Only the best in the minor leagues," said O'Rourke.

So in 1911, Alexander signed with the Phillies, and went south with the team for spring training in Wilmington, North Carolina. There the freckle-faced, sandy-haired rookie puzzled the team's front office with his chutzpah by insisting on working with the veterans, and failing to sweat out many of the same workouts as his young peers. It was okay; there was something about him. At twenty-four, Pete was older than most rookies, but had a presence: "If ever there was a pitcher, that Alexander is one," Phillies coach Pat Moran assured them.

In his first game in Philadelphia—a last spring-training tune-up in the city series against Connie Mack's world-champion A's—Alexander was tapped as the starter, mostly to save the arms of Philly starters. "You'll pitch five innings," Moran assured Pete. "They'll be murder, but you'll learn something."

But doing most of the learning were the A's. Barely pausing between pitches, the twenty-four-year-old Nebraska rookie threw a shutout and walked no one over seven innings. Pete had won twenty-eight games and lost thirteen in 1911 amounting to baseball's greatest rookie season ever by a pitcher. It's even more impressive when one considers that much of what he accomplished was done in the Phillies' bandbox of a ballpark, the Baker Bowl, with its 280-foot right-field porch.

A Philadelphia reporter attributed his success to "torpedo speed and an unhittable curve." With graciousness, Alexander credited Moran, a veteran big-league catcher and later manager of the world-champion '19 Reds, and soaked up his knowledge. "Don't try to strike 'em all out," Moran told the young pitcher. "Use the men behind you. *Be smart. Save that arm.*" Pete's victory total led the National League; so did his shutouts (seven), complete games (thirty-one), and innings pitched (367). His wins included a twelve-inning, 1–0 masterpiece over the Boston Braves and forty-four-year-old Cy

Young in his last season. And they included four shutouts in September, making him an instant favorite in Philadelphia. Back in St. Paul, he became the local kid who made good; hundreds turned out to the railroad station to welcome him home after the season.

"Alex was really an amazing pitcher," Philadelphia teammate Hans Lobert told Lawrence Ritter in *The Glory of the Their Times.* "He had little short fingers and he threw a very heavy ball. Once, later on, when I'd moved to the Giants, Alex hit me over the heart with a pitched ball and it bore in like a lump of lead hitting you. I couldn't get my breath for 10 minutes afterward. [Christy] Mathewson was just as fast, but he threw a much lighter ball."

Just like that, Alexander had become one of baseball's top pitchers. From 1912 to 1914, he was among the National League's best, not topping his rookie heroics, but ranking among the best in strikeouts and innings pitched. Then, in 1915, Pete had a season for the ages, going 31–10 to lead the league in wins, innings, strikeouts, and every other major statistic, among them complete games (thirty-six) and ERA, a measly 1.22. He pitched four one-hitters that season, including a 3–0 win June 5 in St. Louis in which Artie Butler whistled a single past his head with two down in the ninth; it was the closest Pete would ever come to a no-hitter. His performance powered the Phillies to the World Series, and Pete beat Boston's Ernie Shore in the opener, 3–1. But the season's labors had left him exhausted, and Pete dropped game three, 2–1, and Philadelphia lost the Series to Boston in five games.

Pete pitched even better in '16, winning thirty-three games; and in '17, another thirty, giving him an astounding three-year record with the Phillies of 94–35. So just as Christy Mathewson and his catcher Roger Bresnahan had become a celebrated battery in the early part of the century, Alexander and Phillies catcher Bill Killefer became, arguably, as good. Both were quiet, calm, and seemingly without nerves: Often, they worked as if on autopilot, without exchanging signals, which allowed Alex to work even more quickly. Mound conferences were few. "You just throw 'em and I'll catch 'em," Killefer would say to the pitcher, "and we'll get outta the park early today."

One day in Pittsburgh, Pete had a two-run lead over the Pirates in the eighth when two errors and a single filled the bases. He got two quick outs before Honus Wagner strode to the plate, trying desperately to continue the rally. Killefer figured he'd confer with his pitcher.

"Got to strike this bird out," he told Alex.

"Well, I don't figure it would help none to walk him," Pete shot back. He struck Wagner out on three pitches.

"Alexander showed me more different kinds of pitches than any man I ever faced," the great Honus once said after a frustrating at-bat against Pete. "He had the greatest assortment of curves in the world—bar none. Alex has a fast ball, medium ball, slow ball, drop ball, and a curve, all of which he can throw side-arm or overhand. Alex has perfect control and knows how to mix them up. There is no chance to outguess him."

After the '17 season, Alexander was drafted into the army, and sent to France as part of the American force that had recently entered World War I. Fearing Pete wouldn't survive, Phillies owner William Baker committed what baseball historian Jan Finkel calls "one of the most cynical acts in baseball history"—sending Alexander to the Cubs as part of a five-player deal. But Chicago owner William Wrigley earned Pete's lifelong gratitude by sending Pete's wife, Aimee, whom he married just prior to shipping out in early 1918, $500 every other month he was away.

Alexander was gone for about a year—not long in the scheme of things, but the horror of war lingered and was the most likely origin of his long, slow descent into alcoholism. Assigned to the artillery, Pete spent seven frightful months at the front, enduring relentless bombardment that deafened him in his right ear, near the area of his skull where he also took a shrapnel wound. Worse, the war left him shell-shocked and may have also triggered the epilepsy that plagued him for the rest of his life.

Pete had in fact suffered from seizures for years, in part from what Aimee said was a youthful baseball injury that left Pete unconscious for more than two days, and suffering for weeks from double vision. Hans Lobert told Lawrence Ritter that there were several times when teammates held Pete down, grabbing his tongue to prevent choking, and poured brandy down his throat. Sadly, epileptics were scorned in those days, and considered by some to be tools of the devil. For the most part, Alexander dealt with it in his own stoic way, by carrying a bottle of ammonia to bring him back after a seizure, and by drinking to excess. After all, it was more socially acceptable in those days to be a drunk than admit you were epileptic.

Alex's teammates were willing to overlook his troubles. Alexander was a winner and made them better. As a patient man unspoiled by success, he was forever gracious with younger teammates, including one, Stan Baumgartner, a pitcher with both the Phillies and A's, and later a sportswriter with the Philadelphia *Inquirer*. As a twenty-year-old rookie lefthander in 1915 hoping to catch on with the Phillies, Baumgartner was having troubles throwing the curveball one day on the sidelines when Alex volunteered to help.

Tucking the ball deep in Baumgartner's palm, Alex demonstrated how the young pitcher should let it roll off his hand for maximum spin. But Baumgartner still didn't get it, so Alex smiled and took the ball himself with instructions to watch.

Breaking off one of his famous hooks, Alex turned professorial. "Be sure to let the ball roll off the bottom knuckle of the first finger near your palm," he told the young lefty. "You don't have to snap it. Let it roll and it will curve itself."

So incorporating the knowledge from the quick tutorial, Baumgartner tried again. "The ball curved," he said. "I knew I would stick in the majors."

Back from the war in '19 and pitching for the Cubs, Alexander took a while to work himself back to condition, dropping his first five decisions. He finished at 16–11, but then returned to former form in '20, going 27–14 with a 1.91 ERA. He was still near the top of the league, notching twenty-two wins in '23, but not at the level of his big years in Philadelphia. By 1925, the Cubs were in last place, when William Wrigley hired Joe McCarthy, a well-known disciplinarian from the minors, to give the moribund team a jolt. McCarthy and Alexander clashed repeatedly, with Pete grumbling after one such tiff that he wasn't "taking orders from a bush-league manager."

That left the Cubs no other alternative but to waive Alexander. Off to St. Louis, he racked up a couple more good seasons— contributing two World Series wins in '26, twenty-one wins in '27 at the age of forty, and his epic Series heroics in '28. But by '29, the Cardinals had grown tired of his frequent absences and unsteady behavior. With six weeks to go in the season, manager Bill McKechnie sent Alexander home with his record standing at 9–8; that ninth win, by the way, was Pete's 373rd in his career, which tied Christy Mathewson for the most in National League history. Traded back to the Phillies after '29, Alex would never win another big-league game. He pitched nine games for the Phillies, went 0–3, and wound things up for Dallas in the Texas League.

Without the structure of baseball, Alexander went downhill

quickly. He drank more heavily than ever. The shrapnel injury suffered in the war ate away much of his right ear lobe and caused a
hearing loss, and Alex periodically visited V.A. hospitals for relief. In
and out of both hospitals and jails, he was once scraped from the
streets in Los Angeles and identified only by his 1926 World Series
ring. Though he and Aimee remarried in 1931 after he pledged to
stop drinking, his promise didn't stick, and he passed from boarding-
house to hotel, his name occasionally reaching the news when he
was thrown out again for nonpayment of rent or after another arrest.

Pete caught on as manager and a relief pitcher of the House of
David barnstorming team, providing him with a steady income, but
after that job ended in '36, a $50 monthly check from Cardinal
owner Sam Breadon to whomever was caring for him was all that
separated Alex from the streets. Others tried helping, moved by
Alexander's deepening plight, and his kind, soft-spoken demeanor
that had never failed to help a rookie or a youngster in the art of
pitching.

To his last days, Alexander was forever patient with young
pitchers, urging above all that they master control. "Every kid pitcher
wants to set a batter's shirt on fire with every pitch, just to make an
impression," he wrote in a 1939 article in *Liberty* magazine. "They
want to flash into baseball's Hall of Fame by pitching a no-hit game.
Well, I got myself into the Hall of Fame without a no-hitter."

For the most part, Alex was grateful to accept a few dollars or a
temporary job, but then he'd drift on, turning up outside Cincinnati,
where he worked as a guard at an airplane factory, then in Springfield, Illinois, where he took a job as a greeter at a bar, and in New
York at the flea circus. Shortly after his election to the Hall of Fame,
he was offered a job as a guard in Cooperstown, but he never got
around to taking it. As for the sob stories, "Pete shook them off,"

sportswriter Jack Sher said, "the way you shake off a catcher's signal that you know won't send a man down swinging."

Just about everyone in baseball had an Alexander tale, most of them involving alcohol. Perhaps the quintessential Alexander tale came during spring training in the early '20s with the Cubs, before the real rot of alcoholism had taken hold. In a stunt with his old battery mate Bill Killefer squatting behind home plate with a tomato can rather than a catcher's mitt as a target, which he moved after each pitch, Alex fired ball after ball into the opening of the container. That was Alex, a combination of baseball mastery with a touch of mystery and a dash of vaudeville. No wonder Cooperstown was so happy to have him.

◆　◆　◆

Ty Cobb had an idea back in late 1936 when mistakes were found on the first edition of his Hall of Fame plaque. "Ask Frank Menke; he'll know."

Alexander Cleland hadn't thought to consult Menke, choosing instead to consult major league baseball statisticians to clean up various errors on the plaques. But Menke, a New York-based sports reporter for nearly thirty years and the editor of an all-sports encyclopedia, was just the man to see on all matters of baseball minutia, a kind of early Bill James who could clear up any sports argument in a bar. For Hall of Fame organizers intent on spreading the Abner Doubleday myth, Menke's knowledge was downright threatening.

Menke had kicked off his career in 1911 as a wire service reporter with International News Service, and, as many writers did in those days, a sideline as a ghostwriter to pen bylines for star players. As a ghostwriter for Giants pitcher Rube Marquard during the '11 World

Series, Menke kicked up a fuss when he, or rather Marquard, dared criticize the great Christy Mathewson in print. Actually, Mathewson or his ghostwriter, Jack Wheeler of the *Herald,* had started it when they gave Marquard a dressing-down for "a poor pitch" to the A's Frank Baker who hit a home run off Rube to help win game two. Striking back, Menke kept it for days with Marquard's blessing, prompting a real feud between the pitchers. "Marquard was mostly interested in the money he was to get out of it," Menke told Fred Lieb years later. "He was satisfied to have me do the writing . . . saying, 'Don't make it too easy [on Mathewson].' So I didn't."

Part of Menke's regular job was penning a daily sports brief distributed to papers around the country. He included trivia in his reports, and in time, added human interest stories that prompted him to begin digging for sports records and statistics. Menke became the source—the go-to man for stats—and the expert on records. But as Menke dug, he was distressed to discover how little concrete information on sports existed, and in particular, how much of it was inaccurate or flat-out wrong. Pouring through almost two thousand sports books, some of which had to be translated, Menke decided to take a crack at a new project: an encyclopedia of sports to include both statistics and history.

By 1938, just as Cooperstown was moving into high gear spreading the Doubleday myth, Menke's analysis on the origins of baseball were ready—and in direct conflict with the Hall of Fame publicity show. In the April issue of *Ken* magazine, Menke picked up where Henry Chadwick had left off a generation before—with evidence that the beginning of baseball had more to do with the streets of New York City and a shipping clerk named Alexander Joy Cartwright than with Abner Doubleday. Just as Chadwick had insisted decades earlier, Menke argued that pioneer baseball really had evolved from cricket—suggesting that British immigrants had played the game a lot during the colonial era in New York, Boston, and Philadelphia.

Most convincing of all was Menke's suggestion that baseball may have developed simply from generations of boys, who lacked traditional cricket equipment and fashioned their own bats and rules. Now that was plausible, particularly in the evolution of the bat from cricket's flat, paddle model to the thinner, easier-to-make rounded baseball bat that anyone able to use a knife could fashion from a log or a tree trunk. As interest in this new game spread, Menke theorized, so did the number of players and bases, starting with first, then third, and finally second.

Like Chadwick, Menke found the Mills Commission report riddled with errors and guesswork. Baseball, he said, was at least thirty-five years old by the time Doubleday "invented" the game. The game wasn't first played in Cooperstown, but along the Atlantic seaboard, he wrote. And Abner Doubleday, who the Hall of Fame PR campaign had morphed into a village "schoolboy" of 1839, was, as most knew, instead a West Point cadet with little interest in sports.

◆　◆　◆

So who was Alexander Cartwright? And why did he so annoy the organizers of the Baseball Hall of Fame?

Actually, Cartwright's name had floated about the periphery of arguments regarding baseball's origins for some time. In 1910, Alfred Henry Spink, who had founded the *Sporting News*, published a baseball book, *The National Game*, on the heels of the Mills Commission announcement, which he debunked as erroneous. In doing so, Spink became the first prominent writer to champion Cartwright's contributions as the game's inventor. He based his theory on a statement in 1877 by Duncan Curry, the first president of the sport's first club, the Knickerbockers, that Cartwright had appeared one day in 1845 at the club's playing field with his complete set of plans for baseball.

A year after Spink's book, Albert Spalding gave Cartwright a further acknowledgment—sort of—in his book. For all of Spalding's heroics in baseball and business, he didn't have a sense of humor; first, he gave his book the exact same title as Spink's book of the previous year. Next, he stuck to the Mills Commission's reports of baseball's origins and, despite utilizing the archives of his late friend Henry Chadwick, even included a photo and short biography of Abner Doubleday. To his credit, Spalding was gracious in his mention of Cartwright—rightfully acknowledging him as the first to form a team, and mentioning the Knickerbockers as that initial squad.

Thereafter, the question of the Doubleday myth reared up every so often. In 1935, former Cubs second baseman Johnny Evers, he of the "Tinker-to-Evers-to-Chance" infield—questioned the myth in a speech in Amsterdam, New York. Later that year, G. E. Staples, the St. Louis Cardinals director of publicity, wrote to Cleland, seeking guidance on the game's origins for a series of radio broadcasts he was planning; Staples had evidently heard several accounts, some of which credited Doubleday and others, Cartwright.

Where baseball really originated still inspires controversy, much of it good-natured rivalries among cities vying for the distinction. In 1991, a New Jersey man unearthed a notice from the July 13, 1825 edition of the *Delhi* (New York) *Gazette* listing the names of nine men challenging any group in Delaware County, some sixty miles south of Cooperstown, to a game of baseball at the home of Edward B. Chase for $1 per game. Historians have since found other references to early forms of baseball in the New York cities like

Rochester and Geneseo in the 1820s, and there is evidence of early baseball playing in Massachusetts, New Hampshire, and Vermont, and throughout the northeastern states. Even Walt Whitman made reference to baseball, writing about it as early as 1838. Although called baseball, most of the games were experiments with different rules and methods of play that may or may not resemble the game we know today.

More recently, other cities, like Pittsfield, Massachusetts, claimed to have invented baseball. Pittsfield's claim emerged in July 2004 when esteemed baseball historian John Thorn unearthed a city bylaw dated 1791 that outlawed the playing of ball games within eighty yards of the Town Meeting House to protect the building's windows. So could baseball have started be Pittsfield? Remarkably, the wording of the bylaw included "baseball," making the document, if existent, the earliest written reference to the sport in North America. It's entirely possible. On the other hand, Cartwright's contribution included the something Pittsfield's reference did not—a precise set of rules and measurements that formed the basis of the modern game.

Chances are that Walt Whitman wouldn't have recognized the difference between a fastball and a slider, but he was an early and welcome convert to baseball. In 1858, Whitman reported on a game for the *Brooklyn Daily Times*, and in 1867, called it "the American game" in print, generally acknowledged as the first to do so in print. Baseball embodied the "snap, go [and] fling of the American atmosphere," Whitman wrote. A decade later, Whitman went even further in his praise, asserting that baseball was as vital to "the sum of our historic life" as the Constitution. But for all the vigor in which the old poet viewed baseball, he never did register an opinion on where the sport had originated.

◆   ◆   ◆

The few old photos of Alexander Cartwright picture him either as a twenty-something lad, dressed in a kind of boater hat giving him a resemblance to the Dutch (Paint) Boy, or as an old man sporting a long white beard and looking like Walt Whitman. Born in 1820 in New York City, he became a bank clerk and a member of the Knickerbocker Base Ball Club, so named for the fire company of which he was a member.

The brand of baseball, or "town ball" as it was known, as played by the Knickerbockers, was considerably different than today's game. Not a sandlot or semipro team in the modern sense, the Knickerbockers were more of a social club—a kind of nineteenth-century country club. Here was a way for genteel young men of the growing middle class to play the game (thought to be at a field on or near the corner of Twenty-seventh Street and Fourth Avenue in the Turtle Bay section of Manhattan next to Peter Stuyvesant's glue factory) but more importantly, to enjoy the lavish postgame banquets. Nor did they focus so much on how to put more pop into their pitches, as they did proper conduct, as befitting their class.

In one sense, the Knickerbockers were an exclusive bunch. Players couldn't leave the game unless excused by the captain. Those refusing to obey the captain were docked fifty cents, and twenty-five cents for arguing with the umpire. And if the captain left the field before game's end, or neglected his duties in any other way, the fine was a hefty $1. Likewise, profanity was inexcusable. In the Knickerbockers' very first outside match, J. W. Davis swore and was docked six cents—the game's first fine. Ty Cobb wouldn't have lasted a week with this lot.

Frank Menke suggested that Cartwright stepped forth with his suggested baseball rules in 1839, but that date seems doubtful, and may have been a ploy to detract from the Cooperstown myth, which insisted that Abner Doubleday had invented baseball that same summer. Cartwright wasn't twenty years old and probably not a member of any sports club at that point. More likely, baseball got started in its current form about six years later, in 1845, when Cartwright, then twenty-five, stepped forth with his suggestions designed to thrust some life into a game that was still essentially rounders. Knowing that town ball in its current state could be boring for players and spectators alike, Cartwright sought to make some changes.

Cartwright knew that standing in the field waiting to bat while an entire opposing team batted was about as exciting as watching paint dry. He knew that being hit with the ball while on the bases was unnecessary and he knew that positioning a slew of players in the outfield and two catchers behind the plate, typical for the times, was excessive. His greatest contribution: recognizing that basic simplification could turn this old-fashioned game into something more lively.

So Cartwright approached Billy Tucker, an active member of the rival New York Base Ball Club. One of the city's best players, Tucker agreed to become a Knickerbocker. Just as important, he had a roommate, a lawyer named William Wheaton—a ballplayer, a lawyer, and a good man to assist in the club's formation.

Cartwright's rules, thought to be baseball's first published, were the basis for what became known as the "New York game." For starters, it meant a player could no longer be deliberately hit by the ball, the danger of injury lessened considerably, which, in turn, led to the use of a harder ball. That alone led to profound changes because a harder ball travels farther and faster when struck than a soft ball, prompting fielders to develop greater skills and more efficient team-work to create outs.

Cartwright redrew the infield as diamond-shaped, rather than square—setting first and third bases forty-two paces apart. He established foul lines and made pitchers throw the ball underhand, keeping the wrist and elbow straight. Batters got three missed swings before they were called out. The rules were quickly adopted, and the Knickerbockers found a much more spacious and permanent playing field across the Hudson River in Hoboken, New Jersey, at a large, grassy meadow named Elysian Fields, a major improvement on their former field where smells wafted from the next-door glue factory.

Elysian Fields was a lovely spot, ideal for this new game. Filled with flowers, trees, and enough room for picnicking, it "blasted the senses . . . by reeking forth fumes of whiskey and tobacco," an English visitor remarked. So there, dressed in uniforms of blue woolen pantaloons, white flannel shirts, and straw hats—baseball caps wouldn't appear until 1855—the Knickerbockers in October 1845 played the first game of modern baseball—an intrasquad game with seven aside in which Cartwright contributed two hits in an 11–8 loss. Still, the rigors of this new sport didn't keep the team from retiring to McCarty's Hotel for a postgame meal of beer and cigars.

Back at Elysian Fields, on June 23, 1846, the Knickerbockers played the first game of competitive baseball—a four-inning affair in which they were trounced 23–1 by a group from New York, with Cartwright serving as umpire. At least they were cheered on by the polite applause of their friends, with women protected from the sun by a colored canvas pavilion; with no grandstand, spectators without carriages stood.

Thus marked the historic break from the more primitive game of rounders in which wooden stakes projecting four feet from the ground stood for bases and a player was put out by being struck with the ball. The Knickerbockers' rules and club bylaws were formalized in a $2 room at Lower Manhattan's Fijux's Hotel, owned by team member Charles Knickerbocker Fijux, which became the place for all team meetings. It was at Fijux's that the Knickerbockers voted to limit membership to forty; of the names on its roster between 1845 and 1860 were seventeen merchants, twelve clerks, five brokers, four professionals, two insurance salesmen, several "gentlemen," a hatter, and a U.S. marshal. The only requisite for admission: some skill in the game and a certain social standing. A demanding schedule fed the feeling of exclusiveness since only men of leisure could afford to devote every Monday and Thursday, known as Knickerbocker "Play Days," to the new game that would take America by storm.

Through it all the team maintained their customary postgame habits. It soon became standard for New York's growing legion of teams to commemorate the end of each season by, well, celebrating at lavish blowouts. In 1854, the Knickerbockers were joined by the Eagle and Gotham clubs in a memorable dinner at Fijux's, where, according to one account, "the utmost hilarity prevailed and everything passed off in a happy manner." Chances are the celebrants even sang the quaint verse of their club song:

"The young clubs, one and all, with a welcome we will greet,
On their field or festive hall, whenever we may meet,
And their praises we will sing at some future time,
But now we'll pledge their health in a glass of rosy wine."

By then, Cartwright had moved on, leaving New York in 1849 in a Conestoga wagon to prospect for gold in California. Crossing the country, Cartwright traveled with a light ball and an undersized rule booklet with the word "Knickerbocker" stamped on the cover. At most stops, he preached the baseball gospel to fellow travelers, miners, saloonkeepers, and soldiers—writing in his travel journal on April 16, 1849, near Independence, Missouri, that "it is comical to see Mountain men and Indians playing the new game." On reaching California, however, Cartwright soon found that mining wasn't something that suited his more entrepreneurial talents; so in the fall of 1849, he took a friend's advice and set out for Honolulu to study the chances of shipping fruit and vegetables back to the mainland.

Hawaii suited Cartwright, who became a well-to-do merchant, a leading citizen, and a financial advisor to several of the traditional Hawaiian rulers. Along the way, he started an insurance company, founded Honolulu's first fire department, and, secure in his knowledge he had played a major role in the popularity of baseball, enjoyed preaching the baseball gospel. Cartwright never left Hawaii, and so he was understandably disappointed when Albert Spalding failed to stop his team in Honolulu on his Round-the-World baseball tour of 1888. After a long, productive life, Cartwright died in 1892 at the age of seventy-two.

◆　◆　◆

Predictably, the Cartwright-Doubleday rift got a further jolt of attention when Frank Menke's *Sports Encyclopedia* was published in February 1939. Included in the baseball section was his stated belief that it was Cartwright, and not Doubleday, who had been baseball's true father—a theory that got considerable ensuing attention from Bob Considine in New York's *Daily Mirror*, and then in the *Sporting News*.

Considine called Menke's creation theory an "embarrassing revelation" for baseball. The *Sporting News* made a similar assertion in calling Menke, with only slight exaggeration, "the leading iconoclast of the century" whose claim "completely upsets the base on which the anniversary rests."

It all seemed so plausible. Unfortunately for major league baseball, the timing couldn't be worse. No, they weren't about to abandon their own claim that it was Abner Doubleday who had invented baseball—it was just too late with the Cavalcade plan proceeding so swimmingly—but they did have a crisis of sorts, and needed a quick program of damage control.

To the rescue came Steve Hannagan who deftly arranged for an emergency "cavalcade" of his own. With spring training set to open around Florida, he called on a colleague, one Stuart Cameron of the delightful-sounding Miami Beach News Service, to visit the various camps in an effort to talk up the Centennial. Hannagan's plan was sound—a schmooze-a-thon in which Cameron, supplied with Hall of Fame talking points, would emphasize the Cooperstown/Doubleday myth. In response to Menke, Hannagan and crew stressed that Doubleday had been generally accepted as the official "inventor for more than thirty years." No, the Mills Commission "didn't pull Doubleday's name out of a hat," Hannagan wrote—and the baseball bigwigs were more than satisfied with the theory as it stood. It was a tempest in a teapot—and spin control at its best.

Back in Cooperstown, editor Walter Littell of the *Ostego Farmer* could have used a dose of Hannagan's tact. His paper's response to the Doubleday myth was to demonize Menke, writing dismissively that his "poison will pass." Menke belonged to "the class that would belittle Washington, Lincoln, and other men who have played their part in American history," Littell wrote. His real concern was that the Cartwright publicity could endanger the festivities in Cooperstown, leaving some would-be tourists at home: "On this account, it is very

important that Cartwright Day [planned for May] is a real success."
As James Vlasich writes in *A Legend for the Legendary*, "This statement
made the day for honoring the famous Knickerbocker seem more
like a cover-up than a celebration."

But the fact is that early Hall of Fame organizers had reached out
to the Cartwright family, quietly giving due to their famous
ancestor's role in creating baseball. The writers did, too, in electing
Cartwright to the Hall in 1938 as a founder, calling him the "Father
of Modern Base Ball," on his plaque. Most tactful of all had been
Alexander Cleland, who for years carried on a correspondence with
Cartwright's family, who maintained that the onetime Knickerbocker should be credited as baseball's inventor. Cartwright's son
Bruce had been the first to campaign for recognition of the late
baseball pioneer, writing to Spalding back in 1909 after the Mills
Commission report that long after his father had moved to Hawaii,
he had never lost his love for the game. Spalding did not reply.

When Cartwright's grandson Bruce Jr. contacted the Hall of
Fame in late 1935 to see if it might want some of his grandfather's
things, Cleland was receptive. Writing back to Cartwright in Honolulu, Cleland explained that the Hall had obtained very few photos
of his grandfather and would appreciate anything he could donate.
Bruce came through, forking over an early portrait, taken in New
York sometime after 1838, but also two receipts from a Knickerbocker banquet, an extensive family tree, and an early book of baseball history that gave Cartwright his due. In return, Bruce
Cartwright Jr. had a modest request—that his grandfather "receive a
little credit for what he did for baseball." Cleland's response was
more than reasonable, and Alexander Cartwright received both a
special exhibit and his own case, along with a virtual assurance from
Cleland that he would "be among the first to be represented by a

plaque." Albert Spalding would have hit the ceiling. But Cleland's magnanimous response to placate the Cartwright family had deflated what could have been a volatile situation.

It helped that the Cartwrights were some five thousand miles away in Hawaii, slightly out of the mainstream. Despite the Hall's faulty public insistence that it had been Abner Doubleday who was most responsible for the birth of baseball, the Cartwright family seemed satisfied with the baseball establishment's acknowledgment. Alexander Cleland had been a masterful politician in diffusing a minefield. The countdown to the Cavalcade of Baseball could begin after all.

◆   ◆   ◆

The weather in New York had dipped into the teens on January 17, 1939, when baseball writers were dispatched to major league baseball headquarters for the kickoff to the long-awaited Centennial. Today, year-round baseball news is routine, but it wasn't in the days when baseball writers counted on light schedules and long lunches in the off-season. But thanks to the Hall of Fame PR onslaught, that was all about to change.

Events had kicked off two weeks before in Philadelphia, where a dinner termed the "opening gun" of baseball's Centennial featured Connie Mack, Clark Griffith, and the debut of a baseball history film. It was also a chance to beat the Doubleday myth into the nation's conscience. "Just one hundred years ago," American League president William Harridge told the crowd, "Abner Doubleday devised the sport, and throughout 1939 organized baseball will celebrate the event."

Several months of anniversary events were planned for Cooperstown and at big-league ballparks. Starting May 6 in Cooperstown would be a progression of special days. Less than a week later came news about the Hall of Fame balloting in which writers elected three more members—George Sisler, Eddie Collins, and the late Willie Keeler. And a week after that, General John J. Pershing joined the Baseball Centennial Commission, although he was stationed in France, and there was little he could do. Four days later, the Baseball Centennial agenda occupied a big slice of the annual Baseball Writers' Dinner at the Hotel Commodore, where Postmaster General Farley revealed his plans for the Centennial stamp. Those long lunches would have to wait: The Cooperstown PR machine was running on all cylinders.

The stamp got its share of attention, helping Hannagan to fulfill his ambition to spread news of the Cavalcade to people with only a casual interest in the sport. For much of February until mid-April or so, Farley was said to be deep in thought on the design of the stamp. Some urged that he select an image of Doubleday, others wanted Cartwright. But in the end, the politician did the smart thing—compromising with the image of boys playing ball on a town square.

Periodic ramblings about the controversy of baseball's origins continued to crop up. In late April, A. M. Sakolski of New York City wrote to the *New York Times* that "there is no historical evidence that General Abner Doubleday originated the game," reciting the familiar argument that in 1839, he couldn't have been in Cooperstown. Even the *Times* had bought into the myth, responding with a Spalding quote from 1911 that it had indeed been Doubleday's doing. But the very next day, the newspaper caught itself, writing in an editorial on the baseball stamp that Cartwright "appears to have drawn up the first professional baseball code in 1845."

But Spalding still had the last laugh. On May 1, he and five other old-time stars squeezed into the Hall of Fame with just a month to go until the June Cavalcade, generating a whole new round of publicity for the Cooperstown myth. Joining him were 300-game winner Old Hoss Radbourne, Cap Anson, curveball inventor Candy Cummings, ex-Giants catcher Buck Ewing, and White Sox owner Charles Comiskey.

◆　◆　◆

Rain played havoc on the opening of the 1939 baseball season—particularly on the Yankees whose opener against the Red Sox at Yankee Stadium was postponed twice before Red Ruffing out pitched Lefty Grove 2–0 in front of 30,278 fans who spent as much time watching the leaden, threatening skies as they did the game. They managed to watch long enough to cheer the arrival of Babe Ruth, attired in a massive tan raincoat, and watch Bill Dickey launch a home run, and Joe DiMaggio make two spectacular catches in centerfield.

Games were played more quickly in those days—a lot more quickly without the TV timeouts—and after the one-hour, forty-seven-minute game, the Yankees dressed and departed immediately for Washington, D.C., for the Senators home opener the following day. But it rained again in Washington and the game was postponed, leaving both teams to do their part to commemorate baseball's Centennial—traveling in the morning to Arlington Cemetery where they attended a memorial service at the gravesite of Abner Doubleday.

It was big-league baseball's kickoff to the Centennial celebration that would climax June 12 in Cooperstown. The commemoration was the idea of Clark Griffith, whose early interest in the Hall of Fame had been a real boost for Cooperstown. It also marked the official entry of big-league, regular-season participation in the

Centennial in which teams were welcome to improvise in whatever way they chose. Many did by incorporating a series of hokey, Hannagan-inspired stunts from parades to playing exhibitions with rocking-chair umpires and players adorned with old-style handlebar mustaches.

The kickoff coincided with several other publicity-generating events, like Christy Mathewson Day in his hometown of Factoryville, Pennsylvania, where there was a parade and a game between the great Giant pitcher's alma mater, Bucknell, and Scranton-Keystone Junior College. Then came the unveiling in Cooperstown of the bronze bust of the pitcher. Attending were forty members of the Mathewson family, including his widow, Jane, who spoke of her late husband as one whose "life's work can be marked 'well done.'"

Meanwhile, Hall of Fame officials were slapping one another the equivalent of 1939 high fives by making certain to publicize what they considered a seismic event—receipt of a letter from President Roosevelt that recognized the baseball Centennial and that General Doubleday had "invented" the game.

"It is most fitting that the history of our perennially popular sport should be immortalized in the National Baseball Museum at Cooperstown, where the game originated," the president wrote. "Baseball has become, through the years, not only a great national sport, but also the symbol of America as the melting pot. The players embrace all nations and national origins and the fans, equally cosmopolitan, make only one demand of them: Can they play the game?"

⚾ CHAPTER 8 ⚾

"I Hope It Goes Another One Hundred Years"

*P*resident Roosevelt's note, the unveiling of the baseball stamp, and the ensuing publicity campaign were perfectly choreographed to generate maximum attention on Cooperstown. But the warm ovation that greeted Babe Ruth on his entrance to Yankee Stadium on opening day was unscripted—a spontaneous greeting for baseball's most beloved figure. It didn't matter that Ruth was "baseball's No. 1 Forgotten Man," as John Drebinger of the *Times* put it in a reference to the absolute refusal of any big-league team to hire him as manager. The Babe desperately wanted to manage, but no team would take a chance. There was too much baggage, too many memories of the old Babe, the wild man who could follow up an all-night visit to a whorehouse with a game-winning home run.

Former Yankee owner Colonel Jacob Ruppert, who had died six months earlier, may have put it best: "How can you look after others if you can can't look after yourself?" the blunt-speaking beer baron had told him after he had asked for a shot at managing the Yankees.

Therein lay the great dilemma of Babe Ruth in retirement. He was baseball's "Lion in Winter," its greatest and most beloved figure, but at only forty-four, in essence blacklisted from the big leagues. Retired since 1935 when he'd played a few games for the Boston Braves and hit his final three home runs, numbers 712, 713, and 714, on a single last spasm of power on a Saturday afternoon at Forbes Field in Pittsburgh, he'd been told that Bill McKechnie's managerial job would be his for the asking in '36. But the job offer evaporated, as did another from the Tigers. In '38, Ruth headed to Brooklyn as a coach and Ebbets Field gate attraction, thinking he'd have a shot as Dodger manager. But after a seventh-place finish, the Dodgers reached instead for Leo Durocher, whom Ruth detested. Dejected, he retired for good, saying with a touch of pathos, "No matter what the future holds in store, my heart will always be with the great game of baseball."

Ruppert had suggested that Ruth apprentice by managing the International League's Newark Bears, the top Yankee farm team. Ruth refused, pointing to star players who had never managed a day in the minors before landing a position in the bigs, among them Ty Cobb, Mickey Cochrane, Joe Cronin, Rogers Hornsby, Christy Mathewson, Tris Speaker, and Bill Terry. "I gave twenty-two years of my life to big-league baseball," The Babe said at the Baseball Writers' dinner at the Waldorf-Astoria in New York, "and I'm ready to give twenty-five more." Nearly one thousand baseball officials heard his plea, but still, nobody budged.

But wherever he went, Ruth still drew headlines and packed them in, playing periodic exhibition games against semipro teams and putting on pregame hitting exhibitions. Despite his bulging waist and mostly-shot reflexes, The Babe packed a wallop in his bat—drilling a ball 430 feet in the early '30s in St. Louis during a home run hitting contest, further than any of his competitors, which included current big-league sluggers Johnny Mize, Dolph Camilli, and Joe Medwick. Ruth cast a wide smile the rest of the day; bragging that he could still "powder the onion." Still, he was restless—and longed for the action, the attention, and the pace of baseball, from the card games on the long train rides west to the banter around the batting cage and the games themselves. At Yankee Stadium, a reporter asked the Babe how it felt to be in the stands. "Feels funny, funny," he mumbled with a muted smile, putting on a brave front. Invited to pen a column for a vacationing Walter Winchell, Ruth turned it into a job plea, writing that eventually the "baseball bosses" would think of him not as a "hell-raising kid" but as "an old-timer who has learned about self-control."

So Babe Ruth rattled about his eleven-room apartment on Riverside Drive at Eighty-third Street on the Upper West Side of Manhattan, waiting for the managerial call that never came, and carving out a new life, crowded with hosting a radio program along with golf, bowling, and hunting. He plugged Quaker Oats Cereal and continued to visit kids in hospitals and orphanages—always a passion—and in the evenings, generally stayed home, playing cards and listening to the radio. His favorite shows: *The Lone Ranger* and *Gangbusters*.

At least there were no money worries. Ruth, his second wife, Claire, and their two daughters had invested well, thanks to the astute counsel of his shrewd agent-turned-money-manager, Christy Walsh, who had first met the ballplayer in the early 1920s after breaking into his apartment disguised as an ice man. Back then, Ruth blew through dollars like candy, tipping $100 for a 35-cent ham sandwich and loaning his teammates wads that he would never again see. Walsh, with the help of Claire, set up a trust fund for the family, gave Ruth a budget, and wrote him $50 checks whenever he needed cash. The system worked—cutting down on Ruthian spending habits, and granting him financial security for life.

Adding to The Babe's woes was the loss of old friends. In 1938, Ruth jokingly told the crowd at the Baseball Writers Association dinner that he called it the "I Wonder Dinner," as in, "I come here every year and I wonder who'll be missing each year." Among them would be the seventy-one-year-old Ruppert, who died January 13, 1939, leaving the big-hearted Ruth devastated. The two men had clashed repeatedly, but all was forgotten once the hard-nosed Yankee owner, who had always called Ruth "Root" in his German accent, became gravely ill, and Ruth hurried to his bedside at his Fifth Avenue apartment to say good-bye. Emerging from the bedroom, Ruth's eyes were moist. "I couldn't help crying," he said. "It was the only time in his life that he called me Babe to my face . . . he was like a second father to me." Ruth got another jolt later in the spring when Lou Gehrig, obviously not himself, was benched; the "Iron Horse" was headed to the Mayo Clinic for a thorough physical.

Amidst such heartache, Ruth welcomed the trip to Cooperstown for the Hall of Fame festivities. At first, Alexander Cleland and baseball officials had worried that The Babe hadn't responded to repeated requests for equipment and artifacts. They needn't have worried—Ruth was no correspondent and after a lifetime of people catering to him, wasn't used to reaching out. Fortunately, the Hillerich family of Louisville—they of Hillerich & Bradsby Company "Louisville Slugger" bat fame—had stepped forward and donated to

Cooperstown a number of items: The Babe's prized bat from 1920, autographed and including twenty-eight notches around the trademark, one for each home run he slugged before it broke at the handle. The Hillerich family also gave The Babe's mitt and a pair of running shoes.

On the train headed to Cooperstown, and throughout the day, Ruth was in fine fettle—very much himself and, as ever, baseball's biggest attraction. All day long, he drew a crowd, barreling about and accompanied by an ever-present group of children moving with him like a rugby scrum, asking him to sign their scraps of paper and anxious to be at his side. It was all quite familiar to Ruth who basked in the adoration and the attention; The Babe loved every minute, seemingly always headed somewhere and forever in conversation, not with any one person, but with everyone. From the biggest of cities to the most remote locales, he was the most popular, most charismatic athlete of all time. How different from a trip The Babe had taken some years before to Paris, which he didn't care for much because no one recognized him.

Making Ruth the last of the ten immortals to be introduced was another Steve Hannagan idea that worked. Although Ty Cobb, by polling more votes than Ruth, had arguably earned the right to be introduced last, he wasn't in Ruth's league in terms of appeal and popularity; besides, he still hadn't shown up. Spotting The Babe, dressed in what Tom Manning described as a cream-colored "Palm Beach" suit with a button-down white shirt with a wide collar, but no tie (he was the only one of the ten to not wear a tie), the humanity that now covered Main Street, including a barefoot boy who had scaled halfway up a telephone pole for a better view, erupted in applause. With a sense of drama, baseball's big day had left its best 'til last—the main man, the "Sultan of Swat," and the immortal everyone wanted to see. Such was the magnificent charisma of Ruth who had the innate ability to "chat into a mike or in front of thousands," as Ken Smith wrote, "with the utter simplicity of a fellow passing the time of day with a neighbor over a back-yard fence."

How true. Lining up with his teammates one sweltering day in Washington to be formally introduced to President Calvin Coolidge, Ruth waited his turn: "How do you do, Mr. President," Waite Hoyt said. "Good day, sir," said Herb Pennock.

"Mr. Ruth," the president said, shaking hands with Ruth. "Hot as hell, ain't it, Prez?" Mr. Ruth said.

Ruth biographer Robert Creamer may have come closest to summing up Ruth's appeal: "The crudity, the vulgarity, the indifference, the physical humor that bordered on brutality, the preoccupation with his own needs . . . none of that mattered when Ruth smiled or laughed or did almost anything," he wrote in his 1974 biography, *Babe*. "He was so alive, so attractive . . . ingenious, unself-conscious, appealing."

Bursting out from the entrance to the Hall, Ruth strode to the lectern. "I hope that some day some of the young fellas coming into the game will know how it feels to be picked for the Hall of Fame," he started in his trademark deep baritone with a trace of a southern drawl. "I know the old boys—we were just talking it over—worked hard and [made] it. And I made it. And I hope the coming generation—the young boys today—that they'll work hard and also be on it. And as my old friend Cy Young says, 'I hope it goes another one hundred years and the next one hundred years will be the greatest.'

"To me, this is just like an anniversary itself because twenty-five years ago yesterday, I pitched my first [big-league] baseball game in Boston for the Red Sox. So it's a pleasure for me to come up here and to be in the Hall of Fame."

Ruth's reference to history may have caught more than a few by surprise. For all of Ruth's heroics, he could be remarkably forgetful of statistics, dates, and especially names. After Hoyt, the great Yankee right-handed pitcher and his teammate of eight years, was traded to the Tigers, Ruth bid his old friend farewell: "Good-bye, Walter," he said, soberly shaking his hand. When pitching for the Red Sox in the 1918 World Series and ordered to hit Leslie Mann, The Babe drilled Max Flack instead, thinking it was Mann. Turning down a dinner invitation from Mary Pickford and Douglas Fairbanks, Jr., then the biggest names in movies, Ruth was asked who was throwing the party. "Oh, a couple of actors I met in Hollywood," he said. To compensate, The Babe called most teammates and people forty and under, "kid," while anyone older was "doc" or "mom." In his autobiography, Ruth writes of his first wife as Helen Woodring, not Woodford, and he often called Claire, his second wife, "Clara."

With teammates, The Babe bestowed nicknames of his own making, most based on unflattering physical characteristics, among them Horse Nose, Rubber Belly, and Chicken Neck. For a time, he was called "Tarzan" with some good-natured affection by his teammates—that is until Ruth found out that the name was for the "king of the apes." The thin-skinned Ruth threatened bodily harm to anyone who ever called him Tarzan again, and his teammates stopped. But to opposing bench jockeys, Ruth was a baboon, an "ape," a "monkey," and worse, a "nigger," which helped give rise to enduring rumors that Ruth had African American blood, and led in part to a considerable lifelong following among African Americans, many of whom sat and cheered for him in segregated sections of Griffith Stadium in Washington and Sportsman's Park, St. Louis.

It all fed the legend. "Don't tell me about Ruth: I've seen what he did to people," said Hoyt, reminiscing as an old man. "I've seen them—fans—driving miles in open wagons through the prairies of Oklahoma to see him in exhibition games as we headed north in spring. I've seen them: kids, men, women, worshipers all, hoping to get his famous name on a torn, dirty piece of paper, or hoping to get a grunt of recognition when they said, 'Hiya, Babe.' He never let them down; not once."

Indeed, the mists of time obscure the essence of this baseball phenomenon. Most baseball fans can recite key Ruthian accomplishments—The Babe's early pitching success with the Boston Red Sox, followed by his headline-grabbing sale to New York and the sixty home runs in 1927, the 714 lifetime home runs, and the four world championships that his bat helped the Yankees win to become the biggest story in sports. But The Babe was about more than just baseball. "I swing big, with everything I got," he once said in what could be a metaphor for his life. "I hit big or I miss big. I like to live as big as I can." Ruth knew himself well; larger than life, he was a bonafide cultural phenomenon, then as now the game's greatest ever.

◆   ◆   ◆

For starters, the son of a Baltimore saloonkeeper did things on a baseball diamond that will never be matched. But to get at the true legend of Ruth requires deeper examination: Never a poster child, this pear-shaped, moon-faced man-child defied description—eating, drinking, whoring, belching, over-spending, wearing silly hats in photos, wearing silk underwear, and generally attacking life with the gusto of someone just sprung from jail—and in 1920, becoming the biggest phenomenon of the era.

In the fast-moving Jazz Age, Ruth lived life in overdrive—talking louder, staying up later than the others, and eating more, too—commonly stuffing himself with a midnight snack of a half-dozen hot dogs washed down by as many sodas and a fifth of scotch. For a man who burned the candle at both ends, he was as much at home in the ballpark as he was the orphanage, the society cotillion, or the cathouse. Money meant nothing. When a Detroit chambermaid returned a $500 watch Ruth had lost, The Babe was so relieved that he tipped her $500. On a postseason trip to Havana, Ruth is said to have lost as much as $35,000 at the racetrack. Striding into the Yankee clubhouse before a game, Ruth was the main attraction: He wore the best tailored clothes, had his nails done by a manicurist, and occasionally made a stab at answering his voluminous mail. "Open these for me, will ya?" he'd ask a teammate. "Keep the ones with the checks and the ones from the broads." Once, when team trainer Doc Woods sifted through a wastebasket stuffed with Ruth's discarded mail, he found $6,000 in checks and endorsements. "Born? Hell, Babe Ruth wasn't born," said his longtime Yankee teammate Joe Dugan. "The sonofabitch fell from a tree."

The second of two children, Ruth at seven was declared "incorrigible" and moved to St. Mary's Industrial School for Boys, a Baltimore reformatory-turned-orphanage—home, on and off, until the age of eighteen. The few frayed photographs of St. Mary's reveal a bleak, Dickensian-looking place. Ruth's family seldom visited, and the boy seemed destined to become a shirtmaker. But when Brother Matthias, the 250-pound, 6'6" giant of a Xavieran priest in charge of St. Mary's, took a shine to Ruth—recognizing his budding talent for baseball by hitting him fly ball after fly ball—the boy became a star. By eight, Ruth was on the twelve-year-old's team and proving to be a natural at every position.

Years later, Ruth would talk with reverence of Brother Matthias's mentoring, how he would stand in one corner of the ball field and clout towering home runs over the centerfield fence. Ruth would spend hours playing catch with Brother Matthias, and even emulated his batting stance, the well-known pigeon-toed lean into the approaching ball. Supplementing Brother Matthias's imposing size was a quiet but stern presence that earned him the respect and the nickname "The Boss" from St. Mary's boys. Ruth remained a truant at heart and fled the walls of St. Mary's from time to time, but he always went back and was met by Brother Matthias who never scolded or reprimanded him. Ruth would call him "The greatest man I've ever known."

◆   ◆   ◆

Ruth came to personify the fast-moving Jazz Age—and 1920 was the year he struck it big, really big, on America's biggest stage, New York. He had become a phenomenon in 1919 by hitting a record twenty-nine home runs for the Red Sox, but 1920 transformed him into a megastar who transcended baseball and, arguably, *saved* it as the Black Sox scandal shook the game to its core. Ruth hit fifty-four home runs for the Yankees that year—twenty-five more than the year before, more than every major league team save one and thirty-five home runs more than runner-up George Sisler.

The Babe was the sports story of the decade—and he exploited it. "I swing big, with everything I got," Ruth said. "I hit big or I miss big. I like to live as big as I can." On the morning of September 25, 1920, America woke to news that members of the White Sox had told a Cook County Grand Jury about the World Series fix of the year—an extraordinary tale, except for the fact that it was obscured by another baseball event of the previous day: The Babe's fiftieth and fifty-first home runs of the season.

Ruth socked number fifty off the Senators Jose Acosta in the first game of a doubleheader at the Polo Grounds, with the ball striking the roof of the right-field grandstand and bounding back on to the field. The shot, which threw the 25,000 spectators into hysteria, "gave the slugger a whoop and a hurrah he will never forget, the *New York Times* reported. "It was one of those events in sport, which will furnish chatter for years to come. Baseball has never before developed a figure of such tremendously picturesque proportions as this home-run king of the Yankees." And that on the day that America discovered the Black Sox.

The home runs did more than launch the Yankee dynasty; they helped the Bombers become the first team in major league history to draw more than one million spectators at home, and generated a level of unparalleled excitement at a time when baseball sorely needed it. Baseball needed the charisma and bat of Babe Ruth.

The strength of that enduring charisma is apparent every time a slugger chases his records. Roger Maris ran smack into the full force of The Babe's legend in 1961 as he pursued the single-season home run record. The writers were merciless all year, twisting the soft-spoken Yankee's words and making him so miserable that he lost clumps of hair; it didn't help that many thought Mickey Mantle, not Maris, was the anointed one, the man who should have broken the record. When Maris reached the mountaintop, the baseball establish-ment ruled that the number sixty-one would need an asterisk, a ludicrous acknowledgement that he had played a schedule of eight more games than had Ruth.

It was as if big sluggers needed personalities to match. Closing in on Ruth's all-time record in 1974 was Hank Aaron, another quiet man who faced hostility as well, but of a vicious, racial nature. In 1998, Mark McGwire and Sammy Sosa enjoyed buckets of good press in their duel to surpass Maris, but that has all dissipated amidst allegations of steroid abuse. By the time Barry Bonds hit seventy-three home runs in 2001, the biggest story may have been how little excitement the new record generated. Not only was Bonds facing many of the same drug allegations as McGwire and Sosa, but his arrogance and surliness with reporters did little to endear him to anyone.

Red Sox manager Ed Barrow had been the first to recognize that Ruth, who came to the majors as a pitcher, might be of more value with his bat. On April 4, 1919, in a spring training game at the old fairgrounds in Tampa against John McGraw's Giants, Ruth cracked what Barrow called many years later, "the longest home run in history." Batting in the second inning against Columbia George Smith, Ruth sent a pitch high over the right centerfield wall, far above centerfielder Ross Youngs's head, clear out of the fairgrounds and into a neighboring hospital yard. After the game, as Youngs stood where the ball fell, a group of writers watched as somebody used a surveyor's tape and measured the distance to home plate—579 feet.

Ruth had become a slugger—continuing to hit moon shots and acquiring all the quirks, mannerisms, and the swagger of a home run hitter. He used the same dark ash wood bat, carrying it on and off the field himself and not letting anyone, even the clubhouse boy, so much as touch it. Like Shoeless Joe Jackson, the marvelous White Sox hitter whose swing he emulated, Ruth would coat his bats with tobacco juice and lovingly pat them before lugging one up to home plate and bashing another long hit.

One day, when Hooper asked Ruth to lend him the bat once he was finished with it, Ruth said, "I will like hell. I'll keep this baby as long as I live." But a few weeks later, the bat cracked, and after the game, Ruth tried to repair it using a hammer, tiny nails, and tape. A few days later, when he was called out on a third strike, Ruth became so indignant that he slammed the bat like an ax on home plate, cracking it beyond repair.

Ruth turned and walked back toward the dugout, his eyes still "blazing" with anger, Hooper noted. In the dugout, after a few minutes of silence, Hooper again brought up the bat.

"Babe, how about that bat?" he asked.

"Take the sonofabitch," Ruth said. "I don't want to see it as long as I live!"

Hooper took the bat, held onto it, and with a noble sense of history, donated it decades later to the National Baseball Hall of Fame and Museum.

* * *

"He was a very simple man, in some ways a primitive man," longtime Yankee writer Frank Graham said of Ruth. "He had little education, and little need for what he had." Introduced before a game to a man suffering from a cold, Ruth reached into the pocket of his uniform and pulled out an oversized onion. "Here, gnaw on this," he said. "Raw onions are cold-killers." Asked about political unrest in China, "the hell with it," he replied. Asked what he was reading, Ruth said he had given it up. "Reading isn't good for a ballplayer," he said. "Not good for his eyes. If my eyes went bad even a little bit I couldn't hit home runs."

Much of what he said was crude, and Ruth enjoyed intentionally sprinkling his conversation with vulgarities. "Piss pass the butter," he would say to a teammate with an impish smile. Once when relaxing with several teammates and their wives at spring training, Ruth excused himself, saying, "I've got to take a piss." Taken aside by a teammate who followed him to the men's room, he was told that wasn't advisable in mixed company. So The Babe coughed up his apology: "I'm sorry I said 'piss.'"

Ruth proved especially appealing to two groups of people— women and children. There are many stories, some apocryphal, about Ruth's insatiable appetite for sex. Suffice to say he craved sex and bedded down scores of women, from an entire St. Louis whore-house, all in a single night—true—to the women in every American League port of call, many of them willing to visit Ruth's hotel room, often two and three at a time, which was probably true. His sex drive abated only slightly in later years, even after he was married for the second time, to Claire, and she was traveling with the team; to meet his need, The Babe just borrowed keys from his teammates and used their rooms.

It's hard to believe, then, that for virtually his entire big-league career, Ruth was married—first to Helen Woodford, a waitress he met in 1914 at Landers Coffee Shop, which he frequented in his early days in Boston. The nineteen-year-old Babe met the sixteen-year-old Helen, a Manchester, New Hampshire native, within his first six weeks in Boston, and was immediately smitten. One morning, when she was waiting on Ruth at the coffee shop, Ruth said to her, "How about you and me getting married, hon?" So they did, on October 18, 1914, in Ellicott City, Maryland.

One can only imagine how Helen endured her husband's con-stant philandering, most often pursued on road trips. Even so, they seemed to enjoy one another's company and could often be seen bowling or skating, both passions of Ruth's. Helen would hang in there, moving with The Babe to New York City in 1920 and adopting a little girl in '21, but the couple soon separated.

Never, ever suffering from the same sort of strain was Ruth's gen-uine lifelong love affair with children. Essentially a big kid himself, he never tired from their attention, and really did visit all of those orphanages and hospitals in all those cities, often without a shred of attention or publicity. When, in 1918, a fire nearly destroyed St. Mary's, Ruth took to raising funds for his old school.

* * *

Every Ruthian blast fueled the legend—creating a completely new game, based on clout as opposed to the traditional scientific game favored by Ty Cobb and John McGraw. Sportswriters focused on this new game calling it "a whale versus a shark," or the end of the dead-ball era, a whole new way to win a game with a single blast. Said Casey Stengel: "It's a bomb against a machine gun."

Walter Johnson cited Ruth's batting eye and physique as clues to his greatness. "He is tall, heavy and strong," the Big Train said. "His weight is in his shoulders, where it will do him the most good. He is a tremendously powerful man. . . . He grasps the bat with an iron grip and when he meets the ball, he follows it through with his full strength and weight. For his size, Joe Jackson is as hard a hitter as Ruth, but that margin of thirty pounds in weight and enormous reserve strength enables Ruth to give the ball that extra punch, which drives it further than anybody else."

His titanic blasts were so utterly different from what anyone was used to that he was changing the game every time he sent another ball beyond the outfield fences. That he could do it after staying up all night doing things most of us only read about made him even more popular. "Fans everywhere loved him no less for his infrac-tions," wrote Cobb biographer Al Stump. "Vicariously, they were right with him."

The hypercompetitive Cobb predicted Ruth would burn out.

He figured pitchers would soon adjust to Ruth's big uppercut of a swing. He considered Ruth undisciplined at the plate, too great a guess-hitter, and unable to master the curve. Besides, Cobb knew more than most about the stories of Ruth's prodigious appetites off the field. One morning with the Tigers in New York for a series, Cobb was out at 6:00 A.M. for a run along Park Avenue, when he bumped into Ruth returning home after a long night.

"Been having a good time?" Cobb asked.

"Pretty damned good," replied The Babe. "There were three of them."

The cantankerous Cobb would come to admire Ruth—and the two became golfing companions. When it was clear Ruth was anything but a flash in the pan, Cobb started to appreciate his gifts, and get to the essence of what made him special. "After Ruth had been around awhile and no longer pitching, I could see what made him so different," Cobb said in later years. "His pitching made him a hitter [of home runs]. As mostly a pitcher, he didn't have to protect the plate as I did and the other regular hitters had to do. He could try this and that. Experiment. Learn timing. As a pitcher, if he flopped [at bat], nobody gave a damn. Pitchers always had been lousy hitters. . . . Once [Ruth] got smart and grooved his cut, he had a whole new career."

In a sense, Ruth remade what had been a scientific, low-scoring game into an extension of his own slugging lifestyle. One day, while the Yankees were in Philadelphia, Yankee Herb Pennock was asked to attend a formal party in nearby Wilmington, Delaware, and asked Ruth and two other teammates, Joe Dugan and Bob Meusel, to attend. The players were game, and so was team manager Miller Huggins, provided they got back in time for a good night's rest before the next day's game at Shibe Park.

At the party, Ruth was a big hit, politely telling the guests that baseball had come easily to him, though it took hard work to hone his skills. Asked about his swing, he talked of his admiration for Joe Jackson's technique, which he copied. The baseball talk flowed as freely through the evening as the alcohol, and after a couple of hours, Ruth set his roving eye on one of the women, a maid.

"Babe," said the boxing promoter who had arranged for the visit of the players, "you got to get out of here."

"Not without that broad," Ruth said.

"Come on," the promoter reasoned, "I'll get you broads in Philly better than her."

"You sure?" Ruth said.

The boxing promoter kept his word, and took Ruth to a brothel. Hours and hours later as the sun rose over Philadelphia, the promoter, thinking of the Yankee game later that afternoon, reckoned that Ruth should return to the hotel.

Sitting in a lounge chair with a woman on each knee and an open bottle of champagne upside down on his head, Ruth thought it over. "I ain't gonna be leaving for awhile yet," he said.

That afternoon at Shibe Park, Ruth pronounced himself ready to take on the A's. "I feel good," said Ruth, who had probably not slept.

"You don't look so good," said Fred Merkle, a longtime Giant finishing his career with the Yankees.

"I'll hit one," said Ruth.

"Bet?" Merkle said.

"A hundred," said Ruth.

"Wait a minute," said Merkle. "This is an easy ballpark."

"All right," said Ruth. "I'll give you two-to-one."

In his first at-bat, Ruth cracked one into the left-field stands and won the bet. Next time up, he tripled to right. Then, he tripled again, driving a ball over Al Simmons's head in center. In his fourth at-bat, he hit another home run.

In 1927, Ruth and the Yankees put together a season for the ages. Ruth belted sixty homers, his personal record, which was more than every other team in the American League, and hit .356, to help the Yankees win the pennant by nineteen games. Gehrig had quite a run himself, belting forty-seven home runs and batting .373. Then, at batting practice before game one of the World Series against the Pirates at Forbes Field, the Yankees launched home run after home run in an awesome display, unnerving the upstart Pirates, whom the Yankees promptly swept.

By then, the game had spawned a generation of home run hitters —Gehrig, Jimmie Foxx, and Hack Wilson among them—but the mighty Ruth was still king. Ruth's '27 output came in a year when the American League hit 439, meaning he accounted for nearly 14 percent of the league's number. When Roger Maris hit sixty-one home runs in '61, the American League hit 1,534, leaving Maris's share at less than 4 percent.

"There is no other real way to compare one generation with another, but in fairness to Ruth it must be said that no player in history ever dominated his competition to such an astounding degree," wrote Lee Allen, a Ruth biographer. "Ruth hit home runs when no one, with the exception of Gehrig, hit them in quantity."

His 1929 marriage to Claire Hodgson—made possible after his estranged first wife, Helen, died in a Massachusetts fire—settled Ruth down a tad. The couple adopted Claire's daughter from a previous marriage, giving The Babe two daughters on whom he doted. He remained The Babe, a bit pudgier and a carouser when he could get away with it, but still a man for whom the public craved to know exactly how he managed to do what he did. One day in 1930, while waiting to step into the batting cage before a game in St. Louis, Ruth got to talking with Browns manager Bill Killefer.

"Your face is getting fatter and fatter," Killefer said.

"Yeah?" said Ruth, sending a stream of tobacco juice toward the ground. "Well, I don't hit with my face."

"Is the wife on the trip with you?"

"Sure."

"Having a hard time dodging the old phone calls?" Killefer asked, with a smile.

"Oh, go to hell."

"You must do some reading," a reporter said. "Who are your favorite authors?"

"My favorite Arthurs? [Art] Nehf and [Art] Fletcher."

"Not Arthurs. Authors, writers."

"Oh, writers," said Ruth. "My favorite writer is Christy Walsh."

"What is the psychology of home runs?"

"Say, are you kidding me?"

"No, of course not. I just want an explanation of why you get so many home runs."

Ruth spat more tobacco juice. "Just swinging," he said.

"Have you ever had an idol, someone you thought more of than anyone else?"

"Sure," said Tony Lazzeri, standing nearby. "Babe Ruth."

"Go to hell," Ruth said to both. "Excuse me, it's my turn to hit."

CHAPTER 9

A "World Series with the Score Tied Nothing to Nothing in the
Ninth Inning"

There are no figures on how many people in tiny Cooperstown
actually stuck around at home as the introductory ceremonies
concluded. Those who did would have had a wealth of local,
national, and international news to absorb that busy Monday in June.

Just three hours or so south, along the Hudson River at West Point,
President Roosevelt was at that hour telling the 456 graduates of the
U.S. Military Academy, the largest in history, that the United States
sought peace, but recognized the need for revitalizing American
defenses in light of "dramatic illustrations of the fate of undefended
nations." Without naming the growing crisis in Europe posed by Nazi
Germany's recent invasions of Austria and Czechoslovakia, the president paused, adding, "I need hardly to be more specific than that."

The president's speech was a jarring spin back to reality for the nostalgia-drenched festivities in Cooperstown. Roosevelt himself had just spent a long weekend entertaining King George VI and the queen of England at his home in Hyde Park, even introducing the Royal Couple to the American delicacy of hot dogs. From all reports, the king loved hot dogs, enjoyed the hospitality of his American hosts, and helped cement the close bonds between countries that would become so critical to winning peace.

Out west in Kansas City, Lou Gehrig was playing that Monday in his final game as a Yankee—spending three innings in an exhibition contest against the minor league blues and, sadly, demonstrating exactly why he'd been benched. The once sure-handed Iron Horse let a ball go through his legs at first, then dropped a low throw and bounced out in a puny grounder in his only at-bat. If Gehrig's baseball career had quickly unraveled, at least one thing was clear: After the game, he was headed to the Mayo Clinic in Rochester, Minnesota, where he was to undergo a thorough examination to determine, as Rud Rennie put it in the *Herald-Tribune*, "why a man of his age and physique should so suddenly los[e] his ability to field and bat and run."

"I don't know how long I'll be gone," Gehrig told reporters. "If everything goes well, I'll be back."

"Nervous?" he was asked.

"No," said the Iron Horse. "Just anxious to get started."

◆　◆　◆

With the immortals' speechifying finished in Cooperstown, Judge Landis hopped up to the podium again, looking slight indeed next to imposing men like Ruth, Johnson, and Mack. His intent was a brief piece of business but important—to declare the Hall of Fame was open for business. "May it forever stand as a symbol of clean play and sportsmanship," the judge, his oversized Centennial baseball cap now off, grandly proclaimed in what became a mantra for how future generations of members would be elected. In retrospect, the commissioner's stand on "sportsmanship" rings a tad hollow considering his hard-line stance against integrating the big leagues. But considering it was Landis's firm actions against gambling that had restored a dose of integrity to the game, his comments were fitting. How fascinating it would be to get the judge's view on the current debate: Should steroid users be banned from the Hall and from the record books?

And with that, everybody stood for the national anthem, another gig for the Cooperstown High School Band. On NBC Radio, Tom Manning announced "the conclusion of one of the most elaborate and brilliant ceremonies that sportdom has ever known."

"Yes, the folks of Cooperstown are mighty proud and they should be," Manning concluded with a final ceremonial burst of nostalgic improvisation: "And now in dropping out of the air, the password of the day seems to be this: Give your boy a ball and a bat with which to play," he said, "and your worries will be over that he might go astray."

◆   ◆   ◆

But baseball's grand day was hardly finished. First came photos, including the famous group shot from International News that captured so much of the personalities of each man and would appear the next day on the front pages of newspapers around the country. An hour-long reception and brief museum tour for the Hall of

Famers and dignitaries would be next, followed by the day's climax—an eclectic parade of schoolboys, soldiers, and major leaguers marching from Clark Gymnasium to Doubleday Field. There, teams composed of thirty-two current big leaguers, two from each of the sixteen teams, would choose up sides and play an exhibition game that Mel Allen and Arch McDonald were preparing to broadcast nationally.

"Reception" was the organizers' word. The session was more of a baseball scrum, a free-for-all in which the immortals stuck to their makeshift stage as baseball officials and fans closed in with congratulations. Umpire Tommy Connolly, in town to officiate the upcoming exhibition game, cornered Lajoie, Speaker, and Collins—congratulating them on their speeches. "I must say," observed Connolly, who with Bill Klem would be among the first umpires elected to the Hall fourteen years later, "that your language has improved a lot since I was umpiring behind you."

A boyish-looking reporter rushed up to Cy Young with a stream of questions. "What was your favorite pitch when the opponents loaded the bases?" he asked.

"My boy," Young said, "I can't recollect ever having to pitch with the bases full."

The reporter persisted. "How many games did you win, Mr. Young?" Annoyed but still in good humor, Young shot back, "Young man, I won more than you'll ever see."

Many of those at the reception took their Hall of Fame first-day stamped postcards, already signed by Landis and Postmaster General Jim Farley, and pressed close to the stage in order to get the immortals to attach their names as well. They signed their names dozens, even hundreds of times, accounting for baseball's first big outburst of autographing. But few cards survive; today, a complete set of the immortals' signatures on one of the postcards is a valued baseball keepsake, fetching upwards of $10,000 in auctions. Meanwhile, the more innovative had the immortals sign a baseball; in 2005, a ball autographed by all eleven went for $49,500.

Then, amidst the crowds and conversation, an immaculately dressed, middle-aged balding man pushed his way to the top of the stairs of the platform. Heads turned and applause followed him: It was Ty Cobb, the great Georgia Peach, who had, quite suddenly and with little warning, arrived—offering a stream of apologies for his tardiness. So the Cavalcade's last living immortal had finally made it, with word spreading quickly through the crowd. Too late for the composite photo session, Cobb was engulfed from all directions by the other greats, some of whom hadn't cared for him as a player. The reaction moved Cobb, whose eyes grew misty.

Seeing his old rival, Ruth broke into a wide grin. "Hello, rookie," he bellowed, grabbing his hand.

Greeting the other immortals warmly, Cobb immediately fell into conversation. Chatting with Wagner, Cobb was interrupted by Napoleon Lajoie, who had just autographed a book for a little boy. "Now, go get the cream of the crop, son," Lajoie told him, pointing to Cobb, who scribbled his name.

Word was Cobb had been delayed after taking sick in Utica while en route from his home in Menlo Park, California, with two of his five children, nineteen-year-old Beverly, and seventeen-year-old Jimmy. Reporters, eagerly lapping up the scraps of conversation and good-natured ribbing, immediately surrounded Cobb. "Ty's late— just as he always was for spring training," an immortal quipped. The real reason for his delay would emerge some twenty years later when Cobb admitted he had missed the noontime ceremony on purpose. It was to avoid being photographed with Judge Landis, to whom he bore a festering grudge for not clearing his name back in '26 in the alleged game-throwing plot with Speaker. Vintage Cobb.

Though Cobb had played baseball as if driven by demons, he was for now full of gentle humor and platitudes. Stories of Cobb's many feuds, furies, and fights, some with an overly racial tone, were legendary—he was perhaps the nastiest, most cantankerous man ever to wear a big-league uniform. How sad that he remained a bitter man, even in retirement when he'd grown rich, very rich, from Coca-Cola investments. Golf, which Cobb had taken to with the same competitive gusto as baseball, offered some relief as he issued a challenge to Ruth, himself an avid golfer. "I know The Babe slices a lot," he laughed, "so I'm going to pick out a nice, long, narrow course."

"The Babe gets kind of mad at me for kiddin' him," Cobb went on. "Sometimes he actually looks as though he wants to fight me. I wouldn't fight him. I'd run first because I like him. He was the greatest slugger we've ever seen or will see, but I can get his goat on the links."

Time was growing short. With the doors to the baseball museum now officially open, the immortals were taken on a quick tour. Pouring through the artifacts, Ruth paused before a glass case containing the uniform of his late manager, the diminutive Miller Huggins. "Gee, he was a tough little guy," the great slugger said with a sigh, "and the only one who knew how to handle me."

With a half hour to kill before the start of the parade to the ballpark, the old ballplayers and officials fanned across town—some headed back to the Cooper Inn for lunch, while others gathered in coffee shops or took a walk two blocks south along picturesque Lake Otsego. All day long, Cooperstown's few eateries, from the Homeplate Grill at the Tunnicliff Inn on Pioneer Street to Clark's Luncheonette at the entrance to Doubleday Field and Withey's Drug Store on Main Street, had done a banner business in feeding thousands of visitors. No wonder the *Freeman's Journal* correspondent would write later, "No one appeared at Doubleday Field in the afternoon who looked hungry."

The immortal's next destination: the Knox Girls' School gymnasium at the foot of Lake Street by the southern bank of Lake Otsego, where they stepped into the uniforms of their old teams for the parade. Cobb, his mind still on golf and his character forever hyper-competitive, stuffed a note into Ruth's shoes, reading, "I can beat you any day in the week at the Scottish game."

The glow of this day had melted even the friction of these two long-term rivals—and The Babe accepted the challenge. Two years later, they would play a series of matches to raise funds for the U.S.O. in country clubs near Boston, New York, and Detroit, with Cobb edging Ruth two games to one.

The four-block parade to Doubleday Field was another treat, a kaleidoscope of color and pomp. It was also another chance for the locals to mingle with the immortals, who fell in step with the collection of current big leaguers, including Stan Hack of the Cubs and Cookie Lavagetto of the Dodgers, chosen as color guards. Escorting them were a motley assortment of locals, including a thirty-piece band from American Legion Post No. 41 from Syracuse and a thirty-piece drum and bugle corps from Abraham Lincoln High School from nearby Treadwell, as well as a group of Cooperstown High School students, dressed in antique costumes complete with knee pants. Marching as well were a group of soldiers from nearby Fort Jay, dressed themselves in knee pants, all part of an effort to match the bygone uniforms of the Knickerbockers and another great team from the era, the Brooklyn Excelsiors.

Actually, the advertised game featuring big leaguers and the immortals as team captains was the third game of what was billed as a tripleheader emphasizing the evolution of baseball. With most of the 10,000 ticket holders still sidling into the little ballpark, things kicked off quickly with a demonstration of 1839-era town ball. For the event, Hannagan and Stoughton had asked Cooperstown High School baseball coach Lester Bursey to round up a willing collection of twenty students for a demonstration of town ball. Dressed in flat boots, long sailor pants, and derbies, the students gave what the *Freeman's Journal* generously called "a sprightly demonstration" of the old game—scattering throughout the field as batters; with no strike limit, hitting the pitches and heading down the sixty-foot baseline trying not to get hit or "soaked" with the ball. Supervising was an umpire looking like a cross between a nineteenth-century vaudevillian and Abraham Lincoln; dressed in a stovepipe hat, long tight pants, and a flowered waistcoat, he couldn't help but draw snickers from both the crowd and the big leaguers.

Next came the soldiers-turned-Knickerbocker/Excelsior imper-sonators for their version of 1850-era baseball—with its diamond-and-not-square-shaped field and batters taking three swings before being called out. Out to the field trudged the two teams who then lined up, and facing each other, bowed and removed their blue and red caps. At least the quick three-inning game resembled the modern game by reserving the right to argue the call. When a Knickerbocker batter sent a long fly toward center, the Excelsior center fielder, run-ning full tilt with his back to the plate, caught the ball on one bounce—and the umpire, this one adorned with a top hat, a cane, and a red umbrella—called him out. The Knickerbockers pretended to be outraged. So it went in the 1850s, when all batters sending fly balls caught on a single bounce were out. Broadcasting from their table behind home plate, Mel Allen and Arch McDonald did their best to explain the intricacies of the mid–nineteenth-century game, much of it with a smile. Allen took particular pleasure in the old-fashioned "soaking" or drilling of the batter, and the fact that without a mitt, fielders used their caps to catch fly balls.

Not every big-league team had brought their top players. Bob Feller wasn't there. Representing the Yankees were left fielder George Selkirk, a Canadian, and Norwegian catcher Arndt "Art" Jorgens, not Joe DiMaggio or Red Ruffing, prompting a wise-cracking Lefty Grove to observe, "Leave it to [them] to be represented by a couple of foreigners." But many teams did send their best, among them Grove of the Red Sox, as well as American League home run champion Hank Greenberg and Charlie Gehringer of the Tigers; Carl Hubbell and Mel Ott of the Giants; Lloyd Waner and Arky Vaughn of the Pirates; Dizzy Dean and Bill Herman of the Cubs; and Joe Medwick of St. Louis, all future Hall of Famers. Some pretty fair non–Hall-of-Famers were there as well, including the Cardinals Terry Moore; Washington's Cecil Travers; and Wally Moses of the A's. Roaming the base paths was Johnny Vander Meer, less interesting in loosening his arm than commemorating the scene with a nifty portable movie camera.

Despite the all-star cast, "the pace of the game was a clambake affair," Ken Smith called it, "with skill and precision tossed to the four winds." There was the feel of a giant, leisurely picnic, with the newly minted Hall of Famers and the current all-stars there to be seen more than anything. Prior to game time, the NBC radio crew squeezed in interviews of players, most of whom were giddy to rub elbows with the immortals. "This is a thrill being here," Greenberg told Arch McDonald. "It sure was different a hundred years ago; it sure would be nice to be able to call for a low or a high pitch."

Chatting with Allen, Dizzy Dean focused on the immortals. "My remembrance will always be toward those old guys who made it possible for us young fellows to come along and make a living playing baseball," he said. Surveying the scene, Dean had a slightly different take than Smith, comparing the festivities to a "World Series with the score tied nothing to nothing in the ninth inning."

Not exactly. On the diamond, Walter Johnson, improvising as a pinch hitter, warmed up the all-stars by hitting ground balls; after all, the Big Train, with twenty-four lifetime home runs, had been one of the game's finest hitting pitchers. Nearby, Tris Speaker warmed up with Mel Ott. But not all the immortals donned uniforms—Mack stayed, as was his custom, in a suit as did Cobb, who grabbed a seat in the sun behind third base; nor did Alexander, now donning a skimmer, and chased by Vander Meer and his movie camera. Elsewhere, Marvin Owen, the White Sox third baseman, in lieu of warming up, zipped about collecting the signatures of the Hall of Famers on two baseballs—one for himself and the other for his friend Greenberg.

Popping out from the first-base dugout and striding toward a spot behind home plate were two of the immortals, now in baggy uniforms—Honus Wagner, with his distinctive pigeon-toed gait, and Eddie Collins—chosen as team captains and intent on choosing sides. The two Hall of Famers took hold of a black Hillerich & Bradsby bat and picked their players the old-fashioned way, by moving hand-over-hand up the bat handle, with the first man to reach the top the first to choose. No American vs. National League for this game; it was the Wagners vs. the Collinses, as if it were the shipping department taking on the accountants in the company's annual Labor Day softball game.

Dean pitched two hitless innings for the Collins team, striking out two. The Wagners opened the scoring with two runs when Collins reliever Johnny Vander Meer fumbled a bunt from his fellow Red Jimmy Wilson, and gave up consecutive doubles to Marv Owen and Danny MacFayden. At least one spectator had hoped for a big inning, yelling as the game's next batter, Joe Medwick, nicknamed "Ducky," stepped to the plate: "Watch that Ducky clean those bases," the fan yelled. But not this time: Medwick ground back to Vander Meer, starting an inning-killing double play.

The crowd called for Ruth, and in the fifth, they got their wish, with The Babe pinch-hitting for MacFayden. It had only been four years since Ruth had retired, but he barely squeezed into the already baggy uniform he'd worn as part of the 1934 big-league all-star team that had toured Japan. It didn't matter; the crowd recognized the famous number 3 as he stalked to the plate, and shrieked for him to get hold of one. On the mound, Sylvester Johnson blazed a letter-high strike at the knees. But the Phillies right-hander understood his role: just groove one in, about letter high, so The Babe could hack away; such was the routine in virtually every exhibition in which Ruth had appeared. It would be poetic justice to report that The Babe sent the next pitch high over the right-field fence, but he didn't. Instead, he laced into the second pitch and popped it high over home plate.

Springing from his crouch behind home, catcher Jorgens threw away his mask, and with the crowd yelling, "Drop it! Drop it!" quickly pondered the next ethical dilemma: Should he drop it, giving the big guy another chance? After all, he and Ruth went back years, having been Yankee teammates for six years. But Jorgens elected to do his job and make the easy catch. So that was that—and The Babe turned and headed back to the dugout, with the crowd cheering anyway. It wasn't a role to which Ruth was accustomed— time after time he'd come through with towering, dramatic blasts just when his team needed one—and he was angry with himself, knowing he'd gotten a fat pitch to hit. "But I can't hit the floor with my hat," he later admitted.

The Collins team tied the score in the sixth on consecutive singles by Greenberg, Taffy Wright of the Senators, and Jorgens, good for one run, followed by an infield out for another. Then, in their half of the sixth, the Wagners picked up two more runs on doubles from Vaughn, Frank Hayes of the A's, and a single by the Phillies' Morrie Arnovich. With the score 4–2 in favor of the Wagners, the game was called in the seventh to allow the baseball nation to catch special trains headed out of town.

The game itself had taken all of one hour and forty minutes, with most batters swinging at the first pitch, pitchers working quickly, and Collins and Wagner sending in so many substitutions that it was hard to keep track of who was winning. Both Lefty Grove and Dean pitched two scoreless innings, and only one hitter, Hank Greenberg, had more than one hit, getting two singles in two at-bats. There were no home runs, with the day's best hit a blast into the center-field crowd for a ground-rule double coming from Indian Bob Johnson. About the only piece of strategy and intrigue had come as one of Wagner's right-handed pitchers, Clint Brown of the White Sox, was warming up to go in when Wagner ordered him to sit down on account of a sore arm. His arm was fine, Brown insisted, saying later on the train ride back to New York that Eddie Collins may have been the culprit: "I wouldn't put it past that Collins," Brown laughed. "He probably told Wagner that and Hans fell for it."

But the marvel of so many current and future Hall of Famers gathered on one baseball diamond wasn't lost on anyone. Writers speculated how many of the current players on hand would one day make it to the Hall of Famer themselves. Proving particularly astute was Fred Lieb, who in the June 22 *Sporting News* correctly picked out every future Hall of Famer who played the game, as well as others who were there to watch—Pie Traynor, Bill Terry, Rabbit Maranville, and Johnny Evers. Gabby Hartnett of the Cubs and Reds manager

Bill McKechnie were there, too, and they were enshrined. Indeed, the only name Lieb cited for enshrinement who didn't make it was Vander Meer, he of "double no-hit" fame, who appeared headed for Cooperstown until only a month later when he slipped on a wet mound, hurt his back, and struggled for some time thereafter. Though Vander Meer returned to form, he would lose several prime years to military service during World War II, as many players did in that era.

The gate receipts totaled $12,000, which was donated to the Hall of Fame for maintenance, as was an additional $400 from those who had filed through the museum. At the end of the game, PA announcer Caswell Adams introduced two more guests—the opera star Geraldine Farrar, whose late father, Sid Farrar, had been an 1880s-era Phillies first baseman, and another local West Point product, a '29 grad and Abner descendent, Lieutenant Daniel Doubleday. And just like that, baseball stars, old and young, broke for the Cooper Inn to change quickly and head to the little train station for the Baseball Special back to Grand Central Terminal in New York.

Headed back to the station with the late-afternoon sun just starting its descent and again surrounded by well-wishers and all those kids, still clamoring for autographs, the players scratched their names a few more times, shook hands, and waved last-minute good-byes. Baseball's memorable day in Cooperstown was finally over, but the National Hall of Fame had been inaugurated with as fine a series of events and ceremonies as anyone could have imagined. "Today, the weeds begin growing up around the railroad tracks at Cooperstown again," wrote John Carmichael in the next day's *Chicago Daily News*, summing up the feelings of anyone who had been there. "For the big spree is over and now baseball goes back to work on the second 100 years. While Cooperstown prepares to treasure, at its delightful leisure, the memory of a grand party."

✳ CHAPTER 10 ✳

"I Wouldn't Have Missed It for Anything"

As if to compensate for being late, Ty Cobb kept up a running dialogue on the train ride all the way back to Grand Central. "When I was on second and somebody grounded out, I would circle third and draw a throw from the first baseman that made me dive back to the bag," he declared as soon as the train left the station.

Surrounded by old rivals and reporters who scribbled down his every thought, Cobb was in an ebullient mood. "When I got him used to making that throw, I'd cross him by continuing on toward the plate. The timing was in my favor, and I'd seldom be nipped by a throw to the plate."

Cobb kept talking: "Know how I used to cure a batting slump?" he asked, launching into another memory. "I just batted at the pitcher [and] met [the ball] without effort or strain; easy like. [It] brings back confidence."

Nodding in approval nearby but worn out by the day was seventy-seven-year-old Connie Mack. Sighing, he pronounced himself ready for a nap. "This was the hardest day for me in many years," he said. "I must have written my name hundreds of times. My hand is still cramped. But I wouldn't have missed it for anything. Just think of it—all those great players getting together again!"

Never again would this glittering collection of onetime baseball talent be together. Cobb and his two children were headed for some R&R in New York, where he kept talking to just about anyone within range. Taking in a Yankee game, Cobb launched into a riff on how the lively ball had hurt the game. "Players nowadays take the bat at the end and slug," he said. "I used a choke grip, with hands apart, finding I could control the bat better that way." Visiting the World's Fair, a reporter asked Cobb how he would hit against current pitching. "About .320, maybe .325," he said.

"But, Mr. Cobb," the reporter countered, "your lifetime average was .367, and you've always said you felt the pitchers of today weren't as a good as those you faced. Why do you think you'd only hit .320 now?"

"You've got to remember something, sonny," Cobb countered. "I'm fifty-two years old."

◆   ◆   ◆

Cooperstown's small-town rhythms returned. On Tuesday, Miss Hazel Hurst revealed her plans for a foundation to benefit the area's blind. Speaking to the Rotary's Club's weekly luncheon at the Tunnicliffe Inn, Miss Hurst, accompanied by her seeing-eye dog, Babe, revealed her plans to train and supply seeing-eye dogs to the blind. Rotarians, the *Farmer* wrote, "were charmed by the fine and beautiful manner in which she expressed her appreciation of what the Service clubs had done for her."

Moviegoers could look forward to the latest Johnny Weismuller and Maureen O'Sullivan offering, *Tarzan Finds a Home*, down the road at the Oneonta Theatre. Downstate at the World's Fair in New York, a local of sorts—a cow owned by Cooperstown's Iroquois Farms—was making a splash, literally, in producing an impressive average of forty-eight pounds of milk a day. The output of the cow, "Iroquois Sally Castle," was made possible through the rotolactor, a revolutionary merry-go-round milking contrivance on display at Borden's Dairy World of Tomorrow. With her long runway and spacious quarters, "[Sally] is quite at ease in her World's Fair abode, which is strangely different from the surroundings back home," the *Farmer* assured the home folk. That same week came disturbing news that without more milk production in the nearby town of Smyrna the town's Sheffield milk plant would have to close, affecting fifty local farmers.

The warm afterglow of baseball's great day endured. It had been a rollicking good show, the critics chimed in. "We were prepared for a group of great executives and great players, but we had never thought that we were to meet face to face in one place and at one time a galaxy of personalities of world-wide fame whose most impressive quality was character," the *Farmer* editorialized later in the week.

Cooperstown itself celebrated the rest of the summer, with a host of commemorative events and games that included college, high school, and minor league games at Doubleday Field. In July, there was an Independence Day game between high school teams;

American Legion Day and Fireman's Day featuring two of the great Negro League teams of the day, the Mohawk Colored Giants and the Havana Cubans. And on August 26, Hall of Fame officials paid further homage to Alexander Cartwright with a day dedicated to him that featured a parade in old-fashioned garb followed by an amateur game, and pineapple juice and leis presented to players and spectators alike.

By year's end, nearly 28,000 people had visited the National Baseball Hall of Fame and Museum. They included visitors from every state but Wyoming, as well as thirty-one foreign countries. And despite some disappointments—some residents had grumbled that their taxes had gone up to pay for the Doubleday Field renovations, and neither the New York Giants, scheduled to play in Cooperstown, nor Connie Mack, set to return for a day in his honor, made it—those few setbacks were largely overlooked amidst the deluge of attention. Cooperstown, wrote Walter Littell in *the Farmer*, had become recognized as a baseball shrine "from the President down to the most humble fan," with the eventual hope that the town would become recognized "as an ideal American village and summer resort."

Meanwhile, baseball got back to business. June 19 was Lou Gehrig's thirty-sixth birthday, as well as the day that Dr. Harold Habein of the Mayo Clinic concluded his thorough examination of the Yankee star with some devastating news: Gehrig was suffering from amyotrophic lateral sclerosis, an illness involving paralysis of the motor pathways and cells of the central nervous system. Known as ALS, the clinic's finding offered a reason for Gehrig's sudden and baffling deterioration—and sent the Yankees scurrying to honor him. That happened quickly—at the July 4 doubleheader at Yankee Stadium against Washington in which 65,000 people, including Babe Ruth, past and present teammates, and Mayor LaGuardia, gathered at home plate where they heard Gehrig's famous few remarks, baseball's version of the Gettysburg Address, about "a bad break" for "the luckiest man on the face of the earth."

By summer's end, the Yankees had steamrolled to their fourth pennant in a row, easily outdistancing Eddie Collins's second-place Red Sox by seventeen games. With Gehrig gone from the lineup, Joe DiMaggio rose to the occasion, batting .381 for the first of his consecutive batting titles. The World Series that October against the Reds wasn't much of a contest, with the Yanks winning in four games.

As expected, the immortals got to New York, and with the exception of Cobb, scattered back to their homes, never again to be together. Mack, Collins, and Wagner, who were still affiliated with big-league baseball, returned to their teams, getting in at least another decade or so before retiring for good.

Back home in Pittsburgh, Wagner stayed fit by walking five miles a day, and kept spinning his yarns and working as a Pirates coach in spring training and at home games, beloved by all. Ballplayers liked him, wrote Fred Lieb, because "he never made uncomplimentary comparisons," and the writers liked him for making their jobs easy with reams of good stories and good copy.

Newspaper reporters took to celebrating every Wagner birthday, each one adding to the legend of the humble, plainspoken baseball hero. "I don't believe we've ever walked down the street in Pittsburgh [when] we haven't been stopped by somebody who wanted to stop and talk baseball," said his wife, Bessie. "Although he hasn't played for years, it's remarkable the grip he has on the people." It was said that Wagner seldom told a rookie or veteran what he was doing wrong until the player went to him; he just didn't want the others to think that he was butting in because of his age or vast experience.

Finally, in 1951, at the age of seventy-six, Wagner retired. Around then, Bessie fell and broke a hip, so the Wagners' daughter and her family, which included her husband and young daughter, moved in to care for her aging parents. By then, Honus was spending most of his time sitting on his front porch, chewing tobacco or smoking cigars, and playing with his granddaughter Leslie, and her little dog. "She puts you in mind of [former Pirate] Scoops Carey, the way she flies around the yard and she touches all the bases," he said.

Newspaper reporters continued to beat a path to Wagner's house. Attributing the best things in life afforded him to baseball, Wagner was a satisfied man. Without baseball, he'd probably have spent his life in the coal mines, and may never had met his wife. But what he appreciated most of all, he said, were "rich, fine memories and true blue friends. In this respect, I'm a wealthy and contented man."

In 1955, at eighty-one, he watched in tears as an eighteen-foot statue of himself was erected in Schenley Park, just beyond the left-field wall of Forbes Field; the statue was moved to Three Rivers Stadium, and today is outside the Pirates' current park. That December, he died in his sleep, triggering a whole new host of articles and commemorations as the greatest shortstop who ever lived.

That was shortly before Connie Mack died, in 1956, at ninety-three. In contrast to Wagner, his last years had been hard, dominated by a nasty squabble with two of his sons, Roy and Earle, for dominance of the A's. By the late 1940s, Mack's teams, long celebrated for extraordinary highs and equally horrid lows, were mostly just bad. Mack remained in charge, sitting on the bench in his tie and suit, but baseball people didn't dare criticize; that would be like condemning baseball itself or apple pie or motherhood. "When he signals for an obviously wrong move," Bob Considine wrote in 1948, "Al Simmons turns his back on the old man . . . and calls for the right move."

Seven of Mack's last eleven teams finished in the cellar, including his last team, the 1950 A's, which lost 102 games.

By then, the Phillies' Whiz Kids, who made it to that season's World Series, owned Philadelphia, drawing twice the crowds of the A's. It was a time of great flux in baseball circles, as several longtime franchises started moving—including the Boston Braves after 1952 to Milwaukee, and the St. Louis Browns after '53 to Baltimore. Shortly after the A's seventh-place finish in 1954—in its final home game ever in Philadelphia, a 4–2 loss to the Yankees, the A's drew 1,715—the team was sold. Mack's sons said later they tried selling the team to a syndicate that would leave the team in Philadelphia; instead, the A's went to Kansas City.

In return, the Macks received $3.5 million, most of which went to retire the ballpark mortgage and other debts. In bed and ill, Connie Mack signed the final papers with the firm belief that the Yankees had engineered the move, happy to get rid of a team that threatened its fan base. "It's a runaround with an awful lot of pressure to take the A's to Kansas City," a disappointed Mack said. "I'm placing myself on record that I'm not accepting the American League's decision as final. The loss of the A's to our city will be a great one, not only in prestige, but also sports-wise."

The last years were somewhat more restful for Tris Speaker. Virtually immune to injury as a player—playing in more than one hundred games nineteen years in a row—the Grey Eagle still suffered his share of misfortunes over his last two decades. There was the fall from the roof that rearranged Cleland's trip in 1937. In 1942, Speaker caught a cold that developed into pneumonia, all of which were complications that set in from a perforated intestine.

Then, in 1954, Speaker had a heart attack, but was soon up on his feet, popping up at ballparks around the country, as at Busch Stadium in St. Louis, where he was on hand to help welcome Stan Musial to the 3,000-hit club. Visiting his hometown of Hubbard, Texas, Speaker and a friend had just spent a day fishing at nearby Lake Whitney and were hooking their boat and trailer to their car when the seventy-year-old Grey Eagle collapsed. Fishermen lifted him into the back of the car.

Then he opened his eyes and spoke his last words. "My name," he said, "is Tris Speaker."

Larry Lajoie's death, in 1959 at eighty-three, wasn't as dramatic. The Great Napoleon died at his winter home near Daytona Beach, Florida, having spent his retirement much as he'd played: in privacy and shunning public appearances. Not so with Cy Young, who like Wagner, grew more popular with each birthday—commemorated by reporters trekking to central Ohio for his pearls of homespun wisdom.

Turning eighty in 1947, Young had celebrated with eight hundred of his closest friends, public officials, and baseball notables who threw him a party that lasted a day and all night. Young loved every minute, and then announced, "That's enough to last for awhile."

It was—and on his eighty-first birthday in 1948, Young passed the day by doing farm chores at the eighty-acre farm of his neighbor and friend John Benedum, where he had moved after the death of his wife, Robba. "I can still do my work, and I feel good and I sleep good," Young said. "But I'm slipping a little, for I can't see very well."

On weekends, Young held court down at the Elks Club in New-comerstown, where he'd spin the yarns to all within earshot. He'd still catch an Indians game in Cleveland every so often, and always listen to their games on the radio. Death finally came in 1955, at eighty-eight; a year later, Ford Frick, by then commissioner, insti-tuted the Cy Young Award for the year's best pitcher. (The "Cy

Young" was given to the single top pitcher until 1967, when the award was split into two, one for each league.)

Retirement for Walter Johnson came down to two interests— foxhounds and politics. Back home in Maryland, the great pitcher continued serving as a Montgomery County Commissioner, using his platform to launch a bid for Congress in early 1940. His famous name aside, Johnson was no politician, feeling more comfortable above the tumult of campaigning. In seeking the Republican nomination, the Big Train appeared at a few low-key rallies, including one where more than two hundred Republicans played bridge but otherwise did little politicking. Meanwhile, his three competitors conducted spirited campaigns, with one calling Johnson a stooge of the Republican establishment, claiming he would rather go hunting with his foxhounds than dealing with politics.

Johnson won the May primary anyway, news of which he received with typical understatement. "Gee whiz," he said. "The folks certainly have been nice about this whole thing. I'll just tell them that I'll try to do my best and hope they'll believe me."

As the Republican candidate, Johnson attended the 1940 Republican National Convention in Philadelphia, where the *New York Times* reported "the man who had thrilled thousands with his pitching sat quietly and almost unnoticed in a rear seat." The Republicans did what they could; presidential candidate Wendell Wilkie said he hoped Johnson "would begin to throw 'em out in the House of Representatives." Johnson himself promised to go to Washington with the goal of tackling unemployment. Even Ty Cobb endorsed the Big Train, calling him "the kind of man who can be banked on to keep his word to his supporters."

Running against incumbent Democrat William Byron, Johnson ran another low-key campaign. In June, he had a fund-raiser that charged $1.10 per couple. An August watermelon feast at his farm drew six hundred people. But in November, the voters sent Byron back to Congress with a 6 percent margin. Johnson remained a county commissioner.

Johnson seemed too courtly, even *too nice*, for politics. It was back on the farm where he lived as a widower with his five children and raised foxhounds to help him in hunting that he seemed happiest. "He loved the land of his farm with a serene pride," his daughter Carolyn recalled in a 1962 magazine article. "He loved to take us on long walks . . . to gather strawberries and grapes . . . and [watch] the antics of chipmunks and squirrels." Around his farm, Johnson's legendary skills as perhaps the greatest hard-throwing control pitcher in history proved adept at picking off woodchucks and groundhogs. With a rock, Johnson could nail the varmints from a considerable distance.

Diagnosed with a brain tumor in 1946, Johnson grimly hung on, with the Senators and Red Sox playing a benefit game that raised $5,000 for the family to defray costs. When he died that December at fifty-nine, the first of the immortals to go, the dean of Washington Cathedral requested permission to conduct the funeral. The cathedral nave was filled to capacity, with the sidewalks and streets outside jammed with admirers. Crowds lined the streets as the funeral cortege headed to the cemetery in Maryland. At Griffith Park in Washington, the Senators erected a monument that called him "a champion on and off the field."

While Johnson was the first of the immortals to go, George Sisler was the last. Continuing to live in St. Louis where he ran a printing company and then a sporting-goods company, Sisler ached to get back in the game. In 1943, his old mentor Branch Rickey, now with the Dodgers, came calling and six of the next nine years, Sisler worked in Brooklyn as a scout and batting instructor. When Rickey went to Pittsburgh, so did George. When the Pirates took an improbable World Series from the Yankees in 1960 thanks to Bill Mazeroski's walk-off, seventh-game home run, Sisler finally had his share of a Series win.

Two of his sons, Dave and Dick, played in the major leagues, Dick for the 1950 National League champion Phillies, known as the "Whiz Kids," and later managing the Reds in 1964 and '65. Dave pitched over seven big-league seasons for the Red Sox and three other teams. In 1969, during the one-hundredth anniversary of major-league baseball, a panel of experts in his native Akron voted George Sisler the town's greatest athlete. Sisler died in 1973, two days after his eightieth birthday, in Richmond Heights, Missouri.

If Eddie Collins never looked quite like he belonged in a baseball uniform, he looked slightly more convincing as an executive with the Red Sox, with 1940s-era photos showing him sitting behind his oversized Fenway Park desk covered with papers. There was no talk in those days of the Red Sox "curse," but in his years as the team's general manager, Collins got firsthand experience in the traditional heartbreaking losses of his team. Like so many Boston teams through the years, his Sox were good, sometimes very good, but usually lost out to the Yankees and were never good enough to win a World Series. After a second-place finish in 1939, the Sox were again second in two of the next three seasons, each time to the Yankees.

With Ted Williams gone to the marine corps during World War II, the Sox suffered. But back with Boston for '46, Williams put together an MVP season and the Red Sox finally won the American League pennant, but lost the Series in seven games to the Cardinals. In 1947, after Boston finished third, Collins was replaced by manager Joe Cronin, and essentially bumped upstairs as a vice president. But even Cronin couldn't push them over the top; succeeded by Joe McCarthy as manager, his Sox took consecutive seconds—both years losing out for the pennant by a single game. So it went even then with the Red Sox in Boston, where even a trio of Hall of Famers couldn't help them.

Like Sisler, Collins had a son who became a big leaguer—Eddie Jr., who spent parts of three seasons outfielding with Mack's A's, and married Jane, the daughter of Herb Pennock. Collins's other child, a son named Paul, was a minister, who presided over his father's second marriage in 1945. Collins was still the Red Sox vice president when, in March 1953, he was admitted to Peter Bent Brigham Hospital with a heart condition. Two weeks later, at sixty-three, Eddie Collins was dead, with his Red Sox on the way to another respectable but ultimately disappointing finish, in fourth place, sixteen games behind—you guessed it—the pennant-winning Yankees.

◆   ◆   ◆

After the Cavalcade, super-publicist Steve Hannagan made another deft move: returning $35,000 of his $100,000 budget, endearing himself for future projects with the baseball establishment. Indeed, in 1950, Frick approached him to promote the National League's seventy-fifth anniversary, this time sparing no expense, offering a $50,000 fee and a $100,000 expense account. Unfortunately, the contract was cancelled and the plans dropped when National League owners criticized the exorbitant rate.

But even that wasn't enough to slow Hannagan, whose career kept ascending. "A celebrity's celebrity," as the New York Times called him, Hannagan built his business to a staff of sixty-two with offices, not just in New York, but spread out to Chicago, Sun Valley, New

York, and St. Louis. Meanwhile, his ready smile became as familiar in Miami and Hollywood as it was back in New York at his Park Avenue apartment or in the swanky Stork Club, owned by his close friend Sherman Billingsley. After his two marriages broke up, Hannagan was often seen in the company of movie actress Ann Sheridan. How odd, then, that death came far from home—in 1953, at fifty-three, from a heart attack while in Nairobi, Kenya, where he had flown to advise dealers on Coca-Cola sales methods.

Alexander Cleland's baseball career lasted longer, but only slightly. Perhaps the true visionary of the Hall of Fame, remained as its committee secretary until 1941, when he retired. He died in 1954 while living in a nursing home outside New York City; he was seventy-seven.

Similarly, Stephen Clark's baseball career ended for all intents and purposes as the train left the station on Cavalcade day. He stuck close to home, plunging into philanthropic activities that benefited Cooperstown. He helped establish the Farmers' Museum and turn it into a nationally known center of folk art. With his wife, he established rest and recreational facilities during World War II for wounded British seamen. Clark died in 1960 at home; he was seventy-eight.

Meanwhile, the Clark family's good works live on, "benefit[ting] Cooperstown to an extent probably unmatched for a small town," according to a 1989 *Forbes* article. By then, Clark charities spent nearly $1.8 million a year on college scholarships for nine hundred Cooperstown-area students, and continued to underwrite the Clark Gymnasium and provide fresh flowers for Cooperstown's streetlight poles, all of it administered from a small building, looking more like a maintenance shed than a center of philanthropy, on the southern outskirts of town.

Enduring considerably longer in baseball was Ford Frick, who

thrived in a tumultuous business because of his resilience and forti-
tude. In 1947, when members of the St. Louis Cardinals threatened a
strike rather than face the first black man in the major leagues, Jackie
Robinson, Frick stood firm: "If you do this," he warned them, "you
are through, and I don't care if it wrecks the league for ten years. You
cannot do this because this is America." The players backed off.

Frick's line in the sand with the Cardinal players along with his
able guidance of the National League during the Depression and role
in creating the Hall of Fame, all contributed to his election, in 1951,
as commissioner, succeeding A. B. "Happy" Chandler, the flamboyant
former governor of Kentucky. It was Frick's very blandness simply in
following Chandler and before him, the notorious Judge Landis that
branded him, unfairly, with a reputation for passivity.

As commissioner, Frick was asked in the mid-1950s whether the
New York Giants and Brooklyn Dodgers would move west. "It's a
league matter," he said tersely on several occasions, seemingly doing
little to stop the teams from moving. Frick, in fact, oversaw the franchise shifts of not only just the Giants and the Dodgers, to California, which broke hearts all over in New York, but of the A's to
Kansas City, the Braves to Milwaukee, and the St. Louis Browns to
Baltimore. But several new clubs were added on his watch as well—
the New York Mets and the Houston Colt .45s, later the Astros, as
well as the California Angels and the new Washington Senators,
which replaced the team that moved to Minnesota.

But it was Frick's odd decision to create the asterisk on Roger
Maris's new single-season home run mark in 1961 that created long-
lasting controversy. Frick argued that the asterisk was essential
because Maris had broken the record in 162 games, as opposed to
Ruth's 154, as if the new record were tainted. But baseball people
knew the real reason may have been Frick's nostalgia for his old

friend The Babe. Some thirty year later, Maris's asterisk was removed from the record by Commissioner Fay Vincent.

Frick retired in 1965 as commissioner and elected to the Hall of Fame himself in 1970. Never one to speak immodestly, Frick summed up his feelings about baseball in his 1973 autobiography. Its title: *Memoirs of a Lucky Fan*. Frick died five years later, in 1978, at the age of eighty-three.

◆　◆　◆

Grover Cleveland Alexander's final days weren't so restful. From Cooperstown, "Old Pete" continued his itinerate ways, trying to keep body and soul together amidst his enduring alcoholism. In the summer of 1940, Alexander advertised in the *Sporting News* in search of a job. "Seems like I could help with some of the young pitchers," he said. "But they don't seem to want me."

His ad did get a response, though not the one he expected. As a Phillies rookie, Alexander's roommate had been Clarence Lehr, later president of the Detroit Racing Association, who offered him a position as a clubhouse manager at racetracks in Detroit, Cincinnati, and Florida. That didn't last long, and by the spring of 1941, Pete was back in New York, where he was hospitalized for more than a month at the V.A. Hospital in the Bronx.

More troubles were just ahead. Close to midnight on July 27, 1941, a taxi driver found him lying unconscious on a midtown Manhattan street, and took him to Bellevue Hospital, where his wife, Aimee, was the only visitor he was allowed. Word soon got around, and the hospital received hundreds of calls asking after him, and the *New York Mirror* ran a fund for Alex, and raised more than $2,500 to defray his medical costs. Everyone, it seemed, wanted to help a man who couldn't help himself.

Aimee had soon had enough, and in late 1941, divorced Pete for the second time. Alexander continued to look to her for support: "I don't think he ever considered we were divorced," she later recalled.

It was getting hard to keep track of Pete. In 1942, Alexander turned up in Rochester. By '43, he'd moved on to Chicago, where he was fined for disorderly conduct. A year or so later, he was working as a guard at an airplane engine plant outside Cincinnati. Later, he went back to Nebraska, where he roomed in a house before moving again, to East St. Louis, Illinois, where he was supplemented with checks from his old comrade Rogers Hornsby. That was ironic considering that Hornsby was about the only baseball person disliked by Alexander, who always blamed him for spreading the tall tale that he'd struck out Tony Lazzeri back in the '26 World Series while drunk.

Pete's health steadily declined. Deciding to move back once and for all to Nebraska, he rented a room in his old hometown of St. Paul, only thirteen miles from his birthplace in Elba, and as safe a place as any with the local saloons soon cutting off his credit. Keeping tabs on him from nearby Omaha was Aimee, and the former couple kept in touch with visits and letters. They even met at a dance after which Alex wrote to her, "It made me think I was young again and I will never think so again."

Friends paid his way to the 1950 World Series in New York, where he watched the Yankees sweep the Phillies. After the Yankee victory, Casey Stengel ran into him in the hotel press room, and regaled anyone within earshot with stories of Old Pete's greatness—this on the night his team won the World Series. It was Alexander's last hurrah—less than a month later back home in Nebraska, he wrote to Aimee that he planned to get to Omaha soon to see her. "More later," he wrote. "Love, Alex."

But he never got to Omaha. On November 4, 1950, the sixty-three-year-old Alexander suffered a heart attack in his room and died. Some three hundred people attended his funeral, which finished up at Elwood Cemetery outside St. Paul in a plot next to his parents. The Cardinals paid the funeral bill, and sent a giant floral wreath in the shape of a baseball diamond.

Less than two years later, filming started on *The Winning Team* starring Ronald Reagan as Pete and Doris Day as Aimee, who, as a consultant to the filmmakers, convinced them to stress that epilepsy, not alcohol, was the cause of the old pitcher's downfall. That's how it came out when the film was released in June 1952 to generally hostile reviews, including one headline, "Winning Team Fouls Out on Facts." Wrote Old Pete biographer Jack Kavanagh: "Even in death Alex couldn't get a break."

At least Ty Cobb could. Ruth may have been the most popular player of all time, but baseball purists continued to lionize the Georgia Peach, with his lifetime .367 batting average and furious will to win. "It is an inordinate desire to be a little better than any one else, and Tyrus Raymond Cobb carries that desire around with him at all times, whether he is playing baseball or draw poker," Damon Runyon once wrote. "It's what makes Tyrus the greatest of them all." Others agreed, but it did little to mollify Cobb. Lonely, bitter, and estranged from most of his family, Cobb grew ever more paranoid as he took ill with a variety of ailments, and took to carrying a pistol and most of his securities in a brown paper sack. Fighting and cussing 'til the very end, Ty Cobb succumbed to cancer in 1961; he was seventy-four.

Babe Ruth was the other extreme. He continued to play a lot of golf in retirement, forever a presence about the courses of suburban New York City with a driver on his shoulder and the ever-present cigar in his mouth. A doting dad to his two daughters, he roamed about as a goodwill ambassador for American Legion Junior Baseball, attracting enthusiastic crowds with every appearance—and pronouncing himself "happy ... [only]when we have every boy in America between the ages of 6 and 16 wearing a glove and swinging a bat." The Babe remained a magnet for crowds, and reveled, as always, in the attention. Visiting the Far East, he enjoyed meeting the "Eskimos"—make that "Filipinos, Babe," Claire corrected him. In Tokyo, where a half-million people greeted him on arrival, it was as if Elvis, the Beatles, and Michael Jackson had landed at once; his delirious admirers nearly tore the clothes from the man they called "Beibu Rusu."

But in the fall of 1946, Ruth began to suffer periodic pains over his left eye, and his voice cracked. When the pain became intense, he entered French Hospital on West Thirteenth Street for a checkup. The doctors diagnosed throat cancer, but never told Ruth about it. "The termites got me," The Babe told Connie Mack.

Ruth left French Hospital three months later, and had become so weak that he needed help to reach his car. His health declined steadily, and on July 26, 1948, Ruth checked back into the hospital, this time at Memorial Hospital on East Sixty-eighth Street. At 8:01 P.M., August 16, 1948, Babe Ruth's restless, crowded, stranger-than-fiction life ended, not even a decade since he'd visited Cooperstown as part of the Cavalcade. He was fifty-three.

Three days later, at Ruth's funeral, a taxi driver echoed the feelings of the 100,000 or so who lined the rainy streets of Manhattan and the Bronx to watch Babe Ruth's funeral procession: "Even the skies wept for The Babe." Added Arthur Daily in the *Times*: "The Babe would have gloried in it; the final tribute would have left him shining-eyed and choked up because he always had the soft-hearted sentimentality of a small boy."

Their sentiments matched the outpouring of grief at the passing of America's greatest sportsman. There were front-page stories in every newspaper in America, and nearly 80,000 people filed past his coffin in an unprecedented lying-in-state at Yankee Stadium. A mass at St. Patrick's Cathedral conducted by Cardinal Spellman followed, and when the service ended, Ruth's mahogany casket was carried out of the cathedral just as the rain, which had fallen steadily through the morning, suddenly stopped.

The mourners, many of them middle-aged teammates of Ruth, took several minutes to pile into the automobiles for the thirty-mile trip north to Gate of Heaven Cemetery in the Westchester County hamlet of Hawthorne, where The Babe would be buried. The rain held off, only to begin again, once the procession was on its way. Some 250 policemen directed them up Fifth Avenue from Fifty-first Street to 120th Street, on to Madison Avenue and 138th Street, and across the Madison Avenue Bridge into the Bronx. From there, the cavalcade of twenty-five cars traveled north up the Grand Concourse, past Yankee Stadium, scene of so many of Ruth's great moments, and into Westchester County.

The rain continued. Thousands of fans lined the roads, with many removing their hats out of respect. Others watched from rooftops and windows. When the procession reached the cemetery at 1:43 P.M., it was met by another crowd—this one, a tightly packed bunch of six thousand, who had waited since early morning.

The eighty-six-year-old Mack was a pallbearer. So was sportswriter Fred Lieb and two of Ruth's longtime Yankee teammates, Joe Dugan and Hoyt. As the weather cleared and the sun came out, Dugan turned to Hoyt and said, "I'd give a hundred bucks for an ice-cold beer."

"So would The Babe," whispered Hoyt.

As many as possible crowded around the canopied plot in front of the receiving tomb, where the coffin, with "George Herman Ruth" on its silver nameplate, was placed for the brief committal service. Ruth wasn't actually buried until October 26, 1948.

The grave, in the cemetery's hill section, is within two hundred feet of the grave of Mayor Jimmy Walker, an old friend, who once told him, "Never let those poor kids down." Babe Ruth never did.

◆　◆　◆

The pancakes and fried eggs simmer on this early spring morning at the Cooperstown Diner. To one side, the regulars compare notes on the frost—"seems it's sticking around this year," says one—and there are friendly nods and fresh coffee for a newcomer, sidling to a swivel seat at the counter. So it goes on Main Street in Cooperstown, three blocks down from the National Baseball Hall of Fame and Museum.

Spring is a glorious time in Cooperstown. There's still a nip in the air, the promise of a new season just ahead when every team, even the Cubs, are still in the race, and no lines in the restaurants. By Memorial Day, the crowds, many of them families and dressed in the caps or shirts of their preferred big-league team, will have descended on Cooperstown, packing the diner, stores, and hotel rooms. While tourism is the lifeblood of this town—some 400,000 a year now visit—the natives acknowledge that early spring and after Labor Day, when the kids are back at school, can be the most pleasant months to visit Cooperstown.

Cooperstown endures as "a small town" by design. Zoning is strict—there are no neon signs within the town limits, and the brick facades of the buildings along Main Street, and the handsome, sprawling homes about town, many of them summer homes, are a throwback to the era in which the Hall of Fame opened. But don't let the town's charm fool you—baseball and tourism are very big business indeed—and few visitors seem to depart without buying some piece of baseball clothing, or a commemorative bat, or ball.

No wonder Cooperstown is perhaps the most famous little town in America, and the National Baseball Hall of Fame and Museum, its best-known destination. They built it and they came to a museum whose very construction in the depths of the Great Depression is a tribute to American ingenuity. Meantime, they vote—or at least like to argue, as do all sports fan—and discuss every angle of who should be elected to the Hall of Fame, who shouldn't, year-round, just as they have since the day that Alexander Cleland had a quirky idea, Stephen Clark found an old, misshapen baseball, and Ford Frick got to thinking of a way to honor the best ballplayers of the past.

The Baseball Hall of Fame showed that museums could be dedicated to more than art or natural history. These days specialty museums are just about anywhere, including, just down the road in Oneonta, the National Soccer Hall of Fame, opened in 1999. Slightly further afield, in Saratoga, are museums for thoroughbred racing and dance. New York City, meanwhile, is chock-full of specialty museums covering a history of the city's fire and police departments as well as others on skyscrapers, subways, and even tenements.

While the National Baseball Hall of Fame didn't invent baseball nostalgia—Damon Runyon had been interviewing old-time players for years—it honored and legitimized the sport's past. No wonder all those writers kept beating a path to Cy Young's farm; after the Hall opened, celebrating baseball history became common, even expected, on the sports pages—endearing baseball forever in the national conscience. Once an eccentric little idea, the Hall of Fame was also significant in convincing curators of the potential of virtually

any kind of specialty museum. Suffice it to say that the National
Baseball Hall of Fame and Museum lives on, as do the spirits of the
baseball immortals who took up residence within its walls back on
a fine June day in 1939—a great day, actually—in Cooperstown,
New York.

ACKNOWLEDGMENTS

Venture Literary's Frank Scatoni and Greg Dinkin are talented agents who took this project from a concept to reality. National Baseball Hall of Fame and Museum Director of Research Tim Wiles and his knowledgeable staff were there with answers to questions, both big and small, while Bill Burdick, Cooperstown's Manager of Photo Services, was there, as always, to comb for photos. Nate Knaebel of Carroll & Graf is the editor who gave this project shape and substance. My family, Tobie and Julia, put up with my many dinner-table ramblings about Babe Ruth's heroics and Grover Cleveland Alexander's travails, and were always there with support and love. What a team! You're my version of the '08 Cubs, the '14 Miracle Braves, the '60 Pirates. A Fenway Frank for you all—and a heartfelt thank-you.

BIBLIOGRAPHY

Archival Resources:

Collections for Grover Cleveland Alexander, Ty Cobb, Stephen Clark, Alexander Cleland, Eddie Collins, Ford Frick, Walter Johnson, Kenesaw Mountain Landis, Napoleon Lajoie, Connie Mack, Babe Ruth, George Sisler, Tris Speaker, Albert Stoughton, Honus Wagner.
National Baseball Hall of Fame Library, Cooperstown, New York.

Newspapers & Magazines:

American Legion Magazine
Akron Beacon Journal
Baseball America
Baseball Magazine
Buck Magazine
National Pastime
Nebraska History
New York American
New York Archives
New York Herald-Tribune
The New York Times
Oneonta Daily Star

Otsego Farmer
Pittsburgh Press
St. Louis Post-Dispatch
Sporting News
The Washington Post

Books:

Alexander, Charles C. *Breaking the Slump: Baseball in the Depression Era* (Columbia University Press, 2002).

_____. *Ty Cobb* (Oxford University Press, 1984).

Allen, Lee. *The National League Story* (American Book-Stratford Press, 1961).

Broeg, Bob. *Superstars of Baseball* (Diamond Communications, 1994).

Creamer, Robert W. *Babe: The Legend Comes to Life* (Simon & Schuster, 1974).

DeValeria, Dennis & Jeanne Burke DeValeria. *Honus Wagner: A Biography* (Henry Holt, 1995).

Eig, Jonathan. *Luckiest Man: The Life and Death of Lou Gehrig* (Simon & Schuster, 2005).

Gelernter, David. *1939: The Lost World of the Fair* (Avon Books, 1995).

Gershman, Michael; Palmer, Pete; Pietrusza, David; and Thorn, John (eds.). *Total Baseball: The Official Encyclopedia of Major League Baseball* (Viking, 1997).

Katz, Lawrence S. *Baseball in 1939: The Watershed Season of the National Pastime* (McFarland & Company, Inc., 1995).

Kavanagh, Jack. *Ol' Pete: The Grover Cleveland Alexander Story* (Diamond Communications, 1996).

_____. *The Heights of Ridiculousness: The Feats of Baseball's Merry-makers* (Diamond Communications, 1998).

Lane, F. C. *Batting* (Society for American Baseball Research, 2001).

Leitner, Irving A. *Baseball: Diamond in the Rough* (Criterion Books, 1972).

Lewine, Harris & Daniel Okrent (eds.). *The Ultimate Baseball Book* (Houghton Mifflin, 1979).

Lieb, Fred. *Baseball As I Have Known It* (G. P. Putnam's Sons, 1977).

Ritter, Lawrence S. *The Glory of Their Times* (MacMillan, 1966).

_____ & Mark Rucker. *The Babe: A Life in Picture* (Ticknor & Fields, 1988).

Robinson, Ray. *Iron Horse: Lou Gehrig in His Time* (HarperCollins, 1990).

Seymour, Harold. *Baseball: The Early Years* (Oxford University Press, 1960).

Smith, Curt. *Voices of the Game* (Diamond Communications, 1987).

_____. *Voices of Summer: Ranking Baseball's 101 All-Time Best Announcers* (Carroll & Graf Publishers, 2005).

Smith, Ken. *Baseball's Hall of Fame* (A. S. Barnes and Company, 1952).

Vlasich, James A. *A Legend for the Legendary: The Origin of the Baseball Hall of Fame* (Bowling Green State University Popular Press, 1990).

Wagenheim, Kal. *Babe Ruth: His Life and Legend* (Praeger Publishers, 1974).

Ward, Geoffrey C. & Ken Burns. *Baseball: An Illustrated History* (Alfred A. Knopf, 1994).

INDEX

A

Aaron, Hank, 181

Alexander, Grover Cleveland "Old Pete"
    alcoholism of, 144–145, 152, 217–218
    baseball career, 4, 144–145, 146–151,
        152–153, 155
    biographical information, 145–146,
        151–152
    death of, 219
    Hall of Fame vote for, 96, 118
    opening celebration speech, 146
    on opening day, 15
    retirement of, 153–155

Alexander Cartwright Day, 206

Allen, Lee, 188

Allen, Mel, 127, 197–198

Allen, Mel "The Voice," 128

American League. *See also* Johnson, Ban;
    specific teams
    Cobb's batting titles, 59
    competing with National League, 67,
        83–86
    Great Depression and, 73–74
    and Harridge, 29, 167
    home runs per year, 188
    and Johnson, Ban, 67, 81
    Lajoie's batting titles, 65
    radio revenue, 125
    Western League as predecessor to, 37

America's National Game (Spalding),
    100–101

Anson, Cap, 79–80, 96, 168–169

Arlin, Harold, 125

Arnovich, Morrie, 201

A's. *See* Philadelphia A's

autograph collectors, 7, 16, 76, 193–194

B

Babe (Creamer), 176

Babe Ruth. *See* Ruth, George Herman

Baker, Frank "Home Run," 37

Baker, William, 151

Baker Field (Manhattan, NY), 122–123

Barber, Red, 112, 124, 126

Barrow, Ed, 182

Barry, Jack, 37

Bartell, Dick, 74

baseball. *See also* origin of baseball
    "black sox" game fix episode, 28,
        131–132, 180
    dead-ball era, 57–58, 69, 134
    as maker of "The American Spirit,"
        142–143
    New York game, 161–163
    steroid abuse, 181–182
    Whitman's appreciation for, 159

baseball commissioners
    Frick, 216–217
    Landis's term, 6, 28
    Vincent, 217

Baseball Encyclopedia, The, 98

baseball fans
    autograph collectors, 7, 16, 76, 193–194
    loyalty of, 113, 120

memorabilia donations of, 70, 103
and Ruth, 175, 177–178
baseball gloves, initial use of, 80
baseball guide, Spalding's annual, 32–33,
41, 102
Baseball Hall of Fame and Museum. *See
also specific inductees*
Cartwright's exhibit in, 166–167
developing selection criteria, 76–77,
85–86, 97
Frick's idea for, 75
initial members, 39–40, 95–96
initial proposal, 23, 24–25, 71–72
legacy of the visionary builders,
222–224
publicity from sports writers' ballots,
85–86, 99–100
Whiting's design of, 116–117
baseball memorabilia
acquisitions for museum, 70–72, 82,
100–104, 114–115
Cartwright family contributions, 166
Doubleday ball, 64, 69
Hall of Fame first-day stamped postcards and Centennial stamp, 18–20,
140, 168, 193–194
from Hillerich family of Louisville,
174–175
insignificance of, in early years, 75
"T206" baseball cigarette card, 48
Union prisoners playing baseball
during Civil War, 70
Village Club becomes inadequate for,
70–71, 115
baseball nostalgia, 75–76, 141–142
Baseball Writers Association of America,
76–77, 174. *See also* sports writers
Bender, Chief, 38
Benton, Rube, 133
Bergen, Marty, 97–98
Bezdek, Hugo, 49
Big Al. *See* Spalding, Albert
Big Train, The. *See* Johnson, Walter
Blankenship, Cliff, 91

Blue Jays, 69
Boetticher, Otto, 70
Bonds, Barry, 182
Boston Braves
Great Depression and, 74
move to Milwaukee, 209
1914 World Series title, 135
and Ruth, 172
and Young, 81–82
Boston Red Sox (formerly Pilgrims)
and Collins, 136–137
Red Stockings team photos, 71
and Ruth, 180, 182
and Speaker, 57–59
and Williams, 118
and Young, 79, 81
Bradley, George Washington, 100
Brandt, Bill, 101
Braves. *See* Boston Braves
Brewers, 37
Brisbane, Arthur, 72
British origin of baseball (rounders) theory,
30, 32–33, 42–43, 51, 161–162
Brooklyn Dodgers, 73–74, 126
Brown, Clint, 201
Browns, 103–104
Bulkeley, Morgan, 98–99, 118

C
Cameron, Stuart, 165
Cardinals, 74, 81, 153
Carmichael, John, 202
Cartwright, Alexander
Alexander Cartwright Day, 206
baseball rules for Knickerbockers,
160–163, 168
Cartwright-Doubleday controversy,
157–158, 168–169
as "Father of Modern Base Ball," 166
gold fever and on to Hawaii, 163–164
Hall of Fame vote for, 166
Cartwright, Bruce, Jr., 166
Centennial. *See also* opening celebration
ashtrays honoring, 117

as Cavalcade of Baseball, 72, 141–142, 167–170

Cleland first hears about, 22–23

exhibition game of current all-stars, 5, 198–202

Hannagan and Stoughton's publicity campaign, 137–143

postal stamp and first-day covers, 18–20, 140, 168, 193–194

post-ceremony activities, 192–194, 195–196

Centennial Commission

Hannagan and Stoughton's publicity campaign for, 137–143

members of, 120

promotion of Doubleday as founder of baseball, 141, 143

selecting famers from baseball pioneers, 76–77, 98–99, 99–100

Centennial publicity

events pre-Hall opening day, 169–170

Hannagan and Stoughton's campaign, 137–143

in *Sporting News,* 101–102

from sports writers' ballots, 85–86, 99–100

Centennial Special (train), 2–4, 203–204

Chadwick, Henry "Unkle Harry," 29–30, 32–33

Chance, Frank, 96

Chapman, Ray, 59, 89

Chicago Cubs

and Alexander, 151–153, 155

Great Depression and, 74

leader in radio broadcasting, 125

in 1910 World Series, 135

Chicago White Sox (formerly White Stockings)

"black sox" game fix episode, 28, 131–132, 180

and Collins, 131–133, 135–136

and Spalding, 32

Young's first game against, 79–80

Christy Mathewson Day, 170

Cincinnati Reds (formerly Red Stockings)

first place in National League, 8

and McKechnie, 15

Red Stockings team photo, 71

and Vander Meer, 5

and Wright, 99

Civil War, Union prisoners playing baseball during, 70

Clark, Alfred, 12

Clark, Edward S., 10, 11–12

Clark, John, 117

Clark, Robert, 13

Clark, Stephen C., 13, 215

Clark, Stephen C., Jr., 20–22, 61, 103

Clark Foundation, 21

Clark House (Manhattan, NY), 22, 23

Cleland, Alexander

biographical information, 21–22

and Cartwright's role in origin of baseball, 166

collecting memorabilia for museum, 70–72, 100–104

collecting memorabilia from famers, 109–110, 114–115

in Cooperstown five years before Centennial, 21–22

and Frick, 74, 76–77

initial proposal for the Hall and Museum, 23, 24–25, 71–72

retirement and death of, 215

Cleveland Indians (formerly Blues and Naps)

and Lajoie, 67–69

named changed to Cleveland "Naps," 64–65

radio broadcasters of, 125–126

Sockalexis as reason for name change, 102–103

and Speaker, 59–60

Cleveland Spiders, 79–81, 102–103

Cobb, Tyrus Raymond "Ty"

accolades to the end, 219

batting titles, 59

contributions to museum, 114–115
Hall of Fame vote for, 95
and Johnson, 15, 88, 89
Leonard's accusation about, 60
on opening day, 194
personality of, 195
retirement of, 60
and Ruth, 186, 195, 196
storytelling, 203–204
Cochrane, Mickey, 74
Collins, Eddie, Jr., 214
Collins, Eddie "Cocky"
   baseball career, 4, 130–131, 132–134,
      134–136
   biographical information, 130, 134
   death of, 214
   fellow players' view of, 131–132
   Hall of Fame vote for, 96, 168
   Lajoie compared to, 68
   and Mack, 38
   on 1917 World Series, 15
   opening celebration speech, 130
   and Red Sox, 136–137, 213–214
   team captain for exhibition game on
      opening day, 199
Comiskey, Charles, 168–169
commemorative stamp, 18–20, 140, 168
Connolly, Tommy, 193
Connor, Roger, 101
Considine, Bob, 164, 208
Cook, Joe, 6
Coolidge, Calvin, 176
Coombs, Jack, 38
Cooper Inn, 7
Cooperstown, NY
   ban on neon lights, 21
   copyright on term, "Birthplace of Base-
      ball," 118
   farming in, 2, 21
   location, 1–2
   post-opening day, 204–206
   and tourism, 21, 222–223
   train station on June 12, 1939, 3–4, 202
   Village Club, 70–71, 115

Costas, Bob, 124
Coyle, Mickie, 56
Crane, Sam, 62
Creamer, Robert, 176
Cronin, Joe, 213–214
Cubs. See Chicago Cubs
Cummings, Candy, 168–169
Currier & Ives print of match at Elysian
   Fields, 70
Curry, Duncan, 158
Cy Young Award, 210–211
Cy Young Day, 81

D
Daily, Arthur, 220
Daily, George, 85–86
Daniel, Dan, 99
dead-ball era, 57–58, 69, 134
Dean, Dizzy, 198–199
DeBost, Helen, 103
dedication day. See opening celebration
Delahanty, Ed, 96, 97
Delhi Gazette (New York), 158
Detroit Tigers, 125. See also Cobb, Tyrus
   Raymond "Ty"
DiMaggio, Joe, 39, 113–114, 121, 207
Dodgers, 73–74, 126
Doubleday, Abner. See also Doubleday myth
   biographical information, 52–53, 143
   as "inventor" of baseball, 27, 49–53
   portrait of, 70
Doubleday, Daniel, 202
Doubleday ball, 64, 69
Doubleday Field Association, 63–64
Doubleday Field (Cooperstown, NY),
   22–23, 62–63, 119
Doubleday Memorial Fund, 61–62
Doubleday myth. See also Doubleday,
   Abner
   Centennial Commission promotion of,
      141, 143
   challenges to, 158–159
   Clark's desire to promote, 61
   Graves's role in, 49–53, 64, 69–70

media promotion of, 138–139

Menke's conflicting information,
156–157, 164–165

Mills Commission, 41–43, 50–52,
157–158, 165

Doyle, Charles "Chilly," 26, 29, 54

Dreyfuss, Barney, 91

Dugan, Joe, 179

Dunlap, Orrin, 123

E

Ebbets Field, 123–124, 126–127

Edwards, Henry, 83–84, 115

Eight Men Out (movie), 131–132

Elysian Fields (Hoboken, NJ), 70, 162

English origin of baseball (rounders)
theory, 30, 32–33, 42–43, 51, 161–162

Evers, Johnny, 117, 158

Ewing, Buck, 96, 168–169

exhibition game on opening day, 5, 198–202

F

Fabian, Henry "Hennerie," 119

fans. *See* baseball fans

Farley, Jim, 18–20, 141, 168

Farrar, Geraldine, 202

Father of Modern Base Ball, 166

Feller, Bob, 113–114

Felsch, Happy, 132–133

Fields, W.C., 108

Fijux's Hotel (Manhattan, NY), 163

first day covers, 18–20, 193–194

Forbes Field (Pittsburgh, PA), 124–125

Foxx, Jimmie, 74

Freeman's Journal, The, 197

Frick, Ford

as baseball commissioner, 216–217

contributions to museum, 70, 75

as National League president, 73–77

ribbon cutter on opening day, 29

sports writers grilling of, 83–85

stand against segregation, 215–216

support for the Hall, 72, 74–77, 86

G

Gaedel, Eddie, 98

gambling, White Sox episode, 28

Game of Base Ball, The (Chadwick), 30

Gandil, Chick, 131–132

Gehrig, Lou, 94, 121–122, 188, 191,
206–207

Gelernter, David, 112

George VI, King, 191

Giants, 70, 74, 75, 132–133

Graham, Frank, 183

Graney, Jack, 126

Grant, Eddie, 97

Graves, Abner, 49–53, 64, 69–70

Great Depression, 2, 61, 73–74

Greenberg, Hank, 198, 201

Grey Eagle. *See* Speaker, Tris

Griffith, Clark, 70, 91, 169

Groom, Bob, 108

Gunson, Joe, 103

H

Hall of Fame first-day stamped postcards,
18, 20, 193–194. *See also* opening celebration

Hall of Fame for Great Americans (New
York City, NY), 24

hall of fame idea, 75. *See also* Baseball Hall
of Fame and Museum

Hannagan, Steve, 137–140, 141–143, 165,
214–215

Harridge, William "Will," 29, 167

Hayes, Frank, 201

Heilmann, Harry, 74

Heydler, John, 8, 27, 72, 73

Highlanders. *See* New York Yankees

Hillerich & Bradsby Company, 174–175

Hillerich family of Louisville, 174–175

Hitting (Lane), 107

Hodgson, Claire, 188

Holke, Walter, 133

Hollywood, 113

Honus. *See* Wagner, Honus

Hooper, De Wolf, 103

Hooper, Harry, 57, 182–183
Hooper, John, 103
Hornsby, Roger, 96, 218
Hoyt, Waite, 177–178, 221
Hubbell, Carl, 8
Huggins, Miller, 195
Huntington Avenue Grounds (Boston, MA), 81
Hurst, Hazel, 204–205

I
immigration to the U.S., 22
Indians. *See* Cleveland Indians
induction weekends, 5

J
Jackson, "Shoeless Joe," 132
James, Bill, 97
Jazz era, 112–113, 180
Johnson, Ban
  as American League President, 67, 81
  Hall of Fame vote for, 98–99, 118
  and Leonard's story on game fix, 60
  and Mack, 37
Johnson, Bob, 201
Johnson, Walter "The Big Train"
  baseball career, 4, 88–91, 93–94
  biographical information, 90
  character of, 91–93
  Hall of Fame vote for, 96
  opening celebration speech, 87
  on opening day, 15
  political career, 94–95, 211–212
  retirement and death of, 212
  on Ruth's batting skill, 185
  warming up exhibition players on opening day, 199
Jorgens, Art, 200, 201
Journal 72–73
Journal-American (newspaper), 138

K
Kavanagh, Jack, 219

Keeler, Wee Willie, 71, 96, 97, 168
Killefer, Bill, 150–151, 155
Klem, Bill, 46, 99
Knickerbocker Base Ball Club
  baseball played by, 160–163
  as first team, 158
  opening celebration exhibition of, 197–198
  Spalding on, 41
  team photos of, 71

L
Lajoie, Napoleon "Bashful Larry and Peer-less Lajoie"
  baseball career, 66–69
  biographical information, 65–66
  Cleveland "Naps" named after, 64–65
  Collins compared to, 68
  contributions to museum, 114
  Hall of Fame vote for, 96
  opening celebration speech, 65
  on opening day, 8
  retirement and death of, 210
Landis, Kenesaw Mountain
  biographical information, 27–28
  and Cobb, 194–195
  investigation of Cobb and Speaker, 60
  opening celebration announcements, 27, 191–192
  personality of, 6
  special-issue postcard purchase, 18
  and White Sox gambling episode, 28
  Young and, 17–18
Lane, F. C., 107
Lazzeri, Tony, 147, 218
Leatherstocking Stamp Club, 18–20
Legend for the Legendary, A (Vlasich), 166
Leonard, Dutch, 60
Lettis, Theodore, 29
Lewis, Duffy, 57
Lieb, Fred, 103, 201–202
Life (magazine), 121
Life of Emile Zola (movie), 113

Littell, Walter, 63–64, 69–70, 165, 206
Lobert, Hans, 150
Lou Gehrig's disease, 206

M
MacFayden, Danny, 199–200
Mack, Connie
  baseball career, 3, 36–39, 135
  Hall of Fame vote for, 96, 98–99, 118
  "$100,000 infield" put together by, 37,
    132, 135
  opening celebration speech, 35–36
  on opening day, 204
  personality of, 36–37, 38
  retirement and death of, 208–209
MacPhail, Larry, 126
Manning, Tom, 125, 126, 192
Maris, Roger, 181, 188, 216–217
Marquard, Rube, 155–156
Mathewson, Christy
  Christy Mathewson Day, 170
  Hall of Fame vote for, 95–96
  Johnson compared to, 91
  and Marquard, 155–156
  mitt donated to the Hall, 102
  on Wagner, 47
Matthias, Brother, 179–180
McCarthy, Joe, 14–15, 153
McCusky, Frank, 25
McDonald, Arch "The Old Tree,"
  127–128, 197–198
McGillicutty, Cornelius Alexander. *See*
  Mack, Connie
McGinnity, Joe, 135
McGowan, Bill, 38
McGraw, John
  Hall of Fame vote for, 6, 97, 98–99, 118
  on Holke's play in 1917 World Series, 133
  statue of in the Hall, 102
  on Wagner, 44
McGwire, Mark, 181–182
McInnis, Stuffy, 37
McKechnie, Bill, 15

McMahon, Sandy, 24
Medwick, Joe, 7–8, 200
Memoirs of a Lucky Fan (Frick), 217
memorabilia. *See* baseball memorabilia
Menke, Frank, 155–157
Mercer, Sid, 138
Merkle, Fred, 187
Milan, Clyde, 91, 92
Mills, Abraham G., 41
Mills Commission, 41–43, 50–52,
  157–158, 165
Milwaukee Brewers, 37
Moore, Terry, 7–8
Moses, Robert, 111

N
National Baseball Centennial Commission.
  See Centennial Commission
National Game, The (Spalding), 158
National Game, The (Spink), 157–158
National League. *See also* Frick, Ford; *spe-
cific teams*
  competing for the famer slots, 83–86
  competing with American League, 67,
    83–86
  and Frick, 73–77
  and Heydler, 8, 27, 72, 73
  Wagner's batting titles, 44
NBC
  debut of televised baseball by, 122–123
  exhibition game on opening day, 198
  live broadcast of opening celebration,
    26, 128–129
  Manning hired as sports reporter, 126
New York American, 99
New York City and baseball, 111, 125,
  126–127
New York Giants, 70, 74, 75, 132–133
New York Times, 31, 83, 168, 181
New York Yankees (formerly Highlanders).
  See also Ruth, George Herman
  "Babe" and Doubleday memorial
  service, 169

honoring Gehrig, 206–207
Johnson's 1908 shutouts against, 88–89
Mays's beaning of Chapman, 59–60
McCarthy and, 14–15
1927 season, 188
1939 season, 121, 169
record in 1930s, 121
and Ruth, 181–183, 187–188
Newsweek (magazine), 139
1939: The Lost World of the Fair (Gelernter), 112

O

Old Pete. *See* Alexander, Grover Cleveland
old-timers' committee, 98–99
Olympic Town Ball Club (Philadelphia, PA), 33
"$100,000 infield," 37, 132, 135
one old cat game as forerunner of base ball, 33–34, 43
opening celebration
    baseball celebrities at, 39–40
    crowd and crime, 25–26
    NBC live broadcast, 26
    players' arrival in Cooperstown, 1–10
opening celebration speeches
    Alexander, 146
    Collins, 130
    Doyle's speech, 26–27
    Johnson, 87
    Lajoie, 65
    Landis, 27, 191–192
    Landis's speech, 27, 29
    Mack, 35–36
    Mack's speech, 39
    Ruth, 176
    Sisler, 105
    Speaker, 54–55
    Wagner, 43, 46, 47
    Young, 78
origin of baseball. *See also* Cartwright, Alexander; Doubleday myth
Knickerbockers' rules, 160–163, 168

Menke's research on, 156–157, 164–165
one old cat theory, 33–34, 43
rounders theory, 30, 32–33, 42–43, 51, 161–162
Spalding's committee to determine, 41–42
town ball theory, 50, 160, 197
O'Rourke, Patsy, 148
Otsego Farmer (newspaper), 64, 85–86, 116, 205–206
Owen, Marvin, 199–200

P

Parker, Dan, 121
Pershing, John J., 168
Philadelphia A's
    and Collins, 135, 136
    cost-cutting measures during Depression, 74
    deterioration and move to Kansas, 208–209
    and Lajoie, 67
    and Mack, 3, 35, 37–39, 135, 136
    "$100,000 infield," 37, 132, 135
    record of, 35, 37
    World Series wins in 1910s, 135
Philadelphia Phillies, 66–67, 74, 148–151, 209
Phinney, Alexander, 62
Piedmont Cigarette Company, 48
Pilgrims. *See* Boston Red Sox
Pittsburgh Pirates, 4, 37, 45–46, 49, 74
Pittsfield, MA, 159
Plank, Eddie, 38
publicity. *See* Centennial publicity

R

Radbourne, Old Hoss, 168–169
radio, 111–113, 124–125, 125–128
Rainer, Luise, 113
Red Sox. *See* Boston Red Sox
Reds. *See* Cincinnati Reds
Rice, Grantland, 68, 125
Richardson, Hardy, 61

Rickey, Branch, 107, 212–213

Risberg, Swede, 131–132

road games, radio and, 127–128

Roberts, Doak, 55, 56–57

Roosevelt, Franklin D., 61, 110–111, 141, 170, 190–191

rounders as forerunner of baseball, 30, 32–33, 42–43, 51, 161–162

Ruffing, Red, 121

Runyon, Damon, 57–58, 219

Ruppert, Jack, 172, 174

Ruth, Claire Hodgson, 188–189

Ruth, George Herman "Babe"
  baseball career, 40, 176–178, 180–183, 186–189
  batting skill, 185–186
  biographical information, 178–180, 184–185
  and Cobb, 186, 195, 196
  and Coolidge, 176
  death and funeral, 220–222
  in exhibition game on opening day, 200
  exhibition games and pre-game hitting exhibitions, 172–173
  fans' appreciation for, 171
  financial manager for, 173–174, 179
  and Frick, 73
  generosity of, 174, 179
  Hall of Fame vote for, 95
  on Huggins, 195
  opening celebration speech, 176
  on opening day, 3, 16–17, 175–176
  personality of, 171–172, 175–178, 183–184, 186–187
  retirement of, 172–175, 219–220
  and Ruppert, 174
  unfulfilled desire to manage a team, 171–172, 173

Ruth, Helen Woodford, 184

S

Sakolski, A. M., 168

Senators, 36, 87–88, 169

Sheed, Wilfrid, 36

Shelton, Benny, 56

Shibe, Benjamin, 102

Shibe, Thomas, 85

Shoeless Joe Jackson, 132

Singer, Isaac Merritt, 10–11

Sisler, Dave, 213

Sisler, Dick, 213

Sisler, George
  baseball career, 4, 105–107, 108–109, 212–213
  biographical information, 107–108
  death of, 213
  Hall of Fame vote for, 96, 168
  opening celebration speech, 105
  and Rickey, 107, 212–213

Slocum, Bill, 99

Smith, Elmer, 60

Smith, Ken, 47, 198

Society for American Baseball Research, 98

Sosa, Sammy, 181–182

Spalding, Albert "Big Al"
  America's National Game drawings, 100–101
  and Chadwick, 29
  developing sporting goods business, 30–33
  Hall of Fame vote for, 97, 168–169
  on origin of baseball, 33–34, 49–51, 168–169
  and Spink's book on baseball, 158

Spalding Sporting Goods Company, 31–32

Spalding's Official Baseball Guide, 32–33, 41, 102

Spalding's Round-the-World tour, 34, 103

Speaker, Tris "Grey Eagle"
  baseball career, 56–60
  and Cleburne club in Texas, 55–57
  Hall of Fame vote for, 96
  Leonard's accusation about, 60
  opening celebration introduction and speech, 54–55
  retirement and death of, 60, 209–210

Special Base Ball Commission, 41–42
speeches. *See* opening celebration speeches
Spiders, 79–81, 102–103
Spink, Henry, 158
Sporting News, 71, 86, 99, 101–102
Sports Encyclopedia (Menke), 164
sports writers
    Baseball Writers Association of
      America, 76–77, 174
    grilling Frick about list of nominees,
      83–85
    vote results, 95–98
    as voters, 71, 76–77
Spraker, Rowan D., 9, 27
St. Louis Browns, 103–104
St. Louis Cardinals, 74, 81, 153
Standard Oil Company maps, 117
Staples, G. E., 158
Stengel, Casey, 17, 73, 218
Stern, Bill, 123
Stokes, Walter, 102
Stoughton, Al, 137–139, 140–143

T
"T206" baseball cigarette card, 48
television, debut of baseball on, 122–123.
    See also NBC
Tener, John, 8
Tigers, 125. *See also* Cobb, Tyrus Raymond
    "Ty"
Time (magazine), 118
Toronto Blue Jays, 69
town ball as forerunner of base ball, 50,
    160, 197
Tracy, Spencer, 113
Traynor, Pie, 9
Tucker, Billy, 161
Tyson, Ty, 125

V
Vander Meer, Johnny, 8, 16, 199–200, 202
Village Club (Cooperstown, NY), 70–71,
    115

Vincent, Fay, 217
Vlasich, James, 166

W
Waddell, Rube, 37, 45, 57, 96
Wagner, Honus
    on Alexander's pitching, 151
    baseball career, 4, 45–46, 49, 207
    batting skill, 47
    biographical information, 43–44, 46–47
    Hall of Fame vote for, 95
    on Mack, 47
    opening celebration speech, 43, 46, 47
    on opening day, 9
    retirement and death of, 207–208
    storytelling of, 45, 46, 47, 48–49
    "T206" baseball cigarette card, 48
    team captain for exhibition game on
      opening day, 199
Wakefield, Dick, 39
Walsh, Christy, 173–174
Walsh, Ed, 68
Washington Senators, 36, 87–88, 169
Weaver, Buck, 28
White, Deacon, 61
White Sox. *See* Chicago White Sox
Whiting, Frank, 115–116
Whitman, Walt, 159
Williams, Joe, 60, 92
Williams, Left, 132
Williams, Ted, 118, 137, 213
Wilson, Jimmy, 199–200
Winning Team, The (movie), 219
Wood, Harry, 71
Woodford, Helen, 184
Woods, Doc, 179
Work Progress Administration (WPA), 119
World Series,
    1909, 48–49
    1910, 135
    1911, 155–156
    1912, 57
    1913, 57

1914, 135
1915, 150
1917, 15, 132–133
1918, 177
1919, 28, 131–132, 136
1920, 59–60
1921, 125
1924, 93
1925, 93
1926, 147–148, 153
1927, 153, 188
1928, 153
1936, 114, 121
1937, 114, 121
1938, 121
1939, 207
1944, 105
1946, 213
1950, 218
1960, 213
World's Fair (Flushing Meadows, NY),
    109–110

Wright, George, 98–99, 100, 118
Wright, Taffy, 201
Wrigley, William, 151

Y
Yankees. *See* New York Yankees
Yawkey, Tom, 136
Young, Denton "Cy"
    baseball career of, 79–82
    biographical information, 77, 79
    contributions to museum, 82, 104
    Hall of Fame vote for, 96, 97
    on his baseball skills, 78
    Landis and, 17–18
    opening celebration speech, 78
    and reporter on opening day, 193
    retirement and death of, 82, 210
    and Speaker, 58

Z
Zimmerman, Heinie, 133